University of Birmingham

URBAN AND REGIONAL STUDIES NO 1

Recreation Research and Planning

In preparation
Experiments in Recreation Research
BY THOMAS L. BURTON

also by G. E. Cherry and T. L. Burton
Social Research Techniques for Planners

Recreation Research and Planning

A Symposium

EDITED BY THOMAS L. BURTON

LONDON · GEORGE ALLEN & UNWIN LTD

PRINTED IN GREAT BRITAIN
in 11 point Times New Roman Type
BY ALDEN AND MOWBRAY LTD
OXFORD

The Authors

THOMAS L. BURTON, *Editor*

Associate Professor of Urban and Regional Planning, University of Waterloo, Ontario, Canada. Previously Lecturer in Recreation Planning at the Centre for Urban and Regional Studies, University of Birmingham. Author of *Outdoor Recreation Enterprises in Problem Rural Areas* (Wye College, 1967). Joint author of *Outdoor Recreation in the British Countryside* (Wye College, 1965) and *Recreation Research Methods* (C.U.R.S., 1969).

GERARD BROOKE TAYLOR [Tim]

Social Relations Officer at Telford New Town—a post involving social research, community development and information. Filled similar posts at Hemel Hempstead, Peterlee and Newton Aycliffe New Towns from 1947 to 1964. Has spoken and written widely on recreation.

GORDON E. CHERRY

Deputy Director of the Centre for Urban and Regional Studies at the University of Birmingham. Formerly Research Officer in the City Planning Department, Newcastle upon Tyne. Member of the Town Planning Institute. Associate of the Royal Institution of Chartered Surveyors. Vice-Chairman of the Regional Studies Association. Author of *Town Planning in its Social Context*.

BASIL E. CRACKNELL

Economic Adviser at the Ministry of Overseas Development. Formerly Senior Research Fellow at the University of Nottingham. Awarded W. G. Kellogg Fellowship to study rural development and recreation in the United States, 1964.

ISABEL EMMETT

Lecturer in Sociology at the University of Manchester. Formerly Research Director of the Leisure Research Unit at the Department of Physical Education, University of Manchester.

N. J. KAVANAGH

Senior Lecturer in Industrial Economics at the University of Birmingham. Supervisor of research into the measurement of recreation benefits, being undertaken at the University of Birmingham on behalf of the Water Resources Board. Nuffield Research Economist in Cost–Benefit Analysis at the Royal Institute of Public Administration, 1967–69.

L. J. LICKORISH

Chief Executive, British Tourist Authority, formerly General Manager, the British Travel Association. British representative on a number of international organisations concerned with international travel. Publications, *The Travel Trade*, and other economic studies in tourism.

DENIS D. MOLYNEUX

Deputy Director of the Sports Council and Principal Research Officer of the Central Council of Physical Recreation. Formerly Lecturer in the Physical Education Department, University of Birmingham. Author of *Central Government Aid to Sports and Physical Recreation in Countries of Western Europe* (University of Birmingham, 1962). Has spoken and written widely on recreation development and administration.

D. M. WINTERBOTTOM

Senior Planner with Llewelyn-Davies, Weeks, Forestier-Walker and Bor, Planning Consultants. Formerly with the Planning Department, Essex County Council. Associate of the Royal Institution of Chartered Surveyors.

Foreword

This series of URBAN AND REGIONAL STUDIES is intended, in the main, as a vehicle for the publication of the final reports on major studies undertaken in the Centre for Urban and Regional Studies at the University of Birmingham. It complements the series of Occasional Papers and Research Memoranda (published by the Centre) which typically present interim reports or more restricted studies.

The first two series, however, will sometimes include work which, though related to the Centre's research programme, has been carried out in other Departments of the University of Birmingham or elsewhere. The present volume is an example of this. Four of the chapters have been written by the staff of the Centre, two by members (present or recent) of the University of Birmingham, and the remainder by experts from other institutions.

Recreation planning was one of the first major fields covered by the Centre's research programme. This Symposium forms a general introduction to the subject. It will be followed shortly by a volume which will present a detailed account of the studies undertaken in the Centre between 1967 and 1969. An outline and preliminary report on these was published in the Occasional Paper series under the title *Recreation Research Methods* (No. 3, 1969). The Centre's whole research programme is outlined in another Occasional Paper (No. 4, 1969), *The Work of the Centre*.

The Centre was established as an experiment designed to overcome some of the problems created by the traditional organisational structure of Universities and, at the same time, to bridge the gap between research and policy. Its success, or otherwise, has to be judged not only on the criterion of academic excellence but also on the contribution which it can make to the problems facing policy-makers and administrators. It is held that the purpose of urban and regional research is to increase our understanding of social and economic forces in order that policies can be developed to secure an improvement in economic functioning and in the quality of the social and physical environment. It is impossible to draw meaningful boundaries to this field of study. The Centre's role is to bring the skills of a variety of academics from a range of disciplines to bear on a number of selected issues. The subject of the first two volumes in this series—recreation—is one of these. Later volumes will deal with migration, housing, industrial location, urban renewal and urban and regional analysis.

Director, Centre for Urban and Regional Studies
University of Birmingham.

December 1969

Contents

11

Introduction

BY THOMAS L. BURTON

A great deal of attention has been given in recent years to the increasing amount of free time that is becoming available to a large majority of the population of this country. To novelists and playwrights it has presented an opportunity to extend the boundaries of creative imagination and fantasy. To government, at all levels, it has brought a wide range of planning and administrative problems, relating to such matters as the provision of car parks and picnic areas in the countryside, and sports pitches and libraries in the towns. To academics, especially those in the social sciences, it has presented an exciting new field of research and investigation. To almost all it appears, in some sense, as the new millennium—the age of leisure. No one has seriously suggested that we are living in a modern Utopia, in which all work is effectively automated while the population indulges its cultural, recreational and sporting whims. Far from it. But it is generally believed that Britain has reached a stage of technological, economic and social development which allows considerable periods of free time to the majority of the population. It is, moreover, a stage of development at which large sums of money are being invested in the construction of recreation facilities and increasing areas of land are being turned over to recreation uses. In this sense, we are living today in an age of leisure.

But despite this, there has been, until comparatively recently, very little attempt to assess the role that recreation plays within our society; and, in particular, to measure the different ways in which free time is used by the general population. It is true that, in the late nineteenth century, great concern was shown for the provision of public open space within our urban areas; but this was as much the consequence of a paternalist desire to create a better physical environment within the cities and towns as a result of the recognition of recreation needs. By and large, recreation has been considered by society in the past merely as, at best, a creative period of non-working time and, at worst, a period of idleness.

13

With, however, the rapid growth in levels of participation in recreation since the end of the Second World War, this attitude has changed significantly. Government attitudes to sport, for example, have undergone a major change during the past thirty years. The Physical Training and Recreation Act, 1937 was inspired largely by considerations of the social and political benefits of sport for the masses. Sport was chiefly valuable not as a form of recreation, but as an instrument in the training of character and a means of promoting social awareness. The creation of the Sports Council thirty years later, on the other hand, represented, in the words of P. C. McIntosh, 'a major breakaway from the idea of doing good to people and a step towards giving to the people what they wanted in the way of sport and recreation'.* This change of attitudes, which has been reflected not only in respect of sport but across the whole field of recreation, has resulted directly from the rapid increase during the past quarter of a century in the volume of available free time and the growth in the levels of participation in recreation pursuits.

Broadly, there are three main groups of forces which have caused this rapid growth in recreation activity. They are, firstly, physical and technological forces; secondly, institutional forces including certain elements that can be best described as the traditional; and thirdly, socio-economic forces. It would be folly to suggest that these three groups of forces have been operating wholly independently; and even greater folly to suggest that they should be considered independently in future planning for recreation. But, for simplicity of analysis, they may be examined separately.

Physical and Technological Forces

Physical and technological factors have been particularly important determinants of patterns of recreation activity; and, of these, the most significant has been the growth of improved forms of mass communications. This latter development has been along two lines: the movement of people—that is, im-

* P. C. McIntosh, *Sport in Society*, Watts, 1963. His phrase was not, in fact, used in reference to the creation of the Sports Council, but it is appropriate.

provements in methods of transportation; and the movement of information and ideas—that is, the development of the mass media.

Personal and family mobility has been, and still is, a key factor in shaping patterns of recreation. The construction of the railways in the second half of the nineteenth century introduced a degree of convenience, comfort and cheapness in travel, and a means of moving large numbers of people over relatively long distances, which had been previously impossible. It brought many of the fashionable seaside resorts within the reach of the middle classes and, ultimately, the industrial worker. In 1841, Thomas Cook arranged the first public excursion by rail—from Leicester to Loughborough. Ten years later, he organised the transport of hundreds of thousands of visitors from Yorkshire and the Midlands to the Great Exhibition in London. Today, the motor-car has largely taken over from the train: 'The chief value of the car lies in its flexibility in timing and use. The car-owning recreationist is free to drive through the countryside regardless of bus and train routes and schedules.'* A far greater amount of personal belongings can be carried in a car than could ever be taken on a bus or train. The car is, in effect, a room which can be detached from the home and moved away from the home environment, yet retaining many of the latter's important functions. This is especially true for families with young children and old people. But the essential flexibility of the car is not confined solely to excursions into the countryside. It has also proved to be an important element in urban recreation, especially at night when bus schedules tend to be very sparse.

What the train and the car have done for the development of patterns of recreation within Britain, the aeroplane and the ship are beginning to do for the development of international recreation. At present, this latter development is confined almost wholly to relatively small numbers of holidaymakers during the peak summer months. But recent years have witnessed a steady growth in the numbers of people going abroad for their annual holiday and, more significantly, in the numbers of people taking winter holidays abroad. (As was the case with Cook's excursions by rail in the nineteenth century, the improve-

* T. L. Burton, 'A Day in the Country', *Chartered Surveyor*, 98, 7, 1966.

ment in travel facilities is only one element in this development. The other is the organising expertise of travel agents and charter firms—the true descendants of Cook.)

Parallel with these improvements in mass transportation, there has been an equally significant development of communication through the mass media. A recent international study showed that the population of Britain reads more newspapers and magazines per head each day than in any other country in the world.* Even more significant has been the impact of radio, television and the telephone. The latter has proved to be an invaluable means of communication for government, business and private purposes. The radio and television have not only proved to be a means of widening the audiences for established recreation pursuits, such as concerts and plays; they have also stimulated entirely new pursuits, such as panel games, and have widened the dimensions of others, such as photography. Indeed, it has been suggested that they have become recreation pursuits in themselves: in Marshall McLuhan's now famous (or infamous) phrase, 'the medium *is* the message'.†

There are, of course, other physical and technological factors which have had pronounced effects upon the development of recreation activity. One of the most important of these has been the availability of natural resources—for example, mountains and lakes—and, more especially, their location in relation to major urban areas. The studies of outdoor recreation in the United States by the Outdoor Recreation Resources Review Commission (ORRRC) laid particular emphasis upon the location of resources as being a major determinant of recreation patterns: 'Public areas designated for outdoor recreation include one-eighth of the total land of the country, but . . . for reasons of location (or management) much of the vast acreage nominally designated for recreation is now not available for general public recreation use.'‡ In this country, one of our most valuable recreation resources is the coast, with its often striking

* National Publishers' Syndicate (France), unpublished study.

† M. McLuhan, *Understanding Media*, Routledge & Kegan Paul, 1964.

‡ ORRRC, *Outdoor Recreation for America*, US Government Printing Office, 1962.

visual contrasts over very short distances. Inland, there are the lakes, mountains, fells and moors of Scotland, the Lake District, Snowdonia, the Peak District, Exmoor, Dartmoor, Northumberland, the Norfolk Broads, and many others. The growth of mass transport by rail in the second half of the nineteenth century showed itself not least in the development of commercial seaside resorts, such as Southend, Margate and Blackpool. The rapid increase in the ownership of motor-cars during the past decade or so has shown itself equally strongly in the opening-up of the more remote coastal areas and the unique inland regions. These places have always existed; but the motor-car provides much greater ease of access to them than was previously possible.

Institutional Forces

The second group of forces affecting the development of patterns of recreation activity may be described, broadly, as institutional. One of the most important of these has been the law, which has acted as a powerful instrument in formalising the status of a wide range of recreation pursuits. Until quite recently, for example, many forms of gambling were prohibited by law; even now, the legalised forms are quite rigorously controlled. Similarly, the Laws of Sunday Observance, dating back to 1677, still prevent the development of many kinds of professional spectator sports on Sundays. On the positive side, the law has been instrumental in redistributing the balance of time between work and recreation—by a series of statutes which have defined maximum hours of work per week for various categories of workers (one of the earliest of these was the Coal Mines Act, 1842) and, more especially, by laws which guarantee the right of employees to receive various statutory holidays without loss of pay.

Another group of institutional forces consists of the major social organisations themselves—in particular, the Church and the Trade Unions. The Church was an important source of leisure time in the Middle Ages and later, through its designation of certain 'holy days' as non-working days, and by its celebration of major Christian festivals, such as Christmas,

Easter and Harvest Thanksgiving. Many of these festivals have continued into modern times, the statutory Bank Holidays being made to conform with them. The Trade Unions have been equally important. They have negotiated agreements with employers' federations and with individual employers which have provided shorter working hours per week, or longer periods of paid annual holiday, or, simply, increases in basic wage rates—all of which have had pronounced effects on the development of patterns of recreation.

Tradition, too, has been a significant factor. It has long been a tradition in this country, for example, that urban people should have access to large areas of common land and to the open countryside on a simple *de facto* basis, even though they may have no right of access in law. Likewise, the townsman has traditionally had access to public parks and open spaces within towns at no direct cost to himself. Where the law is obscure, tradition is the prime guide to behaviour. Again, in many industrial towns in the Midlands and the North it was customary for all factories and firms to give their employees an annual holiday at the same time, to coincide with the annual town festival—the Wakes Weeks. These had a particularly significant part in patterns of recreation activity; indeed, the importance of Wakes Week in many industrial towns has only declined very recently—as increasing numbers of people have begun to take their annual holiday away from home.

The influence of institutional forces has been seen most clearly in the change in the balance of time between work and recreation, and in the increase in the amount of money that people have had available for recreation purposes. Although the State, at both central and local level, has provided an increasing number of different kinds of recreation facilities, it has also been instrumental in increasing general leisure time, by means of statutes and, occasionally, bye-laws. Similarly, the Trade Unions have systematically increased the amount of leisure time available to their members and have steadily improved basic wages, often through strikes and other industrial action. As a result of these various forces, the length of the average working week in Britain has fallen by about a half in the last century.

Socio-economic Forces

Socio-economic forces have been of three main kinds: demo-graphic factors, income and occupation, and education. The chief demographic factors are age, sex and family structure. The *Pilot National Recreation Survey* in 1965 suggested that these factors are particularly significant in determining the *kinds* and *volume* of recreation pursuits in which people take part.* Together with the American studies of outdoor recreation activity, in 1960 and 1965,† it provides a detailed source of data concerning the relationships between patterns of recreation and socio-economic characteristics. The studies showed that age is the most significant factor of all—particularly for recreation out-of-doors. Maximum participation in outdoor pursuits takes place between the ages of about 18 and 25 years; thereafter, participation tends to decline progressively with age (with one or two notable exceptions—for example, outdoor bowls). This pattern is much less rigid for indoor pursuits, where, as might be expected, participation in some pursuits rises significantly in later years. Sex and family structure appear to have much less effect upon *levels* of participation and much greater effect upon the *types* of pursuits in which people take part.

Income and occupation also have pronounced effects. Income is particularly significant in view of the possibility of sub-stantial increases in levels of personal disposable incomes in Britain during the next twenty years or so. The relationship between income levels and patterns of recreation is not, how-ever, a simple one: 'Certainly, some very expensive pastimes are the monopoly of the wealthy, but many cheap pursuits (not all of them physically demanding) are largely ignored by the lower income groups.'‡ To this it may be added that some low-cost pursuits, such as hill-walking, are highly favoured by high-income groups. But despite these peculiarities, the available data do suggest a strong correlation between income and recreation. Broadly, as income rises so does participation in most recreation

* British Travel Association/University of Keele, *Pilot National Recreation Survey-Report No. 1*, 1967.

† ORRRC, op. cit. *and* Bureau of Outdoor Recreation, US Department of the Interior, *The 1965 Survey of Outdoor Recreation Activities*, unpublished.

‡ *Pilot National Recreation Survey*, op. cit.

pursuits—at least up to a level of about £2,000 per annum. What the data do not show, however, is whether this relationship reflects, primarily, the influence of money as such; or whether leisure patterns are also strongly related to social status. A glance at the evidence suggests that some of the differences between income groups may be attributable to other social status characteristics, particularly occupation, which are closely linked with income.

Education also shows a strong direct relationship with leisure patterns. Levels of education reflect, in part, age factors, since persons with minimal education tend to be the older members of society, for whom compulsory formal education ended at an earlier age than is generally true now. Certainly, the opportunities for these people to undertake further education after leaving school were much more restricted than they are now; and the available data show a clear relationship between further education, especially full-time, and the degree of participation in many recreation activities. People who have received formal education beyond the age of 15 years tend to participate more often in a wider range of activities than those who have not.

Technological, institutional and socio-economic forces have, together and separately, had a significant influence upon the development of patterns of recreation in Britain during the past century. It is difficult to follow, except in general terms, the developments that took place in the years leading up to the Second World War. We know that the last quarter of the nineteenth century witnessed a remarkable growth in day excursions by rail to the rapidly developing coastal resorts. This trend has continued up to the present. The years between the two world wars witnessed a sustained growth in urban recreation and an increase in the practice of giving holidays with pay to employees. Theatres and concert halls were important sources of entertainment in the years before the First World War, but they were patronised largely by the wealthy and upper middle-classes. The music hall was an equivalent attraction for the working-class. In the 1920s and 1930s, however, there was a rapid expansion in the provision of dance halls and cinemas, the latter in particular catering for a much wider cross-section of the population.

It is only with the period since the end of the Second World War, however, that it is possible to be more specific about developments. It has been during this period that recreation has become a major preoccupation within our society. This has shown itself in many different ways: for example, in the increasing share of national income being devoted to entertainment, in the now familiar traffic jams on the roads leading to the coastal resorts on summer Sundays, and in the increasing attention being devoted to recreational problems by politicians, planners and academics alike. Yet, attitudes change but slowly. Recreation is still a 'not-quite-respectable' field of study in many of our universities. The dictum of the Reith Committee on New Towns is still very appropriate: 'that vulgarity need not be the companion of large scale recreation is insufficiently understood in this country'.* We have begun to consider the tip of the iceberg, but there is much yet to be examined beneath the surface.

This book brings together some of the pioneering work that has been undertaken in response to the problems that have arisen from the growth of mass recreation. Its central philosophy is that research and planning are mutually dependent activities in Man's attempt to fashion his environment so as to obtain the greatest possible benefit from the increased leisure that social, economic, technological, biological and medical progress have made available to him. In an age of intense and increasing competitive demands for land and natural resources for a variety of purposes—housing, industry, roads, schools and hospitals, agriculture, forestry and recreation—the need for planning is essential. But planning, without adequate knowledge of the needs and desires of society, is rather like the provision of houses without plumbing—it can be done, but the consequences are likely to be disastrous! Planning, if it is to be a positive force in shaping our environment, requires research. Research, if it is to be something more than an academic extravagance, requires a purpose—to serve as a basis for planning.

It would, of course, have been impossible to include all the recent papers and articles that have been written on the subject of recreation. Clearly, some process of selection had to be made.

* *Final Report of the Reith Committee on New Towns*, HMSO, 1946.

The objective has been, therefore, to include papers which have developed major innovations in concept or approach, or which have demonstrated the essential inter-relationship between research and planning. At the same time, however, an attempt has been made to cover as wide a spectrum of the recreational environment as possible. Hence, attention has been given to urban areas, the countryside, holidaymaking and tourism, recreation administration, and so on. Some of the papers consist of reprints of articles previously published in professional and academic journals and some consist of previously unpublished papers. Most, however, have been specially written for publication in this collection. The result has been to provide a comprehensive overview of current research and planning, but by means of examples rather than a general review.

The collection has been divided into four parts. Part One, entitled 'Demand for Recreation', consists of a single chapter which traces current trends in patterns of recreation activity in Britain. The material has been drawn from a wide range of sources, including many recent national and local research studies.

Part Two, 'Recreation Research', has four chapters. The first outlines a framework for future recreation research and includes a discussion of the problems encountered in attempting to establish an overall policy for recreation research in this country. The second and third chapters tackle two general areas of current research. The first of these considers the field of sociological research in recreation, drawing attention to particular problems encountered in attempting to measure need and opportunity. This is followed, in Chapter 4, by a critical examination of a current and controversial issue concerning the provision of recreation facilities by public authorities—the economic values in relation to the social benefits. The focus of attention here is particularly upon the role that cost–benefit analysis techniques might play in the formulation of recreational investment policies by public authorities. The final chapter in this part of the collection serves as a link with the planning section which is to follow. It considers the ways in which recreation research can usefully serve planning bodies and draws upon the experiences of the author in undertaking research for a local planning authority.

Part Three, 'Planning for Recreation', also has four chapters. The first two, Chapters 6 and 7, consider the problems of planning from an areal viewpoint—considering, respectively, planning in the countryside and in urban areas. In the first chapter emphasis is placed wholly upon the role of the motor-car in countryside recreation and the problems of accessibility to rural areas for urban dwellers. The following chapter devotes its attention to the planning of one particular kind of recreation facility in urban areas—open space—and utilises an experimental method for assessing needs. The remaining two chapters in this part concentrate upon very specific, though quite different, aspects of recreation planning. Chapter 8 examines the problems of planning for tourism, one of the most rapidly growing problems in recreation planning at the present time. Chapter 9, taking a very different tack, outlines the current division of responsibilities for the planning and provision of recreation facilities, as between central government departments, *ad hoc* public and semi-public authorities, local government, voluntary groups and commercial organisations of many kinds.

The final part of the collection is entitled 'Contemporary Issues in Planning for Recreation' and has three chapters. The first of these gives a very personal view of the current controversy about the 'quality' of recreation. The author discusses the issues that arise in arguments about whether planning should be concerned with the provision of the facilities that people want (always assuming that these can be ascertained) or those that it is good for them to have—those which will, in some way, make them 'better' people. This is followed by a chapter which discusses the relationships between various public and voluntary organisations concerned with the provision of recreation facilities. It follows logically upon the discussion begun in Chapter 9 (Part Three) by suggesting changes in the current responsibilities for the provision of facilities. Finally, in the last chapter, the editor takes a highly personal look at the problems of forecasting future patterns of recreation activity. Emphasis is placed upon the current lack of objective methods of forecasting and the consequent need for informed judgments about future trends on the part of planners and research workers. It ends with a cautious look into a crystal ball!

Part One

Demand For Recreation

Chapter 1

Current Trends in Recreation Demands

THOMAS L. BURTON

The years since about 1950 have witnessed five main trends in
the patterns of recreation in Britain: first, a greater interest in
cultural pursuits; second, a growth of social recreation—that is,
groups of people spending an evening dining out or drinking
together, or at parties; third, increased participation in sports
and physical recreation, together with a relative decline in the
popularity of many spectator sports; fourth, increased use of
the countryside for leisure, reflecting, in part, greater participation in outdoor pursuits generally; and, fifth, a substantial
increase in the proportion of the population taking an annual
holiday away from home—resulting in the growth of a large
and economically important holiday and tourist industry within
the country. There have been, of course, other developments,
such as the 'pop music revolution'; but, by and large, these can
be included within these five main trends or else they are of
relatively minor significance. Each of these trends will be considered in detail in the remainder of this chapter.

The Arts

For much of the population of Britain, an interest in culture and
the Arts is identified with class or social status. To many, a
concern with the Arts is a characteristic of upper-class and
professional people; they are presumed to be of little interest to
the working-class. This attitude is understandable; for interest
in cultural pursuits is closely related to levels of education and,
until quite recently, formal education above a very elementary
standard was confined largely to people in the upper strata of
society. As little as fifty years ago, the child of professional
parents could expect to receive a thorough and detailed formal

education, while the child of a skilled or unskilled worker was likely to receive, at best, some basic primary schooling and, at worst, no formal education at all. Today, this pattern is radically changed. Primary and secondary education is now compulsory for all children up to the age of 15 years. Moreover, opportunities to continue formal education up to, and beyond, the age of 18 years, while not unlimited, have been increased substantially in recent years. Again, there has been a rapid increase in the opportunities available for adults to undertake further education in a wide range of studies, by means of courses on radio and television, correspondence courses and, more particularly, evening classes at institutes of further education and university extra-mural departments.

There is little doubt that education provides a greater impetus to appreciation of the Arts than any other social or economic characteristic: 'The place that the Arts occupy in the life of the nation is largely a reflection of the time and effort devoted to them in schools and colleges.'[1] There has been, in recent years, a marked upsurge of interest in all cultural pursuits, at both the professional and amateur levels, among young people who have received more (and wider) formal secondary education than did their parents. But, because of this close relationship between formal education and interest in the Arts, it is important to distinguish between participation in cultural pursuits generally and participation in them for leisure purposes. The Arts can be imposed upon people, as when they are included in schools' curricula, or they can be chosen freely. It is the latter which is relevant to a discussion of leisure, not the former; although, of course, compulsory education in the Arts can lead to an interest which is carried on during leisure time. What, then, are the Arts, and which of them can be considered as leisure pursuits?

Culture may be defined, broadly, as the training and refinement of the mind, tastes and manners; in other words, it has to do with the 'style' of life and, in particular, with intellectual elements in life. For many people, it has come to mean something much wider than this—the whole civilisation, or the pattern of attitudes and values that make up society, or the way in which society as a whole behaves. Thus, we often hear mention of the *American Culture* or the *French Culture* or the *Chinese Culture*.

In a sense, this definition is reasonable: for the attitudes and values of society are, in large measure, reflected in its tastes and manners. But, in another sense, it is too sociological. It stretches the meaning of culture beyond matters of the mind, tastes and manners, to include the organisation and structure of society— the machinery through which values and attitudes are expressed. For present purposes, therefore, culture is given its narrow meaning; and cultural recreation pursuits, or the Arts, consist only of those pursuits which involve the training and refinement of the mind, tastes and manners, when undertaken freely during a person's spare time. They include participation in, or attendance at, concerts, plays, art exhibitions, operas and ballets. Depending upon one's views about *quality* and *standards*, they may also include films, television, pop music and books.

There are two main factors which appear to have stimulated increased interest in the Arts, and in cultural pursuits generally, during the past decade or so: rising income levels and higher standards of education. Broadly, the cost of participation in cultural pursuits is higher than for comparable non-cultural leisure pursuits. The cost of admission to a theatre or concert hall is, on average, greater than that for a dance hall or skating rink (the cinema is an exception to this). A number of British and American studies have shown that the proportion of people who go regularly to plays, concerts, lectures and art exhibitions rises rapidly with increasing income. Interest is negligible in the lowest income groups, but rises very steeply at the top of the income scale.

A similar contrast is found when participation is related to levels of education. In 1955, the number of people over the age of 15 years who were still undergoing full-time education, at school, college or university, was less than half a million. By 1965, the figure had doubled to just over one million; and it is estimated that it may easily double again in the next twenty years.[2] It is these people who are showing the greatest interest in cultural pursuits at the present time: 'In recent years, thanks largely to the patronage and participation of younger people who have enjoyed wider and more secondary education than their parents, there has been a marked upsurge of interest in all the arts, at both the professional and amateur level, both in

RECREATION RESEARCH AND PLANNING

Table 1.1 *Some statistics for the arts*

Cinema attendances	1956	1,101 million
	1966	290 million
	1967	265 million
Numbers of television licences	1955	4·5 million
	1968	15·0 million
Loans of books from public libraries	1955	305 million
	1965	530 million
	1967	590 million
Sales of gramophone records	1960	c. 72 million
	1967	c. 96 million

Sources:
1. J. Barr, 'Free Time Britain', *New Society*, April 15, 1965.
2. British Film Institute. Private communication.
3. British Broadcasting Corporation. Private communication.

audiences and performers.'[3] This relationship with education also largely explains the strong correlation between interest in cultural pursuits and age. Interest is undoubtedly greatest among young people below the age of about 25 years. These are, of course, the people in society who, on average, have received the longest and widest education. If it were possible to be sure that interest would continue for these people into middle age, the prospects for the Arts would be, at once, both exhilarating and somewhat forbidding.

Social Recreation

There is very little that can be said with firm conviction about the second major trend in patterns of recreation during the past two decades—the growth of participation in social recreation. The habit of dining out, or visiting the pub, or going to parties in private homes has remained largely unexplored in research studies of recreation habits. Empirical observation suggests that these are becoming increasingly popular pursuits. But, with a

30

few exceptions, there is very little objective evidence either to support or to refute this view.

Figures of national income and expenditure show that the volume and proportion of family income that is spent on alcoholic drinks has increased slightly during the past decade. In 1968, the proportion was about 5 per cent—that is, about 11 shillings per head per week.[4] The annual per capita consumption is currently about 200 pints of beer, 44 nips of whisky, 48 nips of other spirits, 8 glasses of wine, and 15 glasses of sherry. Of course, some of this is consumed in private homes, but most of it is drunk in public houses and licensed restaurants. In fact, a number of market research surveys have indicated that an increasing number of people spend an evening dining out on an increasing number of occasions each year.[5] This trend is particularly noticeable among middle-income families and among young people between the ages of about 18 and 25 years. It is also most popular among persons with university or college education.

The pattern which emerges from the limited data available is fragmentary and can be assessed only in very broad terms. It is a pattern of people who are gregarious, but only in relatively small groups and in a highly unorganised fashion. It is a pattern which is likely to extend in scope as more people find that they have a larger proportion of their incomes available for leisure spending. It is, moreover, a pattern which fits into the general thesis that people are increasingly preferring to take their leisure in small, often home-centred groups and to spend it in unorganised activities. The general indication is that the numbers of people engaging in these 'social' leisure pursuits will increase substantially in the immediate future.

Participation in Sport and Physical Recreation

Physical games and competitions of one kind and another have figured prominently in religious, social and political life for more than 3,000 years. The Olympic Games in Ancient Greece were an intrinsic part of the festival of Zeus, King of the Gods. Sport in Victorian England fitted in well with social and industrial concepts of intense, though scrupulously fair, rivalry and com-

31

petition. In modern Russia, there is total acceptance of the view that sport and politics are closely interrelated. Sport is, there, used widely as a vehicle for political education. Economics, too, has been of considerable importance in shaping patterns of sport. The first sporting associations in Britain—The Alpine Club (1859), the Football Association (1863) and the Amateur Athletic Club (1866)—drew their membership almost exclusively from the middle-class, those whose economic position and working conditions made it possible for them to engage in sports and other leisure pursuits regularly. Working-class participation did not come till rather later—when the Saturday half-holiday became general practice throughout a wider sector of industry.

Attitudes, too, have varied widely within society. For many people, sport is an end in itself, a means whereby Man can express some of his ideals and aspirations. For these people, sport needs no further justification. For others, however, it is chiefly valuable as a means to other ends: an instrument in the training of character, perhaps; or a method of maintaining a reasonably fit paramilitary force. An enduring feature of British attitudes to sport has been a sustained streak of puritanism. The Laws of Sunday Observance, 1677 and 1871, have endured to the present time, and still prevent the development of much professional sport on Sundays. The debates during the passage of the Physical Training and Recreation Bill through Parliament in 1936 also displayed the puritan attitudes within government—but of a different kind. Considerable stress was laid upon the social and political benefits of sport, little on its leisure and recreative aspects. The benefits would be, as P. C. McIntosh has so aptly put it, 'improvement and discipline rather than unalloyed enjoyment'.[6] Health, fitness and social morality were the prime considerations.

One of the key elements in the development of sport has been the growth of a strong division between the professional and the amateur sectors, and, with it, the distinction between the participant and the spectator. This development has gone farthest in the case of association football. In 1882, the Football Association forbade payments to players, other than expenses and any wages actually lost. Three years later, in 1885, this rule was revoked and the professional game was legalised and brought under the control of the Association. The Rugby Union took entirely the opposite approach. Payments to players were banned completely, offending clubs being expelled from the Union. As a result, there are, today, two distinct rugby associations—the wholly amateur Rugby Union and the professional Rugby League.

Closely associated with the development of distinctions between the amateur and the professional has been the growth of a division between spectators and participants. The professionals attracted to their ranks the majority of top-class players—with one or two notable exceptions. Soon, the professional teams so far outclassed the amateurs that competition between the two became fruitless. In time, separate competitions grew up for the two sets of teams. The advent of the regular Saturday half-holiday brought, at about the same time, growing numbers of people whose main interest in sports was in watching them. These people naturally tended to watch those players who were considered to be the best in the locality; and this meant the professionals. So there grew up the pattern of large crowds of spectators at major professional competitions on Saturday afternoons. This tendency was particularly apparent in the case of association football where attendances at the Football League matches rose to a peak of one million spectators each week during the season 1948-9. Attendances have declined steadily since that season—although the staging of the World Cup competition in England in 1966 appears to have halted this decline, and even, perhaps, to have reversed it a little. In the current season (1968-9), attendances have averaged about 650,000 persons per week. The trend towards large crowds of spectators was also evident in Rugby League football, horse racing and greyhound racing (the latter two providing the additional attraction of gambling facilities).

For many years, the chief sporting interests of both spectators and participants lay in team games, especially association football, rugby, cricket and, to a lesser extent, hockey. But there has been a steady growth of interest in individual and small-group sports, such as swimming, athletics, tennis, skating and golf, particularly during the past decade or so. But, even with these

c

sports, there has been the tendency to channel competition into a team framework. Thus, club matches in tennis and swimming, for example, are based upon teams rather than upon the individuals who make up these teams. Indeed, in tennis, the matches have been formalised into a series of 'rubbers' in which each individual or pair in one club plays, in turn, against each individual or pair from the other club.

The major development in recent years has been in the numbers of people participating in sports rather than watching them, and in the range of sports in which they participate. Age has been, by far, the most significant characteristic affecting

Table 1.2 *Numbers of amateur clubs affiliated to selected National Sporting bodies in Britain, at various dates*

Amateur Athletic Association	1960	1,350
	1968	1,120
Amateur Fencing Association	1960	410
	1968	638
Badminton Association of England	1966	761
	1968	2,800
Football Association	1961	22,685
	1965	25,217
Royal Yachting Association	1960	1,011
	1968	1,491

Sources: Private communications with the various organisations.

this. Participation is concentrated almost exclusively among young people—the only major exceptions being golf, which is very much a pursuit of the middle aged, and outdoor bowls, which is particularly strong among retired people. This relationship is, perhaps, strongest for organised team games and tennis; although not, of course, among people who watch these sports but do not play them. Water sports, too, are largely the province of the young. An exception here is powerboat sailing which draws considerable support from people in the age group 45–64 years—no doubt reflecting, in part, income variations. Among minority sports, only outdoor bowls and, to a lesser extent, horse riding are sports which attract significant numbers from middle-aged and older people.

There is, also, an interesting relationship between levels of participation in sports and income. High incomes are associated with high levels of participation in almost every sport; but this is particularly true for water sports, such as underwater swimming and water skiing, for golf and for many minority sports. The relationship is not, however, based solely upon costs of participation. Indeed, some of the cheapest sports—for example, swimming and organised team games like hockey—are very strongly associated with high income groups.[7] There seem to be two elements here. Firstly, it is clear that participation in sport and physical recreation generally—indeed, in leisure pursuits generally—tends to increase with rising incomes. Most British and American studies have found this to be true. Secondly, there seems to be an element of status involved, linked in part to standards of education. Many sports, such as swimming and tennis, seem to have a high income and high educational status.

The general tendency for participation in sports to decline with increasing age reflects, in large measure, the physical effort demanded of participants and, often, the discomfort and, even, pain associated with this. But there is, also, a direct relationship between levels of participation during leisure time and the degree of 'compulsion' that individuals attach to certain sports. It is rare for sports taught at school to survive long into adult life, except in those cases where the individual has considerable ability. Athletics, tennis and many team sports, for example, suffer a definite loss of interest among adults which is, in part, associated with an identification of these as compulsory school sports. Several studies of the leisure interests of post-school teenagers and young adults have detected this element in attitudes to sport.[8]

Despite considerations of this kind, however, it is clear that sport is a significant and enduring part of leisure patterns in Britain. Contrary to popular belief, organised team games are not losing participants at a rapid rate. On the other hand, many minority sports are attracting more and more adherents. Interest in sport is clearly widening as more 'new' sports are discovered and more people take part in minority sports. There is no indication that interest is decreasing. On the contrary, there are firm grounds for believing that total participation, in terms both of numbers of participants and the amount of time devoted to sport, is rising, and will probably continue to do so in the immediate future.

Countryside Recreation

The fourth significant trend in patterns of recreation during the past two decades has been the increase in the use of the country-side for leisure. Since at least the Middle Ages the British countryside has served as a setting for recreation. But it is only since the turn of the present century that it has come to provide a setting for the pursuits of more than a privileged group within the community; and it is only since about 1950 that it has begun to attract large numbers of the general population. For many years the use of the countryside for leisure remained the privilege of the ruling classes, many of whose activities were exclusive. Thus, general public access to game forests, grouse moors and pheasant grounds was severely restricted by statutes and bye-laws, while restrictive convenants were often applied to fishing areas. This exclusive system has weakened a little during the past fifty years, but hunting, shooting and fishing still remain heavily restricted in many parts of the country. What has changed, however, has been the use of the countryside for other kinds of recreation pursuits.

The years between the two world wars witnessed a slow but unmistakeable growth in the use of the countryside for recreation by the townsman—individually and in groups. Hikers, ramblers and climbers became familiar sights in the countryside during these years. But, in absolute numbers, such people constituted a very small section of the community (although not one which was consciously restricted in class or status terms). Since the end of the Second World War, however, there has been another change. Opportunities for visiting the countryside have now become available to millions, and are no longer the

36

Table 1.3   *The traditional use of the countryside*

Organisation	Year	Membership
1. Youth Hostels Association	1950	210,142
	1960	181,958
	1968	217,842
2. Scottish Youth Hostels Association	1950	37,089
	1960	37,202
	1968	37,825
3. Camping Club of Great Britain	1950	12,000
	1960	48,000
	1968	113,000
4. Boy Scouts (UK)	1950	471,467
	1960	588,396
	1968	530,919
5. Ramblers' Association	1951	9,812
	1960	11,300
	1968	19,000

Sources: Private communications with each organisation.

possession of the favoured few: 'The countryside is being discovered by a new kind of visitor—the car-borne city-dweller, breaking away from his often restrictive urban environment for a day or an afternoon at the weekend.' This has brought a new intensity of recreational movement into the countryside, and new forms of recreational activity which are increasingly superseding the older, established pursuits in terms of their impact upon agriculture, forestry and other productive activities. To the traditional users of the countryside—the hill walkers, youth hostellers, climbers, hikers and horse riders—have been added the car-borne day trippers, coming in large numbers, congregating at well-known beauty spots within fairly close radii of their homes, and relying heavily upon their cars to supplement their recreational needs. In total numbers, these new users far outweigh the others. They make substantial

Table 1.4 *Leisure activities at Box Hill and Berkhamsted Common, 1964*

	Box Hill (per cent)	Berkhamsted Common (per cent)
1. Sitting in the car	17	18
2. Sitting/picnicking by a car	50	55
3. Playing/walking near a car	6	5
CAR-CENTRED ACTIVITIES	73	78
4. Picnicking away from a car	6	3
5. Sitting/walking away from a car	33	14
6. Other activities	*	5
Total replies	112	100
Total interviews	100	100

* Less than one per cent.

Sources:
1. T. L. Burton, 'A Day in the Country: A survey of Leisure Activity at Box Hill', *Chartered Surveyor*, 98, 7, 1966.
2. J. F. Wager, 'How Common is the Land? *New Society*, July 20, 1964.

demands for parking space, toilet accommodation and picnic areas. Moreover, since their numbers appear to be directly related to the ownership of cars, which is expected to increase rapidly in the next decade or so, there is every likelihood that their numbers will increase substantially in the immediate future.

Holidaymaking and Tourism

The fifth major development in recreation patterns since the end of the Second World War is, perhaps, the most well-documented of all. The habit of taking an annual holiday away from home has grown substantially during the past twenty years. Three in five of the population went away for a holiday in 1964, twice the figure for the years immediately preceding the war.[10] The practice of taking short additional holidays, as well as

Table 1.5   *Holiday trends in Britain 1955, 1964 and 1968*

	1955	1964	1968
		(millions)	
Number of main holidays taken away from home but within Britain:	23·5	26·0	26·0
Number of additional holidays taken away from home but within Britain:	2·0	5·0	4·0
Number of *all* holidays taken abroad:	2·0	5·0	5·0

Sources: British Travel Association, *Home Holiday Surveys.*

weekend trips at Christmas, Easter and other Bank Holiday periods, has also increased significantly, at least until 1964 (although there appears to have been a slight fall in numbers in 1968, probably associated with the economic restrictions in operation in that year). The majority of people stick to tradition and spend their holidays at coastal resorts in Britain, but there are growing numbers who venture abroad and to more remote places within this country. This is particularly so among young people: over one-third of all holidaymakers going abroad in 1968 were below the age of 30. One of the key factors in this development has been the growth in the provision of inclusive tours.

Within Britain, developments have been closely associated with the rapid increase in car ownership which has taken place during the past decade. The car has provided the holidaymaker with increased mobility and flexibility, giving rise, in part, to the growth of camping and caravan holidays and the touring holiday, and leading to the development of well-defined holiday regions. The increase in levels of car ownership has also tended to reduce the popularity of the established holiday in a single seaside resort, replacing it with the mobile touring holiday. This latter trend is still a relatively minor one, however, and the developed coastal resorts remain the basic element in patterns of holidaymaking.

Differences in income levels and occupations do not seem to have a significant effect on the taking of holidays. As early as 1955, there were almost as many weekly wage earners going for holidays abroad as there were people in professional and

39

salaried clerical occupations—although, proportionately, there were more of the latter. Where occupation does seem to have an effect, however, is in the timing of holidays. There has been no significant change in the proportion of holidays taken in the peak summer months during the past decade or so. Two-thirds of all holidays are taken in July and August each year. But, for manual workers alone, this proportion rises to about three-quarters; while, for salaried persons, it is about a half.

Perhaps the most significant development since 1951 has been the growth in the numbers of people taking second holidays each year. From approximately $1\frac{1}{2}$ million in 1954, the figure rose to about $4\frac{1}{2}$ million ten years later. There seems little doubt that this trend will continue in the immediate future.

The overall picture which emerges is, then, one of a fairly constant total number of holidaymakers, but who are becoming increasingly mobile as car ownership rises and dependence upon public transport declines; greater numbers of whom are venturing abroad; more of whom are visiting the South and West of Britain, in particular the Cornish peninsula; more of whom are demanding flexible holiday arrangements in the form of camping and caravan accommodation; and more of whom take second holidays each year. In short, the numbers of holidaymakers remain fairly constant, but the numbers of holidays taken continue to grow and patterns of holidaymaking are experiencing significant changes.

Conclusion and Comment

This survey of current trends in recreation demands has, of necessity, been fairly general. The subject merits treatment at much greater depth. Nevertheless, the picture is sufficiently clear to show the major lines along which recreation patterns are developing. The implications of these trends for physical, economic and social planning are substantial. They lead to problems about priorities in the allocation of scarce land and financial resources in the conurbations; to debate and argument about social priorities in the New Towns; to concern about the economic and social well-being of underdeveloped rural areas—such as the Highlands of Scotland—which have been subjected to sudden and intense tourist development; and so on. Some of these problems will be considered in the following chapters of this book. They are beyond the immediate scope of this chapter. Instead, it will be appropriate to conclude this discussion with a brief consideration of the need for recreation planning. Why, it may reasonably be asked, should we plan for recreation at all? If recreation is made up essentially of activities undertaken freely during people's spare time, the whole conception of *planning* for this defeats its purpose. Nobody wishes to be told what they may and may not do with their free time (granted always that they stay within the bounds of the law). This is, of course, an extreme view of planning, and *planning for recreation* would not be remotely concerned with telling people what they may do with their spare time. But all planning implies *control*— and planning for recreation would be no exception. And there is no doubt that control, however slight, of one's leisure time is an apparent contradiction in terms. Why, then, should we plan for leisure?

The short answer is, of course, that it has been forced upon us by circumstances. The tremendous growth in the population of Britain during the past fifty years, the rapid increase in standards of living, the rise in the numbers of private cars in use have all combined to place tremendous pressures upon land and other resources. There is now a fierce competition for land for a wide range of alternative uses—housing, industry, roads, schools and hospitals, recreation, forestry and, not least, agriculture. If all of these competing uses are to be reconciled, and sufficient land is to be made available for each, then some form of planning is essential.

The short answer is, however, misleading. There are very strong *positive* reasons for planning for recreation. Some of our most beautiful countryside areas, for example, derive much of their recreational value from the fact that they are (relatively) wild and uninhabited. The rapid expansion in the ownership of motor-cars means that many of these areas, such as the Lake District and Snowdonia, are now within easy access of very large numbers of people. If some planning is not undertaken to absorb the growing numbers of visitors into these areas, at least visually, then, by sheer weight of numbers, they could destroy

41

the very qualities that attracted them to the areas—remoteness and loneliness. On a different level, many recreation facilities within cities and towns require the investment of very large capital sums; for example, sports halls and ice rinks. Frequently, these facilities are provided by local government authorities and are totally uneconomic to operate. In such circumstances, it is obvious that the authorities should not waste their resources in providing facilities which will not be adequately used (as when, say, there is a similar facility in the area of a neighbouring authority which is of a sufficient size to cater for the population of both areas). In short, then, the case for planning for recreation is that, if carried through successfully it will provide a better overall provision of facilities for leisure.

Notes and References

1. White Paper, *A Policy for the Arts*, Cmnd. 2601, HMSO, London, 1965.
2. *Report of the Committee on Higher Education* (The Robbins Report), HMSO, London, 1964.
3. White Paper, *A Policy for the Arts*, op. cit.
4. Central Statistical Office, *National Income and Expenditure, 1968*, HMSO, London, 1968.
5. Garland–Compton Ltd., *Tomorrow's Leisurbia*, London, 1963.
6. P. C. McIntosh, *Sport in Society*, Watts, London, 1963.
7. British Travel Association/University of Keele, *Pilot National Recreation Survey: Report No. 1*, British Travel Association, 1967.
8. E.g. University of Manchester, Department of Physical Education. *Preliminary Report on a Study in the South East Lancashire Conurbation of Post-School Adolescent's Leisure Activities Particularly in the Field of Physical Activities*, unpublished typescript, 1967.
9. T. L. Burton, 'A Day in the Country: *Chartered Surveyor*, 98, 7, 1966.
10. British Travel Association, *Home Holiday Surveys*, for 1955, 1960 and annually since then.

Part Two

Recreation Research

Chapter 2

A Framework for Recreation Research

D. D. MOLYNEUX

During the last fifteen years in Britain, and particularly throughout the 1960s, there has developed an increasing awareness of the need for recreation research, a response from individuals, units, departments and organisations to undertake it and efforts from statutory and other bodies to co-ordinate and integrate programmes of research in recognisable and manageable sectors of the total recreation field. The major source of initial interest stemmed from an increasing consciousness by planning authorities and conservationists of recreation pressures on the countryside by an increasingly mobile society. During the early 1960s a number of local and regional studies began to emerge. These dealt with recreational pressures on the countryside, tourism and recreation, the growth of water-based recreation on inland waters, and other subjects. The impressive volume of research from the American Outdoor Recreation Resources Review Commission was an undoubted stimulus to many individuals and organisations in Britain who were interested and concerned with problems of countryside (and town) recreation.

The last five years have seen not only a continuing growth in the number and variety of recreation projects but the establishment of teams within university departments, government departments and agencies, and private organisations devoted to research in recreation. Legislation has established clear responsibilities for the conduct of research programmes, including recreation research for a number of statutory bodies, notably the Countryside Commission, the Water Resources Board, the Forestry Commission and the British Waterways Board. Other government agencies, such as the Sports Council and the British Travel Association, have also assumed new responsibilities for recreation research. There have been notable successes in establishing registers of current and recent recreation research, data banks and other information services, and conceptual exercises from which to establish a framework of desirable research in the complex field of recreation.

But despite these considerable achievements, there is still a need to consider all that is involved in establishing a total framework for recreation research embracing all activities, whether urban or rural, which increasingly interest and involve a modern society.

Further, there is a need to review continually the dilemma which faces those who are working in recreation research. The pure researcher, conscious of the total complexity of the factors surrounding the supply and demand for recreation and of the need to grasp the 'prickly nettle' of predicting for its future provision, pleads for time to undertake a wide-ranging programme of research. The planner and the administrator, however, are faced with decisions which must be taken now. Within total land-use allocation, what is the range of recreation facilities which is required? Where should they be sited, to what scale and in what relationship to other types of recreation provision? How should they be financed and administered? The two fundamental needs have to be reconciled. Whilst pressing forward a long-term programme of work which leads to a fuller understanding of the basic factors involved in recreation demand, some answers are required quickly, though more finite answers can only be expected over a period of years.

This chapter has two parts. The first endeavours to describe the various elements which together make up the pattern of recreation demand and supply. A number of questions are posed for which comprehensive answers are required if future planning for recreation is to be truly effective. The second part considers the organisational framework which currently exists for promoting recreation research and discusses possible ways in which it might be improved.

It will be useful at the outset to outline some of the main factors involved in a fuller understanding of the problem. First there is need to clarify our terms. Throughout this essay the term 'recreation' is here given a more precise meaning than in the Introduction to this book; it is taken to mean *purposeful activity*. It is not seen as being entirely synonymous with the term 'leisure'. Leisure can best be regarded as the time available to a person after requirements of sleeping, eating, earning one's living, travelling and basic social and household duties have been met. Recreation centres on activity; leisure is best seen as a component of time. Recreation outside the home, whether taken individually or as a member of a family unit, group, club or society, exerts physical demands in terms of facilities and the use of land. In the urban environment, besides parks, pleasure grounds, sports grounds, allotments and other areas of open space, there is a range of general and specialist indoor facilities —concert halls, libraries, theatres, swimming pools, sports halls, meeting-rooms, museums, workshops, art galleries and so on. Recreation in the countryside exerts a further range of demands —for car parking space, picnic areas, country parks, scenic routes and viewing points; camping and caravan sites; footpaths and bridle-paths; nature trails, field centres, hides and refuges; areas for motor sports and air sports; marinas, boathouses and facilities generally for the fastest-growing band of active recreational pursuits, water-based sports. What are the determinants of supply and demand which can be isolated for the purposes of analysis, but which each act on the other in terms of choice of recreation activity?

Recreation Demand

First, there is the factor of periods of available recreation time, whether evening, half day, whole day, weekend or longer periods, which can be termed holidays. The length of each period of recreation time is more important in determining the choice of activity than the total non-working time in a year; the prevalence of shift working or the staggering of working hours affects the distribution of the working population's total opportunities for recreation. The breadwinner's hours of work may conflict with the leisure time available for other members of the family or the circle in which the individual moves.

Next there is the question of cost, whether for the use of facilities, for travel to the facilities or for equipment required for the chosen activity. Cost is clearly related to disposable income and to the broad occupational groupings of the individual. Two national recreation studies recently completed in this country both throw light on this relationship, and equally suggest further areas of research to secure more clarification.[1] For example, at what stage will individuals cease to use their disposable leisure time in further work and begin instead to participate in recreation activities? The British Travel Association/ University of Keele study reveals that in almost every pursuit, participation increases with income. This increase in reported participation appears to come at different points on the income scale for different activities. The same study, reporting on activity patterns relative to three broad occupational groups— 'executive', 'clerical workers' and 'manual workers'—found that higher occupational groups had a much wider recreational experience than others; 10 per cent of manual workers, but only 2 per cent of 'executives', had never taken part in the long list of activities which were included in this particular questionnaire. There were interesting and not wholly expected variations between particular activities.[2] Overall, while some evidence of value to planning for future provision has been secured, much more research is needed on the influence of income, occupation and 'social class' on the choice of recreation activity. A fuller understanding of expenditure patterns, related to various social and occupational groupings, is clearly necessary if future planning is to be more effective.

A further factor influencing recreation demand is education. The ever-broadening curriculum in formal and further education is introducing young people and older generations to an increasing range of activities. Though the school curriculum, which today includes an ever-widening range of musical, dramatic, artistic and physical pursuits, has objectives much broader than recreation, the experience of these activities is laid. The opportunity exists for a free choice to be made when formal education is over and the young person enters the post-school community. Again, as larger numbers undertake higher education, where the provision of recreation opportunities has grown sharply in recent years and where choice and selection operate through clubs, groups and societies in a way more comparable to the community at large, we can expect an increased demand. A current study at the University of Manchester represents the first major attempt in this country to probe this particular aspect of demand and to follow through the choice of recreation activities into the immediate post-school years.[3] Other projects, perhaps building on the Manchester study, may be required and repeated to assess and keep abreast of this particular influence.

Next, there is the factor of car ownership and the use of the car for recreation purposes. More vividly and tangibly than most other determinants of recreation demand, car ownership has revolutionised society's use of leisure time. The car is essentially a 'recreation tool'.[4] While it may not be surprising that car owners are more active recreationally than others, there is clear evidence that after initial ownership has passed the car is used in a quite selective and purposive way for recreational activities. Moreover, some pursuits are more strongly influenced by car ownership than others. Yet transportation studies, in the main, continue to ignore the recreational use of the motor-car. Those who are planning for recreation must have answers to the distances travelled in different periods of leisure time and, perhaps more significantly, to the time allotted, either consciously or subconsciously, for travelling, whether for active or passive recreation pursuits, in various periods of leisure time. On-site studies which throw some light on these problems must be complemented by studies which are made from the point of origin of journeys for recreation purposes.

After income, occupation and social class, recreation patterns are influenced by life styles and by life cycles. The two are closely linked and, of course, subject to continuing change. The social groupings within which an individual moves at different stages of his career draw him to styles of living which will have characteristic recreational activities. The particular life style will therefore be one means by which a person is introduced to an activity and, depending on the enjoyment and satisfaction achieved, regular participation may develop. Complementary to this, the development from single status, to marriage and various stages of raising a family, has a marked effect on recreation patterns. As one example, the Government Social Survey inquiry highlights the sharp break in sports participation

which occurs with marriage and before the arrival of children. This occurs with both men and women, but especially the latter.[5] The same study suggests that there is a return to active recreation when the family has been reared, a tendency which one can expect to increase in the future if the trend to earlier marriage and smaller families continues. There are changes too within the marriage relationship which are affecting recreation patterns quite radically. Couples are increasingly sharing their leisure time together, where previously the wife was left at home to look after the large family while the husband went out to a football match, pub or other activity. Other signs cumulatively underline that more leisure will be family-centred and home-centred—and that this will extend to second homes whether of the mobile variety, such as caravans, or more permanently based in the country or at the coast.[6] Clearly, these relationships between recreation demands and an individual's constantly changing social and family status must be understood more fully if we are to plan future provision more effectively.

Much more needs to be known of the psychological satisfaction which individuals draw from participation in their chosen activity. Is there a relationship between recreation participation and satisfaction or dissatisfaction with an individual's occupation? The current study of the Institute of Community Studies is the first full-scale attempt in Britain to investigate relationships between occupation, social grouping and family status and patterns of recreation interests.[7] Would fuller understanding of the motivation and satisfaction which attract people to different forms of recreation lead to possibilities of substitution within groupings of activities? If such relationships do exist, then clearly the planning of recreation facilities and their subsequent management and administration contains a degree of flexibility which could be explored and exploited.

Recreation demand in any one community is also conditioned by demographic factors—population size and growth rate, age and sex structure, family size and so on. Regional variations and migration movements may also bring quite marked differences to the total pattern of recreation demand. Similarly, local traditions have a marked bearing on the provision required in any one community. The strength of following for forms of folk-dancing, choral groups, the various codes of football, opera or wrestling, varies greatly between say, the North East, the North West and South Wales and may reach down to quite local district differences. These differences must be recognised in any local provision. There is also the continuing difficulty of misinterpreting real demand for a temporary changing taste. Ten-pin bowling has boomed and declined in Britain within a decade. How permanent is the current interest in skiing on artificial surfaces? What is the future of golf driving ranges in Britain?

Society as a whole is also conditioned by traditional attitudes towards leisure and recreation provision. These attitudes are developed from deep-rooted religious and cultural sources. Public support to establish and run facilities of a recreational nature may be determined by arguments favouring physical fitness, the avoidance of delinquency, developing character and so on. Or opinion may be persuaded by concepts of improved community provision, social welfare and the general quality of life.

Finally, in this brief coverage of elements affecting recreation demand, account must be taken of the effect of the supply of facilities themselves and of the environment generally. To what extent is the explosive demand for recreation space in the countryside a reflection of the town dweller's desire to break free from the city environment? Could the provision of more open space in the towns or the re-casting of existing urban parks siphon off some of the recreation pressures on the countryside? Are there differences between the recreation patterns of people living in densely populated areas of our towns and cities, perhaps in multi-storey tower blocks of flats, and those in low-density estates of detached houses with private gardens? What is the impact on the established recreation patterns of any one community of a new recreation centre, with fine functional facilities for swimming, squash, badminton, music, drama and so on, where no such facilities existed before?

Recreation Supply

The complexity of planning for recreation does not end with

this rapid survey of the factors influencing demand. The equation to be clearly understood must take account of the determinants of supply, which is much more than a mere inventory of facilities. The planner and the economist can regard the same resource in different ways. In terms of land use a stretch of water may include industrial, agricultural, conservation, as well as recreational use, and this will be regarded as of higher importance in terms of land than an urban man-made facility such as a swimming pool. But if other criteria are adopted, such as the capital necessary for development or the numbers of people served by the facility, then a reverse order may apply. Classifications may also be required for differing reasons regarding facilities in terms of their seasonal or all-the-year-round use, their catchment areas or the degree of multi-use they may offer in terms of recreation activities or other uses.

Any consideration of the supply of recreation facilities must consider their effectiveness as a resource. Assuming the acceptance of a natural facility such as a lake or a stretch of coastline for recreation, what will be the effect of spending money on the provision of ancillary facilities? Has the resource an optimum level of development and how can this be determined? Similarly, with older urban facilities—as, for example, a swimming pool built at the end of the nineteenth century—should money be directed towards its renovation and modernisation; or should it be directed to the construction of a new pool perhaps at a different site in the city?

For the user exercising a choice, the effectiveness of a resource will be measured, consciously or sub-consciously, by such factors as its location, accessibility, cost (including travel and payment for the use of the facility itself) and management policies. There is strong evidence from a number of recent studies which suggests that the catchment area for the great majority of users of recreation facilities, such as sports halls and swimming pools, is quite local and that most day recreation journeys into the countryside are about 20–25 miles (one way). The determining factor is probably time for the journey and ease of travelling which will give a variation on distance in different situations. But some recreation complexes with outstanding provision, such as the Billingham Forum, attract regular participants from a much larger catchment area. Within certain categories of facilities, for example, open space seen in terms of local parks, country parks and more remote areas of the countryside, or in various levels of provision of swimming pools with, say, diving facilities, or in theatres or concert halls, with different sized auditoria, there is a need to establish regional and sub-regional policies which transcend the boundaries of any one local authority. It will be necessary to establish a hierarchy of provision within which individual authorities may carry facilities of a certain scale which have a regional and sub-regional significance.

The management and administration of the recreational facilities themselves are also crucial factors in the effectiveness of the total supply of resources. A scenic viewing area, a theatre, a swimming pool, a reservoir, a floodlit all-weather playing surface—each has a carrying capacity which can be different with various types of management policy. A facility capable of varied recreation use, such as a sports hall or a lake, will clearly have several potential capacities for different activities and management policy will decide which will apply. Again management will determine the *effectiveness* of a supply in such matters as the dual use of school facilities or the opening up of under-used private facilities, if this is possible. Pricing policies, which are part of management, may add to or limit supply effectiveness. Equally price mechanisms can be used to even out the demand curve for some facilities, encouraging use at off-peak hours and working in some measure towards a more acceptable saturation level.

In considering the relationship of administration and its effect on the supply of recreation facilities, it is worth noting that suppliers fall broadly into three categories—the public authorities, commercial development, and the private sector (in which one would include the facilities of clubs, societies, voluntary organisations or landowners). The effectiveness of the total supply will depend on the degree to which the three sectors can be related to a comprehensive recreation policy for any one community. Is there overlapping or duplicated provision? As one example, in many local authorities recreation responsibilities are dispersed among several departments of the same authority. Baths, Parks and Education Departments within one County Borough may be providing resources of a similar type and there may be overlapping or under-use (or ineffective use) of finance directed towards recreation provision. If it is argued that some co-ordinating role is required within the local authority such as a new and enlarged department embracing several smaller departments and co-operating with commercial and private facilities to add to the total effectiveness of recreation provision, then it must also be asked at what level or size of authority will the establishment of such a department prove most effective. This is a matter of crucial importance at the present time following the report of the Royal Commission on Local Government; for implicit in both the majority and the dissenting reports is the need for larger authorities spanning present urban and rural authorities.

Finally, and perhaps most obviously, the supply of recreation facilities is governed by finance, both in the construction of facilities themselves and in their subsequent operation and maintenance. What are the roles of the three sectors—private, commercial and public—and how can their total investment be made most effective? Have all possibilities been developed and exploited to utilise commercial capital and expertise? Are there discrepancies in the legislation affecting government aid to local authorities and to the private sector for recreation provision which may lead to a possible imbalance of provision, for example, between countryside and urban recreation development? Is there a case for arguing that the total investment on recreation facilities should be seen as a whole and not in fragmented parts? What should be expected from private clubs and voluntary organisations in future provision, bearing in mind the growth of sports and other recreational activities, which require large capital buildings such as sports halls or arts centres?

A Framework for Research

These, then, are some of the major questions which have to be asked and answered to enable recreation provision to meet more closely existing and future demand. The complexity of the total problem is increased when it is recognised that patterns of recreation are constantly changing and that one is discussing problems in an area of community life where individual choice predominates. Yet accepting the difficulties, the fundamental need in establishing a framework of recreational research is to develop a programme of work to illuminate the basic underlying issues involved, whilst at the same time attempting answers to more pressing problems of immediate concern, particularly to planners and administrators. The two approaches need not be conflicting and are best seen as complementing each other, leading to constant refinement and illumination. Within this dual approach it is vitally important that fundamental work into methods for conducting recreation research, the main object of which will be to refine the tools for use by local authorities and other research workers, should not be overlooked.

It is important also to recognise the considerable volume of recreation research which has been undertaken in very recent years and which is currently in progress. In the sector where research has been most pronounced, countryside recreation, the second edition of the *Research Register* compiled by the Countryside Commission lists no fewer than 177 projects which are being conducted by statutory bodies, local authorities and, predominantly, university departments at post-graduate level.[8] This figure refers to projects in progress as at January 1968 or recently completed. As Greaves notes in a wide-ranging assessment of present countryside recreation research: 'Outdoor recreation is now a fashionable topic for academic study.'[9]

The *Research Register No. 2* is but one tangible sign of the vigorous drive which the Countryside Commission has made in developing a research and advisory service for those working in the field of countryside recreation. In addition the Commission is developing a central recreation research information centre where abstracts of material of all kinds on countryside recreation research can be retrieved.[10] A further notable achievement by the Commission has been to establish the Countryside Recreation Research Advisory Group with a membership drawn from a number of government agencies with research responsibilities in countryside recreation, including the

British Tourist Authority, the British Waterways Board, the Forestry Commission, the Nature Conservancy, the Sports Council, the Water Resources Board and the Countryside Commission itself. CRRAG has as its major objective to facilitate the co-ordination and greater effectiveness of research programmes by greater exchange of information, by co-operation on research projects and by advice on problems of common research interest.[11]

Some efforts have been made to conceptualise an integrated programme of research in major areas of recreation activity. Quite early in its existence, the Sports Council established a working party under the chairmanship of J. B. Cullingworth to map out a programme of specific enquiries in the field of recreation with particular reference to sport and physical recreation. In developing their proposals, the Cullingworth group examined their task within the broad context of leisure as a whole, recognising that it was neither desirable nor possible to isolate completely one aspect of leisure use from others. The group analysed the factors making up the complex pattern of recreation demand and supply and examined what needed to be done to develop methods and techniques of value in recreation research. Their list of research proposals was an amalgam of (i) medium- and longer-term projects tackling fundamental problems for which answers were required, and (ii) other research which would be of more immediate use to planners and administrators.[12] A considerable body of work has been completed or is currently in progress closely related to the Cullingworth proposals.[13]

It is not surprising to find an emphasis in early recreation studies on the use of facilities themselves, whether urban or rural. Most of these studies have concentrated on catchment areas, modes of travel and socio-economic characteristics of the users themselves. Some have probed the capacity of the facility under varying forms of management. While these studies throw some light on the demand for a single facility or for types of that facility, such as swimming pools or indoor sports centres, they remain isolated parts in the total picture of demand.

However, in very recent years, the scope and range of recreation research has widened considerably. Of particular importance are studies into methods and techniques concentrating on pure rather than operational research. The most notable of these is the work, under the direction of T. L. Burton, at the Centre for Urban and Regional Studies at the University of Birmingham. The study, designed to examine critically techniques of assessment, measurement and projection for use in studies of the supply and demand aspects of sport and recreation, has two stages. The first stage, a desk study, has recently been published and analyses research methods developed in Britain and abroad for recreation research.[14] It covers such areas as questionnaire and interview surveys, time budget diaries, methods of data collection through counting devices and observation, and other research tools. The second and experimental stage, now nearing completion, is isolating certain variables in recreation demand in order to throw more light on the usefulness of certain techniques in securing data on recreation types, whilst at the same time establishing guidelines relating to the collection of profile data.

Among other studies adding to our knowledge of research methods is the compilation of a manual into questionnaire techniques for countryside recreation surveys. This will be concerned with assessing the relative efficiency of different survey methods in this field, classifications, and ways of analysing and presenting information on the characteristics, activities and opinions of visitors.[15] A narrower field study of the use of hand-held oblique photography for surveying recreational activities is in progress.[16]

A further development in recreation research in this country in very recent years has been the development of cost–benefit analysis techniques. With recreation provision, like many social services, it may be possible to state the cost of provision, but not to assess the benefit in the same terms. Cost–benefit studies help to clarify issues from which one can begin to determine the values of different alternatives. An example of this kind of study is that by Kavanagh and Smith which examines the problems of measuring demand functions and benefits of trout fishing and sailing on reservoirs.[17] Elements of cost–benefit analysis are also being used in a number of local studies.

A further discernible development in the methodological field has been the interest of a number of research workers in developing graphic and mathematical model building techniques related to leisure facilities[19].

Overall, there are hopeful signs that it is possible to maintain a balance between studies which have as their prime object the refinement of research tools whilst at the same time developing others which can provide some of the answers of value to those, particularly local authority planning departments, who have to make decisions within a limited range of options. But a twofold problem remains. First, there is the increasing difficulty of assimilating the experience of both 'pure' and 'operational' studies, and, secondly, of transmitting the results in practical terms to those working in the field of recreation provision. Perhaps there is need of a 'methods bank' as well as a data bank, if research is to be more effective and cumulative, and less repetitive. But while solutions are being worked out, a great deal can be achieved and research findings made more effective by striving for a degree of standardisation in some elements of sampling and questionnaire design so that comparability of data can be achieved.

The case for large demand studies of such a size that regional and even sub-regional variations can be identified is very strong. But though there is agreement on the need for them, and indeed for their periodic repetition, researchers are divided as to the adequacy of our present development of techniques to begin immediately what will be an extremely costly operation. Perhaps in the interim some concentration should be made on projects which will lead to a clearer understanding of the relative importance of the component factors making up demand, such as income, education, 'social class', occupation and car ownership, if a major national survey is to be fully utilised. Similarly, we need to understand more fully the relative effectiveness of different types of survey methods and of the sample size and sampling framework which may quantify recreation participation on more than a relative scale—for this is the limit of our present state of knowledge. The use of time budgeting/diary-keeping techniques will be of considerable importance in future work.[19] Above all, a major national demand survey, repeated at periodic intervals, should aim to cover the total pattern of recreation activity in the community, not isolating sport and physical recreation and ignoring other pursuits, nor concentrating on countryside interests to the exclusion of urban activities. These segments of the whole may be included in the total design. The need is not only for a closer understanding of 'recreation types' within countryside interests or sport and physical recreation, but of 'recreation types' within total community interests. These studies could be supplemented by a determined effort to analyse in depth from the variety of local, regional and national demand studies recently completed or near completion.

One major area of recreation research remains comparatively untouched, despite the rapid upsurge of interest and involvement of a growing body of researchers drawn from a variety of disciplines. Scarcely any serious work has been undertaken into the socio-psychological and physical factors underlying recreation choice. Social attitudes, personality traits, home and work environment and physical health may, and probably do, determine recreation choice—or, indeed, opting out of any recreational use of leisure time at all. The complexity of these problems is obvious and there seem to be few bidders prepared to explore this particular field. Yet the importance of this field of enquiry may have implications reaching far beyond its effects on social and physical planning for recreation. It could have an important bearing on the total well-being of the community, in the physical, mental and social sense.

Finally, though programmes of work, increasingly co-ordinated and related to a short- and longer-term strategy, are being developed in various sectors of recreation research, such as countryside recreation or sport and physical recreation, there is a need to develop some liaison machinery which spans the whole field of recreation. Research will undoubtedly progress most easily in recognisable sectors of recreation. But there are some limits to the effective understanding of relationships between the sectors. The recreation patterns of individuals are not confined to sport, or driving into the countryside. They operate over a much wider range of choice. Fuller understanding of total recreation patterns, covering towns, countryside and home environment, will come about more swiftly if there could emerge—perhaps through a central government initiative—a liaison machinery to develop a policy of increased integration of the various programmes of research. Such a liaison could reveal the gaps in present research and perhaps rectify them. It might also secure additional finance and other resources to support work to cover the gaps, where no statutory body or agency exists to assume this responsibility. And, by its very creation, it would provide further tangible evidence in government thinking of the importance of well-planned and administered recreation provision, in both town and countryside, viewing the community as a whole.

References

1. British Travel Association/University of Keele, *Pilot .
   Recreation Survey: Report No. 1*, H. B. Rodgers, July 1~~., ~~~
   the Government Social Survey *Planning for Leisure* by K. K.
   Sillitoe, SS 388, HMSO, 1969.

2. British Travel Association, op. cit., pp. 7–19.

3. *Preliminary Report of a Study in the South East Lancashire
   Conurbation of Post-School Adolescents' Leisure Activities
   Particularly in the Field of Physical Activities*, Department of
   Physical Education, University of Manchester, December 1967.

4. British Travel Association, op. cit., p. 69.

5. Government Social Survey, op. cit., p. 44.

6. Peter Wilmott, *The Influence of Some Social Trends upon
   Regional Planning*, Proceedings of the Social Science Research
   Council and the Centre for Environmental Studies joint con-
   ference 'The Future of the City Region', July 1968.

7. Current research project *Family Life, Work and Leisure* led by
   the Institute of Community Studies.

8. Countryside Commission, *Research Register No. 2*, Spring 1969.

9. J. Greaves, 'National Parks and Access to the Countryside and
   Coast. Trends in Research', paper prepared for the *Town
   Planning Institute Calendar of Planning Research* (3rd edition),
   August 1968.

10. *Recreation News, No. 2*, December 1968, prepared by the
    Countryside Commission for the Countryside Recreation
    Research Advisory Group.

11. *Recreation News, No. 1*, November 1968, prepared by the
    Countryside Commission for the Countryside Recreation
    Research Advisory Group.

12. An unpublished report submitted to the Sports Council in
    March 1967. The members of the group were J. B. Cullingworth
    (Chairman), G. E. Cherry, G. Mercer, D. D. Molyneux, D. C.
    Nicholls, H. B. Rodgers, K. K. Sillitoe, and Margaret Willis.
    I am grateful to the group for permission to use in this essay
    sections of their analysis of factors influencing recreation
    demand and supply.

13. See *The Sports Council. A Review 1966–69*, published by the
    Central Council of Physical Recreation, October 1969.

RECREATION RESEARCH AND PLANNING

14. Thomas L. Burton and P. A. Noad, *Recreation Research Methods: A Review of Recent Studies*, University of Birmingham, Centre for Urban and Regional Studies, Occasional Paper No. 3, 1968.
15. J. Greaves, 'Methods of Surveying Visitors to the Countryside'. See Countryside Commission, *Research Register No. 2*, Spring 1969.
16. R. H. Windsor, 'A Study of the Use of Hand-held Oblique Air-photography for Surveying Recreational Activities'. See Countryside Commission, *Research Register No. 2*, Spring 1969.
17. R. J. Smith and N. J. Kavanagh, *The Measurement and Benefits of Trout Fishing; Preliminary Results of a Study at Grafham Water, Great Ouse Water Authority, Huntingdonshire*, Department of Industrial Economics and Business Studies, University of Birmingham, March 1969.
18. Ray Maw, 'Construction of a Leisure Model', *Official Architecture and Planning*, Vol. 32, No. 8, August 1969, pp. 924–35.
19. See also Government Social Survey, op. cit., pp. 32–4.

Chapter 3

Sociological Research in Recreation

ISABEL EMMETT

The existence of a certain pattern of recreation activity is the outcome of a dynamic relationship between the following factors: first, existing facilities; second, differential knowledge of existing facilities; third, time—in particular, the time which consumers have available for leisure; fourth, money—in particular, the money in consumers' pockets available for recreation purposes; fifth, the values of suppliers; and sixth, the values of consumers. This chapter considers briefly these six factors, the relationship between them, and the role of the sociologist in studying them.

Little is currently known about the existing facilities for recreation in Britain. Facilities are owned by: commercial concerns aiming to make money out of people's recreation; voluntary organisations whose purpose is to do good to people in their recreation; employers hoping to do good to their own image by providing for their employees' recreation; educational establishments concerned to ensure the physical and spiritual growth of pupils; private groups of citizens aiming to secure scarce resources for their exclusive pleasure; and local authorities whose main motivation sometimes appears to ignorant outsiders to be to yield to the sheer inertia of going on doing what has always been done.

In the last few years a few county authorities have set out to discover what facilities exist for physical recreation within their boundaries. Physical recreation is of particular interest because it is usually costly in terms of space. These studies had, as a primary aim, comparability of data, but inevitably difficulties arose in attempting to achieve this. The data which they have collected will help everyone who is concerned with the study of recreation; but some local authorities did not co-operate, data

E

about small indoor halls often proved unobtainable and the lack of congruence between demographic fact and local authority boundary diminished the utility of the studies for some purposes. Populations move, swell here, shrink there, travel more, pay rates in entities whose boundaries they do not know they are crossing on the way to recreation. Rural authorities have fewer parks than urban authorities: they are nearer to open country. Does this mean they are poorer in recreational facilities? Lancashire County Council have rated authorities on a combination of facilities available in each. Cheshire, learning from their colleagues, see problems in doing this. The human community which I am currently studying, the conurbation of South East Lancashire, is split by the county boundaries. A comparison can be made between Bolton and Ince-in-Maker-field, because they are both in Lancashire; but, at present, it is difficult to compare Bolton to Stockport, which is what I want to do, because although both towns are part of the conurbation, one is in Lancashire and one in Cheshire.

An admirable beginning has been made in attempting to compile an inventory of existing facilities;[1] some of the problems are being exposed; but we do not have anything like a complete picture of what facilities exist in many parts of Britain. It is hardly surprising, therefore, that knowledge of existing facilities varies between consumers and varies as to different types of facility. In the current research in the South East Lancashire conurbation, young people have been subjected to a lot of questions about what they do in their spare time. It seemed fair to try, in return, to answer their questions about recreation. In this way we learned that it is time-consuming and costly for a research unit to find out where a boy living in Oldham can go to learn judo or archery, and it is much more difficult for the boy to find out himself. Commercial establishments intent on making profits advertise places and times at which people can see films, dance, play bingo, drink and eat. Employers and educational establishments usually let their own protégées know what facilities they have. If a private golf club wishes to expand, it privately makes efforts to do so. Public money is contributed to courses in the kinds of recreation activities which are not widely catered for by commercial concerns and to the provision of facilities to do them; and the Central Council of Physical Recreation, other voluntary organisations, committees of local authorities and governing bodies of sports produce pamphlets and posters which are sent to schools and put up in some public buildings. But it seems that organisation speaks to organisation. Many individual people do not know where they can learn to play squash or what steps they need to take in order to find out where they could learn.

Thus, people who are active in organisations have better knowledge of facilities than do other people; everyone has better knowledge of commercial provision than they do of other provision; and articulate, pushing, middle-class people with the right social networks are better able to find out about public provision and their rights in regard to publicly owned facilities than are less articulate people. This is part of the explanation of the finding reported in the *Pilot National Recreation Survey* that high-income groups use cheap and free facilities more often than do working-class people.[2] Another reason is that pursuits which are cheap in money terms are often costly in terms of time, and middle-class people often have more time available to engage in recreation pursuits than do manual workers.

Gross variations in the distribution of free time and money, in fact, contribute significantly to the continuing maintenance of class differences in recreation pursuits and, in spite of the comforting assurances heard from time to time that class differences are dead or dying, it does not look that way to most students of British society. However, the major division with which this chapter is concerned is one which, while it is affected by social class, is itself distinct from social class divisions. This is the division between the suppliers and the consumers of recreation goods and facilities.

The values of suppliers are those that lurk behind every planner: the values of those who control education and those who finance the building of future towns. If it were simply a question of ensuring that growing bodies—which might one day be needed for the army or the police force—got regular exercise, the easiest way to provide for this might be to have lots of rock-and-roll played everywhere and young people would look after the rest, cheaply and with pleasure. But even when energetic forms of dancing to pop music were in vogue, jiving was not widely regarded as a sport conducive to the improvement of character, although the rather unenergetic practice of rifle shooting was (and still is).

In the field of physical recreation, the aim of the suppliers is seldom to find out what people say they want to do, and then to provide facilities for them to do it—an aim which might be called the simple democratic aim. This is partly because it is realised that supply very often creates a demand: sometimes and in some places, the more swimming pools you build, the more people go swimming. People do not always know what they want to do until they actually try it. So the simple democratic aim expands into the utilitarian one: to find out what people would enjoy doing, if they knew how and where to do it, and enable them to have that enjoyment: that is, the greatest happiness of the greatest number, taking into account latent demand.

But, as was suggested earlier, a further aim is commonly linked to this, and that is the paternalist aim: to find out what gap exists between the things people enjoy doing and the things it is thought desirable for them to do, with a view to persuading them to do what is 'good for them' in the view of the suppliers. The publicised, group-held values of most of those concerned with the provision of facilities for recreation result in a combination of the utilitarian aim with the paternalist aim, the latter often in heavy disguise. It has been clearly demonstrated that, in the case of some sports in some places, if facilities are increased and better publicised, increasing numbers of people participate and find pleasure in them—which makes it look as though providing more and more facilities is the way to achieve the greatest happiness of the greatest number. It has not been demonstrated that sport is conducive to 'good', but a belief that sport is good for you is widely prevalent. The two beliefs are easily confused because they tend often to point to the same policy: an expansion in the provision of some facilities. Thus, when we find that half as many girls as boys like sport, few conclude that half as much provision should be made for girls as is made for boys. When we find that middle-class children are more active in their leisure than working-class children, few conclude that grammar schools and middle-class suburbs should continue to get more open space than secondary modern schools and slum districts. The information is more often used in a plan to redress the balance, to make opportunities more equal, and to convert the unwilling to do the sport that is thought to be good for them.

Conflicting with and diluting this strain of values among the suppliers of facilities is a strong, though more privately held sense of rightful privilege and self preservation. The providers include some privileged consumers who do not want others to use, overcrowd, commercialise and vulgarise *their* facilities; and they are always busy rationalising their objections to school and university facilities being opened to a wider public; golf, boating and rugby clubs being less expensive and exclusive, and so on. This is the mixture on one side: a population with healthy bodies and characters developed by the right kind of recreation, but not at the expense of gentlemen's preserves, is the aim of the suppliers.*

On the other side are the values of consumers. Different sets of values are more easily discernible among these than among suppliers, partly because more is known about divisions among consumers, and partly because there are more consumers than suppliers. Consumers' values can be seen as a series of differential views of the universe: and these views complicate the relationship between supply and demand. In London, in the 1930s, children were taken, in primary and secondary school, to swimming baths each week and for this and other reasons they saw and knew London and indeed the universe—as endless tarmac buildings, dotted with swimming pools; and they *saw* water as something to swim and play in. In North Wales, there are pools, streams and sea all over the place, but most of the population do not know how to swim and see all that water as something to wash sheep in, to keep out of when you are blackberrying, and to sell to English tourists. A minority of English grammar-school children, introduced to rock climb-

* This is a gross oversimplification: not all of the people who want to keep their 'happy hunting grounds' or golfing grounds three-quarters empty most of the time are gentlemen—and commercial providers on the whole have less tangled motives than do other providers.

ing by enthusiastic teachers, see Snowdon, Tryfan and Cnicht as thrilling edifices, challenges to the soul, poetic inspiration. They pay good money, save and fiddle holidays to go and climb; forgo courting, dancing and proper treatment of their girlfriends, to buy rope, tackle and boots—while labourers who live within easy reach of the mountains curse as well as love living among these same peaks and, walking halfway up Snowdon and down every day for weeks to dig ditches, wonder at the mad fools who do it for fun and then feel proud of themselves for having done so.

The North Welsh do not see water as something to swim in or climb mountains for pleasure. It may be argued that chilly mountain pools are not facilities and that the true moral of the story is that if heated swimming pools were provided, with changing rooms and regular swimming lessons, the values of a whole community could be changed overnight. This is, however, doubtful: the factor of time becomes important. It is certainly true that when a sports hall including squash courts is built, it not only meets the demands of people who know what squash is and know they want to play it; but it also introduces some people to squash who did not previously know they wanted to play it. And if one knew that providing more squash courts, or publicising those that exist, would result in more people playing squash, the situation would be relatively simple. The values of the suppliers could be tapped (ignoring, for the moment, that these change and conflict). The archbishops, or the Cabinet, or a popular referendum could be invited to decree what games people should play—for the benefit of the country, for the benefit of people's bodies and souls, or for the benefit of the Exchequer. The necessary amount of facilities could be built for those games all over the country, a good advertising campaign programmed and then people would start to play. But, in the short run, supply does not necessarily create demand. It is possible to provide facilities, at no direct charge to the public and find that no one uses them. The values which are currently held intervene, and it takes even longer to change values than it does to build swimming pools.

In the Lancashire conurbation study[3] school-leavers were asked if they owned a bicycle, motor-scooter, motor-cycle, or if anyone in their family owned a car. It was thought that owner-ship of vehicles would make a difference to the availability of facilities; a car turns a three hour bus ride to the countryside or badminton club into a feasible trip. But it was not like this. Car ownership did not differ between the families of sporty children and non-sporty ones, except in so far as playing sport is tied to social class and car ownership is tied to social class. Sporting children more often owned bicyles, but the chances are that they were not active in sport because their bicycles enabled them to reach facilities they would otherwise have been unable to reach, but that they had bought or acquired bicycles because their love of physical activity contributed to them wanting a bicycle.

If a person wants to play squash and lives in a community where (or has as his main reference group people to whom) playing squash is permissible or admirable, then his mental image of his physical environment will stretch out to include a squash court; or, if he does not know of a squash court, it will contain gaps with question marks in it so that from time to time he will mention to people that he would like to play squash, until he discovers some place where he can play it. And he will use a vehicle if he has one, but get there anyway if he has not.

More sporty than non-sporty children lived near to open country, to parks and swimming pools. But what their answers meant was not that the nearer one gets to facilities the more one likes sport, but that they perceived the world differently and because they used facilities, they knew where those facilities were: the facilities were part of their universe.

Another question that was asked in the Lancashire study was why children did not play the sports, games or outdoor activities which they had thought of taking up regularly. Most often the answer was that there were no facilities, or facilities were too far away. Part of the reason for this reply is that asked for a reason, the children felt they had to give one. They may have heard that the Duke of Edinburgh thinks there are too few playing fields; they may have seen the slogan painted on the walls 'playing fields not battle fields'. For those who did not know what to say, 'no facilities' was a way out. When a child sees on television a sport which looks pleasant to do or when he is more or less forcibly introduced at school or at camp or in the army to a sport which he then finds it is pleasant to do, he sometimes follows up this experience, finds out where he can do it and goes on to do it. But far more often he does not. For the bulk of the children who have this experience, the thought 'gymnastics looks fun from what I can see from this television programme; I would like to do it myself', or 'I enjoyed that horse ride; I wonder if I can go regularly', dies the moment it is born because it is unthinkable to him that he should say to his friends the next day 'I am going to join a gymnastics club tonight', or 'I am going out horse riding on Sunday morning.' He and his group do not perceive the world in such a way that these actions are seen as possibilities.

But what are seen as possibilities are not static for his group: fashions arise and fall not only in what providers think is good for consumers, but also more importantly, in what people are ready to do. People can afford cars so they stop cycling; they can afford Majorca so they no longer camp in Devon; they can look at Engelbert Humperdinck on television so they do not go for a walk to look at the moon. Changes in fashion are *social* phenomena; they move through and affect groups of people; and the likings for and antipathies towards different recreation pursuits which matter, are experienced by groups.

It is this which provides the particular role of the sociologist in studies of recreation. A sociologist looks at people in groups standing in relation to other groups and studies the ways in which their behaviour is influenced by their membership of groups. People are very largely creatures of their social environment and the social forces at work on us do not always make themselves apparent to us when we practise insight—though, as Max Weber and other writers have emphasised, insight helps. And since it is difficult to be aware of the social forces as they affect ourselves, it follows that what people say they like or say they will do does not always coincide with what they actually do. An important concern of sociology is the gap between appearances and reality: the gap between what people say and what they do.

When at the beginning of this chapter, it was suggested that values of suppliers and values of consumers are two of the six primary factors determining existing patterns of recreation, the term 'values' was shorthand for the history of groups of people who are divided and aligned in certain ways, as this history is expressed in preferences for this or that recreation pursuit. And in trying to assess those values the sociologist must start with a study of the social forces at work on young people (I say young people since that is the section of the population in which I am particularly interested) and anticipate that such things as social class, sex, type of school attended, and the teenage subculture influence young people's behaviour in ways of which they themselves are not always aware. He must interpret answers and other data he acquires in the light of his knowledge of these social forces.

The purpose of this chapter, as stated at the outset, was to discuss briefly the main determinants of patterns of recreation; the relationships between them; and the sociologist's role in studying them. It would take a paper twice as long as this one to consider the relationships between each factor, and yet such a consideration must at some time be made. What would be the effect of increased time and/or money on the preserves of the privileged few? How would more widespread knowledge of existing facilities affect the values of consumers? How are the values of suppliers being affected by the impact now being made by the teenage subculture? To what extent is the moral code of public schools, with its belief that participation in sport leads to the development of such virtues as selflessness, discipline and clean-mindedness still being spread in schools, the Army and the club, and to what extent is it succumbing to the onslaught of the modern fashion of debunking, or at least seriously questioning, those things unquestioningly accepted as sacred by a previous generation?

All of these questions are worth asking but here attention will be given to a very small area of this field, which particularly concerns adolescents. This is the relationship between two of the things which contribute to young people's values and activities today: social class and the adolescent subculture.

The provisional results of the Lancashire study show, amongst other things, that more middle-class children than working-class children are actively interested in sport; that this is more true for girls than for boys; and that the sports favoured by middle-class children are different from those favoured by working-class children. Fewer 'with-it' children are less interested in sport than 'square' children; and fewer solitary children than gregarious children.

There is some evidence that working-class people emulate middle-class recreation activities and, after a time lag, catch up. Thus, golf, skiing, sailing, rock climbing and mountaineering have spread their appeal down the social scale in the post-war years. The money, time and curiosity needed to try new things are all more commonly found among middle-class than among working-class people. At the British Sociological Association's conference on leisure in 1967, Madame Nicole Samuel reported that some of those working in the field of leisure in France based future plans partly on an assumption that what middle-class people did with their leisure today would be done by working-class people with their leisure in the future.

Most young people will not spend their leisure time in ways which they consider to be square. This is not simply a way of saying that people do not like what they do not like: if an activity gets a reputation for being square, some people who like doing it stop and others who like the look of it do not try it. Squareness may be seen as one extreme of a continuum ranging from square through with-it to way-out and finally to sick. What is with-it in one group is square in a second, and so on. The judgment changes from group to group and over time. Cliff Richard was way-out to many people when he first appeared on the pop scene and was screamed at by a minority; in time, he became with-it; and is now pretty square. Drugs were sick; are now way-out; and to some groups (these groups themselves way-out to the majority) have become with-it. The time sequence is not inevitable—what stops most sick things from becoming widely with-it are limits set by ordinary young people's need for survival. What the rockers did with their motor-cycles was too dangerous to become widely copied; and what drug addicts do will remain way-out for most people for the same reason. But there is enough of a pattern in these changes over time to make the concepts worthy of planners' attention; just as the initiation and transmission of fashions and trends among young people is of interest to sociologists.

If the squares are going to copy the way-outers and the working-class are going to copy the middle-class, it is worth looking at how the two trends are related. The total adolescent subculture crosses class barriers, but social class plays a role in articulating the various stages of change in fashion over a period of time. The working-class has produced, out of local groups in the big conurbations, initiators and opinion leaders who stand on street corners, meet in dingy pubs and cellars, and distinguish themselves from the adult world with styles of speech, dress and music which are copied. But until a local following provides them with financial support, they cannot get a national following and once they have a national following they have effectively moved out of their class of origin. So that while the commercial pop culture and the swinging middle-class London set associated with it are to some extent parasitic on local working-class youth cultures, there is also a strong feed-back down the social ladder, and upper- or middle-class way-outers act as models for the bulk of with-it youth, most of whom are white-collar workers in shops and offices. Lord Harlech's children and Marianne Faithfull as well as Mick Jagger, can afford time, money and disapproval from the conventional world of adult employers and home providers, to make the kind of experiments in fashion which for a time will be way-out. The models in university towns are often students. They live away from home; the university demands little conformity from them, compared to that demanded by most employers and schools; and there are enough of them grouped together to give moral support to eccentricities.

The working-class may provide ideas and initiate fashions, but to become widely influential they must join the middle-class which by and large provides the model for working-class behaviour. Thus the tendency for working class people, as they become better off financially, to emulate middle-class people in leisure pursuits as in other things, is somewhat reinforced by the routes which changes in fashion take among the young, although the traffic is not all one way. Whilst active participation in physical recreation is not a with-it pursuit at present, some sports and games are more with-it than others; the way-out sports will become with-it; and this should help us at some stage with prediction.

In general, to make predictions about future patterns of recreation it is necessary to break down the population, the country, and kinds of recreation activities in meaningful ways. We need to know what facilities exist and how they are expanding. We need to be aware of differential knowledge of existing facilities and to anticipate whether or not government, educational, voluntary and local authority bodies will try to diminish differential knowledge, perhaps by copying publicity techniques from the commercial sector. We need to be aware that commercial concerns will not accept a particular sphere of entertainment and leisure as mysteriously appropriate to their endeavours, but will continue to try to anticipate changes in fashion and to meet unsatisfied demand over the whole field. We need hard data, rather than optimistic speculation, about whether or not hours worked are actually diminishing for different sections of the population; and whether or not real spare time is actually increasing; and similar hard data about trends in real income. Perhaps most important of all, we need to be aware that it is not only the values held by consumers which matter, but also the values held by suppliers, and we need to be aware that both sets of values will change.

The sheer complexity of this task, and the shifting nature of the factors involved, suggest that flexibility must be one of the key aims of all those working in the field of provision for recreation.

Notes and References

1. The initial appraisals of the ten Regional Sports Councils in England and Wales.
2. British Travel Association/University of Keele, *Pilot National Recreation Survey: Report No. 1*, 1967, p. 6.
3. University of Manchester, Department of Physical Education, *Preliminary Report on a Study in the South East Lancashire Conurbation of Post School Adolescents' Leisure Activities Particularly in the Field of Physical Education*, 1967.

Chapter 4

Economics of Water Recreation*

N. J. KAVANAGH

The concentration of the population of Britain into urban communities has been a feature of British society since the beginning of the last century. Today, eight out of ten persons in Britain are classified as living in urban communities compared with just three out of ten in 1801. Urbanisation, though associated with a rising standard of living, has not been without its social and economic disadvantages: urban renewal, distribution of industry, town planning, traffic congestion, air and water pollution are prime examples of problems of our urban society that are familiar to most of us and have been, and continue to be, the subject of public debate, enquiry or parliamentary legislation.

A new aspect has been added to the urban phenomenon: compared with the inter-war years, urban communities are now becoming more affluent. Affluence combined with greater mobility of travel and the availability of more leisure time makes a powerful force for promoting an increased demand for outdoor recreation facilities. The provision of these facilities is a major issue facing modern urban communities. Public policy in Britain recognises that the provision of recreation amenities is desirable, and legislation passed by Parliament with the objective of developing outdoor recreation facilities emphasises water resources as important sources of supply of such facilities, both actual and potential. The feasibility of using water resources, particularly resources designed to supply potable water, was, at one time, a matter of controversy. This controversy has subsided, and it is now generally accepted that there are rational

* This is a revised version of a paper which appeared in *Water and Water Engineering*, October 1968, and which was based upon the author's report, *The Recreational Uses of Rivers and Reservoirs*, prepared for the Water Resources Board in 1966. The author alone is responsible for the contents of the chapter.

78

arguments for and against developing the recreation potentialities of water resources.[1] What Knetsch had to say about the use of natural resources for recreation in the United States is not without relevance to the British situation: 'The time has passed when we can profitably debate whether outdoor recreation should be properly acknowledged as a rightful use of natural resources. The propriety of this use is no longer an issue.'[3] This sentiment is echoed in the White Paper, *Leisure in the Countryside*, which, at the same time, reminds us of the multi-uses of natural resources and the possible conflicting nature of demands: 'Given that townspeople ought to be able to spend their leisure in the country if they want to; that they will have more leisure; and that in future they will be able to buy cars and boats and otherwise spend money on their weekends and holidays, the problem is to enable them to enjoy this leisure without harm to those who live and work in the country, and without spoiling what they go to the countryside to seek.'[4] By and large, major obstacles on the supply side have been removed, though on the demand side there are some important issues still to be resolved: the type of facilities to develop, the size of future demands, the benefits of outdoor recreation. All of these issues can be subsumed under the heading 'measuring the demand for outdoor recreation'. This paper is largely concerned with the measurement of demand for a particular outdoor recreation activity, and thereby its benefits, as viewed by the economist using methods developed by resource economists in the United States. The approach treats recreation as an economic commodity, the demand for which is subject to the influences of consumers' tastes, commodity prices and household incomes, like any other of the large number of commodities demanded by millions of consumers in Britain today. Before providing an exposition of the method, observations will be made on general trends in outdoor recreation demand and supply in Britain and America, followed by brief references to developments in public policy in both countries.

Public Policy and Recreation Demand

The rate of growth in the demand for outdoor recreation is

likely to increase in a community experiencing a rise in its real income per head, associated with more leisure time and possessing relatively inexpensive and convenient forms of transport. In the United States, according to Clawson, 'The use of outdoor recreation areas has been increasing rapidly, for many years. For the period since the war the rate of increase from year to year has been around 10 per cent for many types of areas, higher for some, lower for others. . . . The major factors behind the persistent, steady, relatively rapid rise in the use of outdoor recreation areas have been increased total population, higher real income per capita, greater leisure and more travel. Since each of these factors is expected to show higher values for the future than today, the trend towards still greater use of outdoor recreation areas presumably will continue.'[5]

The upward trend in leisure time spent in certain primarily outdoor recreation activities in 1960 in the United States is shown in Table 4.1. In Britain the trends are similar, though a

Table 4.1   *Estimates of leisure time spent in certain primarily outdoor recreation activities, 1900–1960: Indices of man hours (1900 = 100)*

1900	100·0
1910	216·7
1920	700·0
1930	1776·7
1940	2616·7
1950	4066·7
1960	7024·0

Sources: Based on data given in Clawson and Knetsch, op. cit., page 25.

satisfactory statistical picture has yet to be drawn. The underlying factors are summarised succinctly in a Report of the Civic Trust which stresses the role of water resources in outdoor recreation: 'Today people start work later in life and retire earlier. The average working week ranges from 38 to 48 hours and we can see a universal 25-hour week as a future possibility. Our prosperity is also growing. Production during the industrial revolution rose typically by 1½ per cent per head per year. A sustained rate of twice or three times this during the new technological revolution could transform our society, provide an ample income for most of us and give us more than enough leisure. Change over the next half century would be more dramatic than over the last. . . . The demand for space is already urgent and unsatisfied. Thirty million people now take holidays. We have eighty thousand active athletes, one million golfers, nine million amateur gardeners. National organisations representing forty-two sports are affiliated to the Central Council of Physical Recreation. The demand for playing fields for traditional games is insistent and hitherto restricted sports (sailing, skiing, climbing, golf) are becoming more popular every year. . . . A further most significant comment from America is this: The focal point of much outdoor recreation is water. Rivers and lakes provide not only the fresh water for camping and picnics, but also the surface and the element for sailing, rowing, skin-diving, boating, swimming, fishing and water skiing. They form fine scenery and habitat for aquatic plants, animals and birds. To complement these, we need the urban playground, the general areas of outdoor recreation on the very doorstep of the big cities where most people live.'[6]

A high rate of growth in demand for outdoor recreation is therefore likely in conditions of rising total income per head of the population and increasing leisure time. Trends in the economy at present may not appear favourable to a high rate of growth in demand, but one must not be too pessimistic about trends in demand in the 'downswings' of the economy. Experience in the USA in this respect is worth noting. Clawson has observed that during the downswings of business cycles in the USA, use of recreation areas was not adversely affected and, in the case of some minor downswings, there was even a slight increase. In the long term the important point is the recognition that outdoor recreation is a matter of economic welfare and that the allocation of resources for the provision of new facilities and the removal of institutional barriers to the use of existing facilities are likely to lead to a more efficient use of a nation's resources.

Since 1962, it has been agreed policy in the United States to take into consideration in water project formulation and evaluation, recreation benefits.[3, 7] Consequently, recreation benefits are now counted along with long-accepted benefits of water resources, such as hydro-electric power, flood protection, navigation, irrigation and the supply of potable water.

In Britain, the Water Resources Act, 1963[8] and the Great Ouse Water Act, 1961[9] are important landmarks in the legislative field concerning the inclusion of recreation in water resources' development. The former gives powers to river authorities in England and Wales to make provisions for recreation facilities at reservoirs and other inland waters and to make charges for the use of such facilities; it lays down provisions with regard to expenditures and the limits of such expenditures by river authorities. The Great Ouse Water Act, relating to a specific body of water resources, makes provision to protect existing recreation facilities and gives power to the Great Ouse Water Authority to provide others.

A recent development in the legislative field was the Countryside Act, 1968,[10] the main purpose of which is to provide for the improvement of facilities for the enjoyment of the countryside by the public in England and Wales. Section 22 empowers statutory water undertakers to take steps to facilitate the use of their reservoirs or other waters for recreation. The Act gives legislative effect to the policy statement contained in the White Paper, *Leisure in the Countryside*. The White Paper, in advocating the wider use of rivers, canals, reservoirs and gathering grounds for recreation comments: 'Although many water undertakers have found it possible to allow their reservoirs to be widely used for recreation, access to many reservoirs is still restricted and sometimes forbidden without sufficient reason. Subject to proper safety measures, there is no reason to deny public access to reservoirs used solely for river regulation or compensation. Public access to reservoirs from which water is taken directly into public supply involves greater hazards, and the first essential is the safety of the public water supply. Methods have been developed by which the hazard from many recreational activities can be eliminated.'[4]

These legislative changes and policy statements recognise that rivers, lakes and the reservoirs are social assets, the potentialities of which can only be developed within a multi-purpose framework; thus, for example, the use of river water by industry without due regard for other users of the same supply can lead to a misallocation of resources. Furthermore, they add a new dimension to industrial location and town and country planning policies, and represent an end to a past policy tending to accept that the industrial growth of Britain must inevitably be associated with the destruction of the recreation amenities of rivers. Whether it was inevitable that past industrial growth could only have been achieved by ignoring the recreation aspects of water resources is a moot point. But it certainly can no longer be accepted. Similarly, reservoirs are no longer to be fenced off from potential consumers because of prejudice or the untested fears of managers of water undertakings. On the other hand, the rights of the water consumers must not be infringed. To reconcile these divergent uses, some guiding principles need to be formulated. Fortunately, such a body of principles is already available, from a report of the Institution of Water Engineers in 1963:

(1) The prime duty of water undertakers is to provide an adequate quantity of safe and suitable water.

(2) Water undertakers, and more particularly those promoting new schemes, are being increasingly urged to allow the public to enjoy the facilities for recreation and enjoyment that reservoirs and gathering grounds can provide.

(3) It rests with the water undertakers to decide for themselves, in the light of their knowledge of local circumstances, whether, and if so, what recreational activities should be allowed on reservoirs or adjacent works.

(4) Although the water authority may decide that such use would endanger the works or the purity of the supply, it is not now accepted as sufficient to deny these requests without giving reasons for the decision.

(5) The difficulty facing those responsible for such decisions in the past has been mainly the lack of information on the effect of recreational use.

(6) There is, however, a growing volume of technical knowledge arising from the experience of authorities whose works are used by the public for recreation purposes.[2]

The wide acceptance of these principles should go a long way towards broadening the use of social assets in water supply and thereby lead to an improvement in community welfare. Another aspect of the wider use of reservoirs for recreation concerns investment needs. The stock of reservoirs represents the sacrifice of consumers of yesterday. To develop new supplies of water recreation to meet a rising demand, whilst existing reservoirs are not fully exploited, involves an unnecessary sacrifice on the part of today's consumers. That is to say, the price of recreation demand may be higher than it need be.

General Considerations in the Measurement of Demand

The provision of a supply of water resources for recreation presumes a consumers' demand. To engage in the provision of facilities without reference to the determinants of consumer demand can result either in the development of facilities which will be under-utilised or in the provision of insufficient facilities. Both situations lead to a misallocation of resources. Gauging consumer demand is not an easy task in the case of a commodity like outdoor recreation, the supply of which has been determined by non-market criteria.

The following are considered to be the important determinants to be considered by water developers in project formulation in the United States:[7]

(1) Population within the zone of project influence.
(2) Proximity of the project to centres of population.
(3) Social and economic characteristics of the population, including disposable income, age and mobility.
(4) Leisure time and recreation habits that reflect changing consumer preferences, as indicated by trends in hunting and fishing licenses, sales of recreation equipment and trends in total recreation demand.
(5) The recreation use-potential of the project, as reflected by its ability to provide for uniqueness, diversity and access.
(6) Availability and attractiveness of existing and potential alternative recreation opportunities.

It will be noted that there is no explicit mention of prices as being a determinant of demand, though they are implied in item (3).

Prices are, however, used in project evaluation, but these are planners' (not market) valuations used to 'achieve uniformity in treatment of recreation in planning of projects'. Two classes of recreation are distinguished for planning purposes and each is allocated a price. The classes are (i) a general outdoor recreation day, and (ii) a specialised outdoor recreation day; a recreation day is defined as a standard unit of use consisting of a visit by one individual to a recreation development or area for recreation purposes during any reasonable portion (or all) of a 24-hour period. The distinction between the two types is as follows: 'A general outdoor recreation day involves primarily those activities attracting the majority of outdoor recreationalists and generally requiring the development and maintenance of convenient access and adequate facilities, e.g. swimming, picnicking and boating, whereas a specialised outdoor recreation day involves those activities of which opportunities are limited; intensity of use is low and often may involve a large personal expense by the user.'[7]

Monetary values are imputed to each type of recreation day within the following price ranges—$0.5 to $1.5 for a general outdoor recreation and $2 to $6 for a special outdoor recreation day. These prices are presumed to measure the amount that users should be willing to pay, *if such payments were required*, to avail themselves of the project recreation resources; and are to be used in order to achieve uniformity in treatment of recreation in planning of projects. They are *simulated* prices determined on the basis of informed judgment, and departure from the range of values provided is permissible if a full explanation is given. The justification for this approach is that: 'The recreational services of public water and related land resource development are currently provided to the users free of charge or for a nominal fee, usually covering only part of the cost. Thus, although it is known that there is a large and growing demand for these services, there is, in the formal sense, no well-established market for them and few data are available on market prices that reflect the values of the service provided by public projects. Under the circumstances, it has become necessary to derive simulated market prices.'

It is intended to use these prices until improved pricing and benefit evaluation techniques are available. These values, it must be noted, are arbitrary, even though they are considered to reflect the consensus judgment of qualified technicians. As planners' prices, their use may make for uniformity in project appraisal, but it is questionable whether they are meaningful measures of the value of a recreation day. A uniform price for a particular recreation in the United States is most unlikely and the distinction between 'generalised' and 'specialised' is largely a social one. It would be interesting to see to what extent local project planners in the United States have tended to depart from them because of local demand. If these prices fail to reflect local demand, then there can be situations of under- and over-supply of facilities, with consequences noted above, and biased estimates of recreation benefits.

If planners' prices are rejected, how do we proceed to put a monetary valuation on recreation reflecting consumers' demand? Subject to certain qualifications the market mechanism can provide monetary valuations of recreation demand reflecting consumers' demand. Traditionally, outdoor recreation, unlike most other commodities, has not been supplied subject to market valuation, and consequently the requisite historical data are not available. In devising methods or techniques of measuring demand this lack of data is only a hurdle to be overcome and should not be considered a permanent obstacle. This point of view is reflected in water resources policy in the United States where it is intended to use planners' prices until improved pricing and benefit evaluation techniques are available.

The rudimentary state of methods of measuring the demand for outdoor recreation is not unique in the history of economics, and we can take hope from what Clawson and Knetsch have observed happening in the case of agricultural commodities: 'The analysis of demand for outdoor recreation may be at roughly the same stage of development that analysis of demand for agricultural commodities was forty or more years ago. In the early 1920s the demand curves of theory were well known amongst economists, but many doubted that empirical demand curves could ever be estimated with any accuracy. During the 1920s various methods for doing this were developed. Later many of the earlier empirical results were revealed to be in error. . . . Better data were needed and gradually came into existence as well as more sophisticated and efficient methods of analysis. But, today, the demand for all agricultural commodities is fairly well known, and different workers have obtained numerical measures which are quite consistent. Although the debate on agricultural policy may rage, there is a general agreement on the basic underlying demand relationship.'[11]

Though their references are to agricultural commodities, what they say is relevant to a wide range of commodities. The development of quantitative economics as the result of the work of econometricians has produced a spate of results for a large number of commodities from a wide range of countries, including the United Kingdom, and in the case of outdoor recreation a few studies are available using data from the USA. The results of econometric studies are often used in policy making, agriculture being the prime example. Later, we will illustrate the use of econometric studies in policy formulation in the field of outdoor recreation using a sports fishery study as an example. Before discussing the underlying theory, however, we pause to emphasise the purpose of measuring recreation demand in terms of money, in order to answer some criticisms of this approach.

There is a general agreement that outdoor recreation is, in essence, a good thing. It is a source of satisfaction; it gives immediate pleasure to the participants; it provides long-term benefits of both a physical and mental kind; and, from the social point of view, there are also benefits to the country as a whole from having outdoor recreation facilities. All of these benefits extend from the unique quality of being endowed with natural characteristics, such as water in scenic surroundings.[12] To expect a monetary valuation to reflect all of these characteristics is considered by some to be impossible, whilst others reject the view that recreation demand should be left to market forces. The view taken in this paper, however, is that all of us have subjective views on the benefits of outdoor recreation, but that what is important when it comes to decision-making about the quantity of resources to be devoted to recreation, is an objective view. We can express objective views by the prices we are willing to pay. This does not imply that market prices ought to be the sole determinant of what is an objective valuation of recreation. To ignore price valuations, however, is to neglect the use of an indispensable piece of information necessary for decision-making. How such valuations can be used will be discussed later. In the meantime, we can proceed to discuss some of the conceptual aspects of measuring the demand for outdoor recreation.

Some Theoretical Aspects of Demand Measurement

The commodity 'outdoor recreation', conceptually at least, can be treated like any other economic commodity. According to economic theory, normally the quantity demanded of a commodity per period of time is inversely related to the price per unit, with a *caveat ceteris paribus*. The immediate use of such a formal framework in the case of a commodity like outdoor recreation is not without difficulties as to what is the unit of measurement of the commodity and the nature of the price variable. An approach which seems to offer an operational way around these difficulties has been developed by Clawson.[5]

According to Clawson: 'the whole of outdoor recreation is, to a large extent, a package deal; it must be viewed as a whole, in terms of cost, satisfaction and time, for all members of the family as a group [and] the demand curves must be derived first for the whole experience.' The whole recreation experience involves five identifiable phases and each of these phases is important in decision-making by the recreationists. These phases are: (i) planning or anticipation, (ii) travel to the recreation site, (iii) on-site experiences, (iv) travel back and (v) recollection. It is the combination of these experiences which leads to the satisfaction for the recreationists.

Following the Clawson approach, to find the demand relationship we estimate demand data for the whole recreation experience and from these data we derive the demand data for the recreation experience *per se*—for example boating or fishing.

The demand data for the whole recreation experience are assumed to show an inverse relationship between the number of recreation days and a *proxy or surrogate* price variable, encompassing such costs as travel, food and other expenditures associated with a journey to and from the recreation site. With these data, demand data for the recreation experience *per se* can be derived using *simulated* prices.

The method of approach is as follows: suppose we wish to estimate the demand relationship for an outdoor recreation, such as boating, on a large reservoir close to an urban population. We assume for convenience of exposition that the population of the area is, say, located in four concentric zones and, further, that these zones are homogeneous with regard to population and socio-economic factors. These assumptions are

Table 4.2 *Hypothetical schedule of visits and travel costs (price) to a recreation area*

	No. of recreation days	Price of visit per day
Zone A	300	5s
Zone B	200	10s
Zone C	100	15s
Zone D	0	20s

made for simplicity of exposition and would have to be relaxed in practical cases. The visitor and travel cost (price) data, assumed to have been collected using statistical methods, can be summarised as in Table 4.2. These data constitute a schedule of the demand for the recreation experience as a whole when there is no charge at all for the use of the facilities, and their values constitute points on a curve, called the demand curve, for the total recreation experience. It is from this schedule or curve that we can derive the demand relationship for the recreation *per se* —in this case, boating. The procedure is as follows. Suppose a price has to be paid for the use of the boating facilities and that this price is 5s per recreation day. It is possible to trace the effects of this price, collected as a user charge, on the number of recreation days demanded. Suppose that a charge of 5s per recreation day is made. Recreationists in Zone A would now have to pay 10s per boating day, made up of 5s in travel costs and 5s in user charges, that is the travel cost to the site for users in Zone B without boating charges. We assume that recreationists in Zone A at this price of 10s demand the same number of boating days as recreationists in Zone B, that is 200. It now costs recreationists in Zone B 15s for a boating day made up of 10s in travelling costs plus 5s in boating charges. At 15s a day we assume that they demand the number of boating days recreationists in Zone C demand at 15s per day without boating charges, that is, 100 boating days. Similarly for Zone C the boating cost of 5s raises the total cost of a boating day to 20s, and at this travel cost there is no demand for boating days from Zone C. Thus, at a boating charge of 5s per boating day, the total number of boating days falls from 600 at zero user charge

Table 4.3   *A hypothetical Clawson demand schedule*

Price of boating	Number of boating days from each zone	Total number of boating days
zero	300 + 200 + 100	600
5s	200 + 100	300
10s	100	100
15s	zero	zero

to 300 at 5s per user charge. We can estimate the number of boating days making the same assumption for other boating charges. In our example we take 10s and 15s. The results, summarised in Table 4.3, constitute a Clawson demand schedule for the outdoor recreation *per se*, that is, for the boating.

The Clawson approach uses a proxy or surrogate price variable, measured in terms of transportation, lodgings and food costs above those incurred if the trip were not made. The definition of price is not uniquely defined and the use of such a variable leads to difficulties of conceptual interpretation when it comes to measuring economic benefits, but may be very useful for the purposes of predicting future demand. Both schedules have negative slopes; that is, the rate of change of quantity demanded with respect to price is negative. The Clawson demand data are subject to bias as they tend to underestimate the

90

demand for recreation because of an assumption about the value of time for each zone. Recreationists are faced with two constraints: income and time. Those living furthest away from the recreation site will have higher travel costs and use more time in getting there than those in adjacent zones. The dual constraint will result in a lower use rate for distant zones, because of the high travel costs and because of the longer travel time needed to get to the site. Suppose we could eliminate the price of travel for recreationists in all zones. Such a welcome situation would not necessarily lead to outer zone consumers of recreation adopting the visit patterns of their counterparts in zones adjacent to the recreation site. The value of time may well differ from zone to zone. High time valuations work in the direction of pushing down visit rates for distant journeys to the recreation site. In drawing the demand schedules, it has been assumed that the time constraint is the same for all zones. Such an assumption is unlikely to be true in general. However, this is a matter to be tested in individual cases. The true demand schedule, therefore, should be to the right of the Clawson demand schedule. The extent of the bias involved depends on the type of recreation and the time involved in getting there. In the case of a weekend recreation it might be important but where a holiday trip is involved it is likely to be less serious.[13] The Clawson schedule also suffers from another distortion: it makes no allowance for the people who make a conscious effort to reside near the recreation site in order to bridge the time factor.[14] Finally, the Clawson demand data provide only a measure of the *primary* benefits of outdoor recreation.

The demand for a commodity is influenced by many factors. These require that the economist's restrictive assumption of *ceteris paribus* be relaxed. The price of the commodity is an important variable influencing demand, but there are also other variables, such as the incomes of recreationists and the prices of other commodities, affecting the quantities demanded per period of time. Knetsch has suggested other determinants of the demand for outdoor recreation being incorporated in the cost function of visit. The other determinants he specified were the income of the recreationists, the availability of substitute areas, and some measure of congestion. Income is a fundamental variable in any demand function, and the types of outdoor recreation in any area will reflect it. A reservoir surrounded by a low income area might be used for one type of fishing, but at higher income levels might be used for another. Thus, rising income may well bring about changes in the type of recreation demanded. This is the old dichotomy between the rich and poor man's sports, the distinction being based upon income and not social position. The availability of close substitutes has an important influence on the volume of visits and the sensitivity of visits to changes in user charges. If one reservoir has a higher permit charge than another, say for fishing, this is likely to make the higher permit fee reservoir less attractive economically, thereby reducing the number of recreationists using it. Location, size and quality of a particular site can, however, counteract the effects of differences in user charges. Congestion can cause the demand schedule to shift downwards, thereby reducing visits from all zones. A judicious use of user charges can be helpful in arriving at an optimum visit rate. An important factor influencing the demand schedule for recreation in which water is indispensable is the quality of water. Deterioration in the quality of water can result in a reduction in the number of recreationists. This is clear; but how to incorporate water quality as a variable in the demand function requires further investigation.

Some Empirical Results in the Measurement of Demand

An important characteristic of the Clawson demand function is that, given appropriate data, parameters of the function can be estimated and statistical hypotheses concerning recreationists' behaviour tested. Empirical studies, until recently, have been few in number, but the position is changing rapidly, both in the USA and Britain. It is not proposed to review here the statistical methodology needed for the purpose of data collection and for estimating the parameters, nor to survey the literature to date.[15] Rather, we confine ourselves to a few studies which serve to illustrate the feasibility of the Clawson approach and several features and uses of the methodology.

The first application of Clawson's methodology was made by

Clawson himself. He plotted visitor days and travel cost data on graphs for a number of National Parks in the USA. These graphs confirmed his hypothesis of a downward-sloping relationship between the two variables. The graphical approach is useful in preliminary exercises but does not lend itself to rigorous estimation of parameters of demand equations. To estimate parameters there is a need to use econometric methods, that branch of quantitative economics concerned with the formulation of economic models and their empirical verification.[16] Knetsch[3] in a study of Kerr Reservoir in North Carolina and Virginia, using a simple econometric model, estimated a relationship between visits and dollar cost of travel per visit which supported the Clawson hypothesis. Clawson and Knetsch have reviewed their results in a further recent work.[1] Smith and Kavanagh, using a model with similarities to that of Knetsch and employing data on trout anglers at Grafham Reservoir, Huntingdonshire, England, provided further support for a Clawson demand analysis.[17]

A more sophisticated model has been developed by Stevens, using data relating to three sport fisheries at Yaquina Bay, Oregon.[18] His study is a *bio-economic* model of recreation demand; he outlines a methodology for estimating direct recreation benefits from water pollution control. His model is of relevance to the problem of the effects of river pollution on anglers' behaviour. This aspect of Stevens's work will not be developed; instead emphasis will be given to his results and their uses.

Stevens established estimates of Clawson demand functions for total recreation experiences for bottom, salmon and clam fisheries, using econometric methods. The variables in each function were the number of angler days, a proxy price variable, family income of anglers and distance. A number of interesting results of economic interest were found. These have to do with the relationships between the number of angler days, proxy prices and family incomes. For each fishery, a negative relationship between the number of angler days demanded and the proxy price variable was found. This result, statistically significant in the case of the salmon and bottom fisheries, lends support to the argument that the demand for sports fishing can

93

be viewed in the same conceptual manner as the demand for other goods and services. The influence of anglers' income on the number of angler days was found to be positive in the case of salmon fishing and negative in the other two cases.

From demand functions, we can derive various measures which are of relevance to policy-making matters, such as the effects of user charges on the number of angler days, forecasting the number of angler days and measuring the value of benefits of fisheries for inclusion, say, in a cost–benefit study of a water resource project.[19] [20,] [21] Some of these can be examined in the context of Stevens's results.

Table 4.4 *Estimated number of angler days taken at alternative increases in the price paid to fish at three Yaquina Bay sports fisheries*

Price increase per angler day	Bottom fish	Salmon	Clam
$0.00	28,372	10,236	6,446
$0.50	20,207	7,204	3,592
$1.00	14,332	5,075	1,998
$1.50	10,244	3,589	1,113
$2.00	7,238	2,558	620
$3.00	3,682	1,275	54
$4.00	1,854	564	*

* No estimate made.
Source: J. B. Stevens, op. cit.

To estimate the effects of user charges, we need to derive the demand schedules for the recreation experiences *per se*—that is: bottom fishing, salmon fishing and clam fishing. Table 4.4, given by Stevens, was derived in a manner similar to the hypothetical demand schedule shown in Table 4.3. The effect of increases in user charges is to reduce the number of visits. This is in agreement with *a priori* expectations. Without user charges the number of angler days at the bottom fishery is 28,372 and at $4 per visit the number of angler days had dropped to 1,854 visits. In the case of clam fishing at $4 the number of anglers is almost zero. Similar patterns can be drawn from the data concerning the behaviour of salmon fishermen. Thus, we have employed information about the effect of user charges on total attendances at the fisheries on the assumption that the *only* variable changing is the user charge.

A useful way to summarise an economic characteristic of consumers is by means of the concept of elasticity. One kind of elasticity is *income* elasticity of demand, which can be defined as the percentage change in the number of angler days per time period divided by the percentage change in anglers' family or personal incomes. The range of values of the measure is from zero to infinity. Commodities with an income elasticity greater than unity are often described as 'luxuries', while 'necessities' are defined as commodities with a value between zero and unity. For both *luxurious* and *necessitous* commodities the numerical value of the elasticity is positive in sign. We can have negative income elasticities—cases in which increases in the incomes of consumers are associated with a decline in quantity demanded. Commodities with negative elasticities are sometimes called *inferior* goods. (It is well to emphasise that this inferiority is not inherent in the good itself, but reflects tastes and the social attitudes of consumers.) Stevens provides estimates of income elasticities for the three fisheries. We recall that the income variable showed a negative relationship between the number of angler days and anglers' family income for the clam and bottom fisheries. This characteristic is reflected in the values of income elasticities given by Stevens and shown in Table 4.5. As far as the anglers of the Yaquina Bay Fisheries are concerned, clam and bottom fishing are considered to be *inferior* goods. Thus, as the incomes of fishermen rise, then the expectation is that the anglers will shift away from clam and bottom fishing. Such information is, therefore, of importance in selecting fisheries for future development. With an expectation of increasing incomes, and assuming other factors unlikely to change, the manager of a recreation site with such demand characteristics would be ill-advised to rush into the development of these types of sports fisheries.

Stevens uses his elasticities to make predictions for the year 1975. Making predictions about human behaviour is, of course, an exercise full of hazards and one which requires many

Table 4.5   *Income elasticities of demand at mean income*

Fishery	Value of elasticity
Salmon	+0·258
Bottom fishing	−0·038
Clam digging	−0·144

qualifications (as is made apparent in Chapter 12 of this book). Assuming no increase in the price variable Stevens estimated that the total number of angler days in the salmon, bottom and clam fisheries could be expected to increase by 59·6 per cent, 13·2 per cent and 0·6 per cent respectively by 1975. His projections made no allowance for any reduction in the quality of fishing at Yaquina Bay, though the importance of water quality is not ignored in this study.

An important question often asked is: 'What is the "value" of a fishery or what are the "benefits" of sports fishing?' The empirical demand functions can be used to provide monetary measures of such 'values' or 'benefits'. The area under the demand curve relating recreation days to the prices consumers are willing to pay provides a measure of benefits. This is the approach of the consumer surplus theory of economics: it is considered by some to be useful in cases where the adjustments are something less than total in nature, for example, in a water pollution problem involving partial destruction of the fishery.[22, 23] However, in the case where a total destruction of

Table 4.6   *Gross revenues accruing to a non-discriminating monopolistic owner of three Yaquina Bay fisheries (in dollars)*

Price increase per angler day	Bottom fish	Salmon	Clam
0.50	10,103	3,602	1,796
1.00	14,332	5,075	1,998
1.50	15,366	5,383	1,670
2.00	14,476	5,116	1,240
3.00	11,046	3,825	162

the fishery might follow from, say, a particular method of waste disposal, Stevens suggests the non-discriminating monopoly approach as the measure of value. Here the value of the fishery is viewed as the total rent that anglers would be willing to pay for the opportunity of fishing or digging clams. The value is estimated by finding that price which maximises total revenue, where total revenue is price per angling day multiplied by the number of angling days. Table 4.6 shows a schedule of gross revenue to a non-discriminating monopolistic owner of the three fisheries. It can be seen that maximum revenue in both the bottom fish and salmon fisheries is found where a price per angler day of $1.5 is charged, while in the case of clam digging this is found at a price of $1 per day. Total revenue is thus $22,747 per year, that is $15,366 for bottom fish, $5,383 for salmon and $1,998 dollars for clam digging. Suppose some method of waste disposal results in a total loss of aquatic life, the benefits of preventing this loss would be equal to $22,747. If the cost of waste treatment were less than this amount, it would be more efficient from an economic standpoint to treat the wastes rather than to destroy the fishery. No allowance is made for other benefits in this valuation. If we were to make the assumption that the loss of aquatic life is irreversible, the validity of which is a matter to be determined by the biologist, we would then have to discount the benefits from the fishery to estimate the capital value of the fishery.[24]

The few empirical studies discussed above show that progress has been made in the methodology of measuring recreation demand since Clawson and Knetsch wrote in 1963 that 'the analysis of the demand for outdoor recreation may be roughly at the same stage of development that the analysis of the demand for agricultural commodities was forty or more years ago'. From current research proceeding in both the USA[25] and Britain,[26] we can look forward to more and better information on recreation demands to be incorporated in cost–benefit studies of water resource projects.

References

1. M. Clawson and J. L. Knetsch, *Economics of Outdoor Recreation*, John Hopkins Press, 1966.

2. *Final Report of the Council on the Recreational Use of Waterworks*, Institution of Water Engineers, London. The Draft Report, together with discussion, is to be found in the *Journal of the Institution of Water Engineers*, Vol. 17, No. 2, March 1963. Also relevant is *Safeguards to be Adopted in the Operation and Management of Waterworks*, Ministry of Housing and Local Government, August 1967.

3. J. L. Knetsch, 'Economics of Including Recreation as a Purpose of Water Resources Projects', *Journal of Farm Economics*, December 1964; and Resources for the Future, Inc., Reprint No. 50, Washington, 1965.

4. *Leisure in the Countryside, England and Wales* (Cmnd. 2928), London, 1966. See also a sequel, *Use of Reservoirs and Gathering Grounds for Recreation*, Ministry of Land and Natural Resources, Circular 33/66, September 1966.

5. M. Clawson, *Methods of Measuring the Demand for and the Value of Outdoor Recreation*, Resources for the Future, Inc., Reprint No. 10, Washington, 1959.

6. *A Lea Valley Regional Park—An Essay in the Use of Neglected Land for Recreation and Leisure*, Civic Trust, London, July 1964.

7. *Policies, Standards and Procedures in the Formulation, Evaluation and Review of Plans for Use and Development of Water and Related Land Resources*, 87th Congress, 2nd Session, Senate Document No. 97, Washington, 1962; and *Evaluation Standards for Primary Outdoor Recreation Benefits*, Supplement No. 1, Washington, 1964.

8. *Water Resources Act, 1963*, Eliz. II, Ch. 38.

9. *Great Ouse Water Act, 1961*, 9 and 10 Eliz. II, Ch. xiii.

10. *The Countryside Act, 1968*, Eliz. II, Ch. 41.

11. M. Clawson and J. L. Knetsch, 'Outdoor Recreation Research: Some Concepts and Suggested Areas of Study', *Natural Resources Journal*, Vol. 3, October 1963; and Resources for the Future, Inc., Reprint No. 43, Washington, 1963.

12. For a more expansive and critical discussion see Ruth P. Mack and Sumner Meyers, 'Outdoor Recreation' in Robert Dorfman (Ed.), *Measuring Benefits of Government Investments*, Brookings Institution, Washington, 1965.

13. J. L. Knetsch, 'Outdoor Recreation Demands and Benefits', *Land Economics*, Vol. 39, No. 4, November 1963.

14. J. A. Crutchfield, 'Valuation of Fishery Resources', *Land Economics*, Vol. 38, No. 2, May 1962.

15. References to these studies can be found in Robert J. Smith, *Select Bibliography on the Economic Analysis of Recreation*, Department of Industrial Economics, University of Birmingham, November 1967, and Robert J. Smith, *The Measurement of Recreational Benefits: A Critical Survey of Literature and of Development of the Theory*, University of Birmingham, Faculty of Commerce Discussion Paper, Series A, No. 101.

16. A. A. Walters, *An Introduction to Econometrics*, Macmillan, 1968.

17. Robert J. Smith and N. J. Kavanagh, 'The Measurement of Benefits of Trout Fishing: Preliminary Results of a Study at Grafham Water', *Journal of Leisure Research*, Autumn 1969.

18. J. B. Stevens, 'Recreation Benefits from Water Pollution Control', *Water Resources Research*, Vol. 2, No. 2, 1966.

19. A. R. Prest and R. Turvey, 'Cost–Benefit Analysis', in *Surveys of Economic Theory: Resource Allocation*, Vol. III, New York, 1967.

20. M. Feldstein, 'Cost–Benefit Analysis and Investment in the Public Sector', *Public Administration*, Vol. 42, 1964.

21. (a) F. L. Arden and N. J. Kavanagh, 'Modern Management Techniques', *Journal of the Institute of Water Engineers*, Vol. 22, No. 6, August 1968.

(b) N. J. Kavanagh, 'The Development of Cost-Benefit Analysis', CBA/68/67, *Royal Institute of Public Administration*, 1968 (mimeo).

22. Emery N. Castle and William G. Brown, 'The Economic Value of a Recreational Resource—A Case Study of the Oregon Salmon Steelhead Sport Fishery', Paper presented before the Committee on the Economics of Water Resources Development of the Western Agricultural Economics Research Council, San Francisco; California, 1964. Conference Proceedings, *Economics in the Decision Making Process—Economics of Water Based Outdoor Recreation*.

23. Arthur Maass *et al.*, *Design of Water Resource Systems;* Chapter 2, 'Objectives of Water Resource Development', by Stephen A. Marglin, Harvard University Press, Cambridge, Mass. (and Macmillan & Co. Ltd., London), 1962.

24. Kenneth J. Arrow, 'Criteria for Social Investment', *Water Resources Research*, Vol. 1, No. 1, 1965.
25. A. V. Kneese, in *Problems in Public Expenditure Analysis*, edited by Samuel B. Chase, Jun., The Brookings Institution, 1968, pp. 65–71.
26. Countryside Commission, *Research Register No. 2*, Spring 1969.

Chapter 5

Research by Local Planning Authorities

GORDON E. CHERRY

In recent years, 'two main changes have taken place in the state of recreation research in Britain: first, an enormous growth in both the volume and variety of topics studied and secondly, an increase in the number of research organizations and individuals involved'.[1] In this expansion local planning authorities have been prominent, and this chapter reviews the nature of the research contributions they have made. By way of introduction, some of the reasons for the growth of interest in recreation research are examined. Then follows an indication of the problems facing local planning authorities in their involvement in research programmes. The main body of the chapter deals with a review of the range and types of research undertaken by, or on behalf of, local authorities and concludes by drawing attention to the fields of study which so far have been inadequately explored.

Background Factors

Research work in local authorities has been stimulated by a number of factors. First there were the influential reports of the early and mid-1960s. A major example was the 27-volume study of outdoor recreation in America by the Outdoor Recreation Resources Review Commission (ORRRC) in 1962 which, in presenting the scale of the problem, suggested the likely future explosion of recreation activity in this country. Michael Dower's *Fourth Wave: The Challenge of Leisure* reflected popular concern in Britain, while the *Pilot National Recreation Survey* of 1965, undertaken by Keele University in association with the British Travel Association,* provided the first set of national

* Now called the British Tourist Authority.

101

statistics. Subsequently, the 'Countryside in 1970' Conferences have served to provide more information and to stimulate further interest. More direct pressure on local authorities has been applied through the Sports Council and its Regional Councils; the Technical Panels which serve these have all, at least, made inventories of facilities in their regions.

Additionally, there has been the effect of recent legislation. In particular, we should mention The Countryside Act, 1968; this was 'an Act to enlarge the functions of the Commission established under the National Parks and Access to the Countryside Act, 1949, to confer new powers on local authorities and other bodies for the conservation and enhancement of natural beauty and for the benefit of those resorting to the countryside and to make other provision for the matters dealt with in the Act of 1949 and generally as respects the countryside, and to amend the law about trees and woodlands, and footpaths and bridleways, and other public paths' (preamble). Through this Act local authorities are empowered to provide country parks, greater scope is made for the provision of facilities in National Parks, water undertakers are empowered to permit the use of their reservoirs and waterways by the public and to provide facilities, and the Forestry Commissioners are also permitted to provide facilities on their land. These and other provisions are intended to enhance the enjoyment of the countryside by the general public, and a new era of local authority endeavour in recreation planning has been initiated. Research has not been forgotten, even by legislation, and in this connection it is pertinent to refer to section 98 of the Town and Country Planning Act 1968: 'The Minister may, with the consent of the Treasury, make grants for assisting establishments engaged in promoting or assisting research relating to, and education with respect to, the planning and design of the physical environment.'

Next, we might observe that the diverse nature of the subject of recreation has made it particularly suitable for multi-disciplinary research and has thereby further encouraged research in local planning authorities. Specialists outside local government have commented on issues and raised questions to open up a very wide range of studies for the recreation planner. At the same time there is a rich variety of background situations

102

and topics, not to mention staff from very different professional outlooks, within the local authority. This is mostly a result of a diverse legislative background. In the countryside there has been some measure of unified approach because of powers for the provision of facilities which stem from the National Parks and Access to the Countryside Act, 1949. But in urban areas, provision for sport and physical recreation is made through at least three departments of the local authority (Baths, Parks and Education), and sometimes more.

A long history of separate legislation has created a division of administrative responsibility for the provision of facilities, with the result that co-ordinated planning, allocation of resources and any serious attempts at comprehensive research over the whole field of recreation by local authority staffs is almost impossible. At the same time, however, pressure to provide recreation facilities (and thereby to stimulate research activities) has come from a number of sources, and this variety in stimulus, while perhaps leading to fragmentation of interest, has still been of significant value. The Baths and Washhouses Act, 1846, was originally concerned with personal hygiene, but now a Baths Department's responsibilities extend beyond swimming to many other forms of recreation and public entertainment. The provision of public parks stems from the Public Health Act, 1875, which gave powers to local authorities to make provision for public walks and pleasure grounds. The Keep Fit campaign of the inter-war years stimulated the demand for physical fitness through outdoor activities, organised games and exercise, and new local authority provisions were made through the Physical Training and Recreation Act, 1937. Now Parks Departments cater for a wide range of active recreation and entertainment events, and the traditional use of the Victorian park is under pressure from conflicting interests and a changing pattern of utilisation. Education Departments, operating under the Education Act, 1944, provide many facilities including sports grounds, swimming pools, gymnasia and sports halls. These three departments, together with Planning Departments acting as co-ordinators or, perhaps, as initiators of policy, have all focused attention on provision of facilities, and research has been stimulated by this activity.

Another factor in the increase in recreation research in local authorities stems simply from the need for planning. As far as the countryside is concerned there is the need to plan in a more positive way than was envisaged in the 1949 Act. As Molyneux reminds us: 'Very few people in the immediate post war years when this Act was formulated and passed could have foreseen the growth of a general countryside recreation movement on the scale made possible by rapidly increasing car ownership. Nor could they have envisaged the explosive growth of active recreation particularly in water-based sports; but the growth in actual numbers, and the increased conflict among recreationists themselves and with other users of land and water, sharpened an awareness of a deteriorating situation.'[2]

In urban areas the need to plan more effectively has a somewhat different context. The early Development Plans were concerned essentially with land use and arbitration between competing uses, their role in terms of recreation planning being to provide allocations for a range of different facilities according to various standards of provision. Hence provision was made for open space, both public and private, allotments, and public buildings such as swimming baths.

More recently, however, there has been the growing realisation that planning for urban recreation entails much more than this. It involves 'not only designing, siting, and administering facilities so that they can serve the varying needs of different sections of the community—clubs, groups, individuals of all ages and the special requirements of schools, but developing also a hierarchy of provision within categories of facilities. Communities will require sports complexes embracing a number of different sizes of halls and other specialist facilities; but they will need also other indoor provision perhaps situated in schools, community centres, industrial premises and so on' (Molyneux op. cit.). A process of planning for urban recreation based upon the submission of separate policies and proposals for each of a series of uses or activities has been shown to be inadequate. In the desire to see recreation planning on a new basis, there has been a departure from relying on national standards, and the search for new criteria of provision has opened interesting research fields.

Further, we should acknowledge the part played in local authority affairs by the Sports Council, established in 1965, and its Regional Councils. The latter, with areas co-terminous with the Economic Planning Regions, have found it convenient to recruit manpower for their Technical Panels from the constituent local planning authority offices. In most cases the Chairmen of the Technical Panels are Chief Officers of prominent planning departments and this ensures a weighty contribution of staff resources to ongoing projects. A large volume of work by local planning authorities in recent years on recreation matters has stemmed directly from this source. Through this involvement with the Sports Council local authorities now share a growing appreciation of a rapidly developing and complex situation. Because of the work with the Regional Councils, town planners have become prominent in taking up the challenge to plan positively for recreation. (In a sense this is almost surprising, because it has brought the planner to develop a specialist interest somewhat removed from the traditional land use orientation of his profession. It could have been, for example, that the educationalists would react to this challenge and keep the all-embracing planner at bay, but this was not the case.)

The variety of work stimulated by the Regional Sports Councils has helped in the recognition of the need for much more data both on supply and demand, together with greater survey material in almost every branch of recreation research. We are beginning to know much more about the relative importance of such characteristics as income, social class, mobility, age and marital status in influencing participation in recreation activities, but much more enquiry is needed. The following topics, for example, have been suggested by a recent working party of the Sports Council: '. . . the capacity of a sports facility—its optimum use and the way this is affected by design, management and administration—is clearly important in calculating needs, yet assessing the capacity presents complex problems. Similarly, more research is needed before advice can be given on the location and siting of facilities. We need greater understanding of the relationship between public and private provision, and between the size of community and the range of sports played; of the extent and strength of regional differences in participation, and their causes; of the impact of vigorous leadership, for instance from a youth leader or recreation officer; and of methods of assessing the needs of casual, unorganised play.'[3] Some at least of these are suitable studies for local authorities.

Finally, we might note that the importance of local authority involvement in the research field also stems from its increasing role as a provider of facilities. The role of private facilities, owned by local voluntary clubs or those associated with industrial or business concerns, is not expanding, and while the number of commercial facilities has shown a marked increase in recent years, for example in the form of ten-pin bowling centres or golf driving ranges, public facilities are increasing even more rapidly in number, especially swimming pools, sports grounds and sports halls. Moreover, it is likely that most large recreation facilities will be provided in the future by local authorities and this puts increasing emphasis on the need for an overall planning policy for provision, an awareness of the dangers of overlap— not only between neighbouring authorities but between departments in the same authority—and a recognition that the social motivations in the projection of demand are as yet imperfectly understood. It is against the background of such factors as these that the development of recreation research in local authorities has to be seen.

Research Problems for Local Planning Authorities

There are, at present, many organisations either carrying out research themselves or liaising closely with others on their studies. These include the Countryside Commission, the Nature Conservancy, the Forestry Commission, the Water Resources Board, the British Travel Association, and the Sports Council. Meetings between representatives of these bodies have led to the establishment of a Countryside Recreation Research Advisory Group (CRRAG). Additionally there are universities, government departments and private consultants. Quite apart from all these, we have already suggested that a considerable onus of responsibility lies on local authorities to conduct research or, at least, to stimulate the researches of others in view of their considerable role in providing facilities. What are the chances that local authorities will effectively meet this challenge?

As far as research within local authorities is concerned, a primary difficulty must be the shortage of skilled human resources. Most planning departments have by now developed an important tradition in local government for case studies on a range of planning problems including recreation; but, if recreation planning is to become something more than work on an inventory of resources or measurement of use (the more popular of contributions to date) a more substantial input of contributory, multidisciplinary skills is required. It must be doubtful whether local authorities will be able to recruit research teams on a sufficient scale to make much impact by themselves. One solution however might lie in the amalgamation, via secondment or voluntary co-operation, of a number of planning department representatives within a region in order to form a bigger team. Personal experience would suggest that, given goodwill and an equal readiness from all partners, there is considerable scope in this idea; the numerous research publications of the North Regional Planning Committee[4] attest to this.

Even granted a collection of skills, however, an 'internal' difficulty remains for the recreation researcher, namely the risk that his work might not be taken sufficiently seriously because it does not rank with other priorities in a departmental work programme. Certain authorities, both rural and urban, have developed research teams which are more than just statistical manipulators, but so far there are relatively few instances of departments where research, as a separate section with a leader on a par with other senior officers, makes its full contribution by linking directly with policy-making. Where this is not so there is the danger that because the research leader's status is depressed *vis-à-vis* other sections of the department, his team's work does not form a coherent part of a committed total programme.

Another problem for recreation research workers in a local authority situation is the gap between research and implementation. This, of course, applies to planning research generally, but it may be most pronounced in the field of recreation. It is likely to cause a work frustration to which local authority planners are very sensitive. This is largely peculiar to them and is not an emotion experienced so much by academic researchers, who are not 'committed' people, in the sense that planners are, in their desire to achieve practical results. Given this frustration based on the feeling that research in a local planning department leads to little immediate positive action, this could result in lack of initiative in launching new enquiries.

Finally, there are the difficulties stemming from a lack of continuity. The best research is undertaken where there are no breaks in ongoing studies and where a number of different aspects of work provide an invaluable support for other related activities. In this situation there are long-term benefits to be derived, and investment in resources is maximised; new projects can be launched quickly, and there are available staff who have an up-to-date background knowledge of essential data, and an awareness of issues, based on wide reading, on which to start work. Where research teams are allowed to run down, and where there is no continuity of work, these advantages are dissipated and it is an even harder task to begin a particular study effectively. In local authority departments this must constitute one of the greatest hazards for research.

On the other hand there are certain advantages to record. Research costs money and when undertaken by academic bodies or consultants, for example, the budget has to be clearly indicated. In a local planning authority these costs are largely hidden, and a good deal of work can be carried out which involves the time of a range of staff internally within the department (secretaries, draughtsmen, clerks/statistical helpers, and even student labour) with little need for precise budgeting. The composition of the department's annual budget is sufficiently flexible for quite large research needs to be met if required. In this situation what is of paramount importance is the initiative of the research workers and the sense of commitment by the Chief Officer. The recreation researcher becomes used to working on shoe-string budgets, but on due reflection the local authority research worker may consider his access to funds rather easier than in other organisations.

A second advantage is his access to other resources. Consider, for instance, computers in the Treasurer's Departments: good working relations with key members of staff can provide some very important facilities, for example, availability of computer time and the technical services of programmers. There is also the ease with which surveys can be carried out because of the co-operation secured from other Departments of the local authority. For example, there is the assistance of the Engineer or Surveyor in car parking and traffic counts, or the Parks Superintendent in surveys of parks and open spaces, or of the police, who should always be notified when surveys involve stopping people in public places for data collection. Additionally, there is the wide range of data which is already available in a number of Departments; for example, the Clerk has the Register of Electors, a most useful sampling frame; the Treasurer has information on rateable values; the Planning Officer has land use and other records; and the Baths Superintendent, the Parks Superintendent and the Education Officer have relevant data on sports facilities.

But whatever the arguments in favour of setting up local authority recreation research teams might be, the research field is too wide for simply one organisation; and, in any case, it is desirable for relationships to develop with a range of bodies for maximum exposure to experience and cross-fertilisation of ideas. It is perhaps likely that an increasing amount of research work will be undertaken in universities and in other organisations outside local authorities, or by local authorities in conjunction with these bodies, including market research firms. It is as well to be realistic about the problems of this situation. If the maximum feedback to local authorities, as both providers of facilities and planning bodies, is to be achieved, three things are desirable.

The first is that the planning officers should have the time and energy to read, and act upon, an ever-increasing output of published material, findings from which will be of relevance in some degree or other to their own local or regional situation. The second is that there should be a receptiveness by planning officers to ideas, and suggestions, about recreation planning from outside bodies. Local authorities (like any other body) *can*

109

be inward-looking and cautious about the usefulness or relevance of ideas developed outside their own court. A local authority reaction based on 'who do those people think they are, telling me what to do?' is by no means uncommon. On the other hand, non-local authority commentators must strive to become more aware of local government situations and the political tactics of getting across a point of view. The third concerns the relationship between local authorities as clients and consultant organisations as paid advisers. The politics of this situation are that local authorities 'use' consultants and this can apply to consultants in recreation planning studies as in any other field. They can be used to advantage or to disadvantage. They are used profitably when a proposal following a survey is accepted by the Council more readily than if it were put forward by the authority's own officers. On the other hand, relationships with a consultant can degenerate dangerously when confidence in the competence or straightforwardness of either party is in question; an effective steering committee between the local authority and the consultant is one remedy, provided that a clear and unchanging view of the research project is held from the outset.

The Scope of Local Authority Studies

A number of local planning authorities have in recent years made substantial direct contributions to recreation studies. Among the prominent authorities have been counties such as Bedfordshire, Durham, Gloucestershire, Hampshire, Lancashire and East Sussex; Brent among the London Boroughs; the Greater London Council; Coventry, Liverpool and Newcastle among the Boroughs; and the Northern Region among groups of authorities who have acted with Regional Sports Councils.

The type of work undertaken can be identified under four main headings:

   (i) surveys concerned with the use of facilities, and reviews of patterns of leisure activities;
   (ii) case studies of recreation planning at particular locations;
   (iii) regional studies; and
   (iv) demand studies.

Without in any way attempting a comprehensive summary of the work carried out, we can review the scope of these studies and draw attention to particularly important examples.

(i) *User Surveys*

Surveys which examine facilities and their use have been especially popular. At their worst, these have reflected planners' readiness to collect data, often in a relatively unstructured way, by way of problem-oriented studies with limited goals and little 'spin off' for future research; consequently, they mostly become additive studies contributing little beyond a stock of knowledge, the usefulness of which ultimately is very debatable. But, at their best, they have contributed new insights into the changing use of leisure time and have drawn attention to the planning implications involved. Favourite approaches have been to collect basic data either by 'turnstile' surveys, collecting information at source of activity, or by surveys of a sample population by self-administered or interview surveys. Data from sports clubs have also proved to be easily obtainable.

A particularly well-documented study of this type is the *Surveys of the Use of Open Spaces*[5] in Greater London. The requirement was to provide detailed information on the use of, and demand for, open space facilities in Inner London, and three separate but complementary surveys were carried out in 1964. The first was a home interview survey to establish overall patterns of open space usage and attitudes to open space. A sample of 2,015 adults was interviewed in a stratified random cluster sample of thirty-three wards in the former County of London. The second was a survey in selected parks to examine (i) the ways in which parks of different functions and sizes were used, and (ii) the extent of their influence. Thirteen parks were selected and a sample of approximately 160 adult visitors to each park was interviewed, with a questionnaire content similar to that of the home interview survey. The third was a survey of schoolchildren aged 11–16, an age group not covered by the other two surveys, to examine the usage of parks in the context of all leisure activities.

The wealth of data obtained from these surveys provided a

useful insight into social characteristics which have helped considerably in establishing planning goals. Reference to the Report should be made for full appreciation of the analysis; but certain statistical findings related to the open space visiting habits of the adult population make fascinating reading. It was found, for example, that there was 'an average weekly visiting rate of 1,040 visits per thousand population aged 15 and over, with the highest visiting rates among those in full time education, those possessing a dog, those in areas exceptionally well provided with open space, those with jobs in a professional and intermediate category, those with larger gardens and those aged 15–19' (op. cit.). Complementing these data, we might note that as far as young children were concerned, 81 per cent of children aged 18 months to 9 years had visited a park in the last month, including 46 per cent in the last week; over half the children visiting a park on the previous day had been accompanied by an adult.

The importance of surveys of this type is that they contribute to a body of knowledge which provides relevant material on which realistic planning policies might be based. For example an important conclusion of the Greater London survey was that 'The differing patterns of demand . . . indicate that an ideal park system has to perform a variety of functions and that these functions can be supplied at different distances from home and in different sizes of park. The close relationship of a park's size, facilities, location and function all suggest the need for a hierarchical system of different types of parks. Certain sections of the population may be dependent on one element in the hierarchy, while those who are more mobile or have more time may make use of many elements in the hierarchy at different times. A goal of open space planning would therefore be to give to each individual the opportunity of access to a range of open spaces arranged so that major and more specialised demands are adequately met in terms of size, facilities and accessibility.' This flexibility based on real knowledge of a situation constitutes a very large step forward from the former rigid adherence to defined standards of provision, expressed in acres per thousand population.

Another type of general study is into leisure activities over a wide range, without a focus on the use of any particular facility. An example of this was the study in Newcastle in 1966, a modest undertaking compared with the Greater London project, but important in its own way to furthering recreation planning.[6] This was a pilot survey into the leisure activities of a small sample of adults above 17 years of age in Newcastle, held during March 1966. Postal questionnaires were sent to 239 households eliciting information about actual leisure activities on a previous weekday evening and the previous Saturday afternoon and evening, and what might have been considered likely leisure activities for a weekday evening and Saturday afternoon and evening the previous summer. Three groups of activities were recognised:

  (i) home activities (such as TV, radio, records, reading, resting, hobbies, visiting friends, etc.);
 (ii) indoor activities (cinema, theatre, dancing, club, pub, bingo, meetings, games, etc.); and
(iii) outdoor activities (sport, gardening, visits to coast and country, camping, walking, etc.).

Once again, it is the contribution to planning policy which should be the criterion for evaluating the importance of this research. Take, for example, the degree of participation in outdoor games. It was found that only 10 per cent of the sample admitted to playing an outdoor game on a weekday summer evening. We should recall that the National Playing Fields Association standard of 6 acres of playing space per thousand population affirmed by the Ministry of Housing and Local Government in 1955 was based on the assumption that 200 in every thousand population were neither too young nor too old for organised games and other outdoor physical recreation; the Newcastle evidence suggests that the 6 acres would be excessive. Further evidence from Winterbottom, in respect of a survey at Colchester, confirms this: 'less than 2 acres [open space] per thousand population are needed in winter, as against the not ungenerous provision of $2\frac{1}{2}$ acres for summer use'.[7] With the addition of a central park and children's play spaces this gives a total provision of perhaps $3\frac{1}{2}$ acres per thousand population.

Such a reassessment, in principle, is supported by Burnett[8] following his survey of open space in New Towns. He concludes not only that 'a simple ratio of acres per thousand population is a very imprecise measure', but that 'it is also questionable whether open space is an element where precise measurement is practicable or even desirable'.

A variation on studies designed to examine usage of facilities has been a national survey of a sample of local authorities, from the point of view of one particular facility. One example is the playground study by the Council for Children's Welfare.[9] The objective was to study a sample of playgrounds and the use made of them by children, the popularity of activities and facilities and their catchment areas. The survey was carried out during the summer of 1965 in the following English towns: the London Boroughs of Brent and Camden, Bristol, Leicester, Liverpool, Newcastle, Southampton, Swansea and Worcester. A total of 123 playgrounds were studied during 12-hour days; during this time 14,000 children were interviewed, 83 per cent of whom were aged between 5 and 14 years.

An analysis for each local authority was obviously important, but this is a case where an aggregate of a number of different types of playgrounds provided new data for the formulation of standards of provision for average situations. Important information was provided, for example, about the effects of equipment and 'competitive' parks on attendance; these findings together with the activity rates of children attending playgrounds (that is, the attendance as a proportion of children of appropriate age groups living within the catchment area) should prove particularly helpful to local planning authorities in this aspect of recreation planning. For instance, information on the average distance travelled by children to play should suggest the basis of a policy for the ideal distribution of play spaces. Fairly obviously, most children were found to travel short distances while a few went a long way, but important new data suggested that the distance travelled varied very little with children's ages. The mean for all children was 467 yards, but there was surprisingly little variation from this norm: 494 yards for under fives, 459 yards for 5–9-year-olds, and 496 yards for 10–14-year-olds.

(ii) *Local Case Studies*

The second contribution by local authorities or by bodies working on their behalf, has been in respect of case studies of recreation activities and potential in particular geographical areas. Examples have included a planning appraisal of outdoor recreation in the Great Ouse and Ivel valleys in Bedfordshire, a survey of the coastal landscape of Durham and its use for recreation activities, a survey of the New Forest by Colin Buchanan and Partners as part of the South Hampshire study, and a survey of the recreation potential of the River Tyne.

The study of recreation and tourism in the Loch Lomond area, with particular emphasis on Balloch, by Nicholls and Young for Dunbarton County Council[10] can be selected as a particularly good instance of a localised, problem-oriented study, with a significant research content. There has been a long-standing proposal for a National Recreation Centre near Balloch, and in 1964 a special study was commissioned to examine trends in the demand for tourist, recreation and leisure facilities and to advise on the nature and extent of the facilities which could be provided in the area. The published report not only forms a model case study of considerable importance to the local authority and a number of other bodies in the area but it is also of relevance to the examination of other areas and situations which indicate similar problems.

Planning for future needs requires an analysis of the determinants of present demand, and for that reason an examination was made of the various social and economic factors affecting the use of leisure time and, thereby, the demand for recreation and tourist facilities. The factors studied included population, education, occupation, income, mobility, hours of work and holidays. But a detailed study of current patterns of recreation was also necessary: information was obtained from users; 3,000 people being interviewed during the summer of 1966 at a large number of locations throughout the area. Additionally, there were surveys of facilities and services to determine the extent of the supply, the size and nature of demand and possibilities for the future. These surveys subsequently supported the idea of a recreation centre at Balloch: it 'appears to be valid in principle', the reasons being 'existing and probable future increases in demand for recreation facilities in the area, and the desirability of concentrating demand in a few places to minimise pressure in others' (op. cit.).

(iii) *Regional Studies*

The third kind of local authority research consists of regional studies, frequently stimulated by the Regional Sports Councils. The first work in this direction was the straightforward inventory of resources which has been carried out in varying degrees of thoroughness in most regions. The second approach has been to develop studies in depth in relation to a number of facilities, in particular swimming baths and golf courses, but also water sports, and, latterly, indoor sports centres. There has been a number of significant contributions by local authorities, working together within a regional framework.

The first such area of study was on swimming baths and we should refer particularly to a joint report of the North Regional Planning Committee and the Northern Advisory Council for Sport and Recreation,[11] which outlined a method for evaluating the demand for additional swimming baths in the North East by 1981. The need for this study was prompted by the fact that, because the only standard of provision seemed to be the 'rule-of-thumb' of one bath to 40,000 population, a political situation had arisen in which new baths were being provided more as a result of the fortuitous energy of a particular council rather than a realistic evaluation of local or sub-regional needs.

A formula was devised based on certain assumptions relating to the capacity of pools: for non-swimmers, 10 square feet of surface area of water, and for swimmers, 36 square feet of surface area, with an extra allowance for divers. There were further assumptions (and these are now being tested by work carried out by the Sports Council) relating to the average time spent by each person in a pool, and this enabled a hypothetical total weekly and monthly capacity to be calculated. At this point it was assumed that the month with the highest proportionate attendance from the latest figures available might retain this share, and this enabled a total yearly capacity to be

116

calculated. Thereafter refinements were made to take into account hourly variations during the day and seasonal variations in weather which affect attendances. Data concerning swimming pools were collected and, from a formula, hypothetical capacities calculated in respect of each. Where existing attendances were in excess of the hypothetical capacity, a degree of over-use was assumed, this being evidence of need for additional facilities. A 50 per cent increase in visits per head of population was taken as reasonable to reflect extra demand to 1981 in a 'boom' sport. Using five sub-regions in the North East the regional number of additional baths was calculated. Not allowing for replacements, the scale of the problem appeared to be of the order of twenty-three new baths, and the report concluded by suggesting approximate locations. This technique for estimating the scale of future provision was subsequently adopted with variations by other regional bodies in the country.

The Northern Region was also prominent in an early report on demand for golf.[12] A survey found typically heavy pressure on facilities. The situation was that there was room on the region's courses for only one-third of the region's golfers at any one time, and over a thousand names appeared on club waiting lists. Only one club in eleven had any space on its course at weekends, and weekday capacity was probably very small. In order to assess the demand, a postal questionnaire was sent to all club secretaries during 1966 for data on membership and capacity, and a detailed supplementary survey made of seven clubs. Estimates of demand were made on the basis of trend projections of membership figures. Membership was found to have increased by 61 per cent over the previous nine years, and at this rate of simple increase 48 new courses would be needed in the region by 1981; this might be considered a minimum assumption as to demand. Making allowance for population increase and a rise in level of participation (as might be reflected in a growth sport) 105 new courses would be needed by 1981, double the present number. This simple research finding was of value to the formulation of regional planning strategy: 105 new courses would require about 10,000 acres of land, and their provision would form a major element in the pattern of land use in a region or sub-region.

(iv) *Demand Studies*

The fourth type of local authority research has concerned studies with a focus on demand. These have been fairly common. One of the objectives of the New Forest Survey, 1965, was to estimate the increase in recreation pressure which might be expected up to the end of the century, and county recreation surveys (for example Gloucestershire and Lancashire) have been devised round the determination of future requirements of recreation provision. Similarly, there has been a number of urban Planning Department studies of demand, particularly concerning the need for open space and the possible reassessment of standards. We have already referred to the GLC *Surveys of the Use of Open Spaces*;[5] this developed a technique for estimating demand for open space based on a relationship with size and distance. Elsewhere, for particular facilities, simple trend projections have been used.

By and large, studies of demand have not been particularly well developed and there is a need to work on new techniques. The Newcastle pilot survey[6] suggested a relationship between patterns of recreation activity and a variety of social criteria, and this correlation has been the basis of a much wider study in the Northern Region. It might be supposed that the use of leisure time is in some way predetermined by a number of factors, including age, sex, marital status, family size, educational level, occupation, economic status, income, car ownership, and type of residential environment. If the variables could be identified over a given area at a particular time, then, by altering selected variables, a reasonably firm basis of prediction might be secured.

In 1967 the North Regional Planning Committee, on the basis of data from a sample of 4,000 households, collected by National Opinion Polls during the summer, undertook such a study. It was designed to examine the pattern of current outdoor leisure activities in the Northern Region in relation to certain profile data and to evaluate the future pattern of activities with particular reference to coastline and countryside. The findings are yet to be published.

Implications and Assessment

How might we assess the contributions of local planning authorities to recreation research? One way is to set the achievements against the need and point to the omissions which appear. Palmer[13] has suggested five areas in which more research is needed: studies in methodology, measurement of regional need, measurement of demand, cost–benefit analysis of investment in recreation, and measurement of capacity of recreation facilities. It was not suggested that these categories were all suitable for local authority research, and the shopping list has to be modified accordingly, but it is a convenient starting point.

Our own review might suggest the following conclusions. There has been some modest progress in developing techniques of survey and analysis; much more needs to be done, but it is likely that the local authorities' contribution will be small and there will be some dependence on academic institutions.[14] Regional studies on the other hand have made very big strides, and this is a field very suitable for planning authorities. With regard to measurement of demand all the indications are that statistical skills will increasingly be required and it is debatable what further progress will be made by local authorities alone. A similar conclusion would apply to cost–benefit analyses. Capacity studies remain to be developed and it is likely that local authorities will have a good deal to contribute through local case studies.

In view of the difficulties experienced, planning departments as a whole can be well satisfied with their total research progress during the past five years or so. There has been an accumulation of data concerning the use of recreation facilities, and certain sports in particular have been well covered. There has been a fuller appreciation of the effect of the motor-car on leisure habits; it is significant that the survey by Furmidge[15] in East Sussex in 1967 complemented that by Burton[16] at Box Hill in 1964. There is also more information on the whole range of activities undertaken in leisure hours; again, conclusions are very similar, in that for a large proportion of people outdoor recreation away from the home is still very much a minority element in leisure time budgets.

119

But, as reference to Palmer's list suggests, there are a number of important areas relatively neglected. There seems to have been little work undertaken on capacity of resources. The problem is well known: for instance, the over-use of a stretch of countryside or coast where the very environmental quality (perhaps dependent on solitude and quietness) which makes it attractive and sought after is destroyed by the uncontrolled incursion of visitors. The difficulty lies in the assessment of over-use and the selection of measures to overcome it; more local authorities need to develop case studies in this direction. As one guide, Furmidge[15] has suggested, criteria for the environmental capacity of picnic areas in Ashdown Forest.

Another omission is the study of the economic benefits of recreation, particularly of tourism. There are a number of issues which local authorities might study for Tourist Boards or Regional Authorities. It would be useful, for example, to identify the level of returns in selected areas of investment in order to contribute to a realistic tourist policy for a particular region.

'Before and after' studies are now beginning to be undertaken, but many more are needed to fill in some very large gaps in knowledge. This type of study is best carried out on a limited geographical basis to determine the impact of a major facility on the recreation patterns of the population in the catchment area concerned. As more and more new facilities are provided, local case studies are presented as ideal opportunities for local planning authorities. An indoor sports complex is a particularly useful example in view of its range of activities.

We might also mention studies under the broad heading of administration and management. Again, local case studies would begin to open a field which is under-explored. There is a need to identify the causes of inadequate provision and to consider the appropriateness of various forms of administration. In conjunction with this there are the problems of management and one might consider a study of the possible role of the price mechanism in regulating the use of a facility.

Not all fields of investigation are, of course, convenient for local authorities to undertake, because of the particular skills required for the investigation. An obvious example here would be studies into leisure attitudes and factors which influence an individual's use of leisure time. Psychological techniques of investigation might be required into motivation, and one would surmise that local authorities would not be able to provide the necessary skills. One aspect of this field of study might however be taken up as a local case study, and this is the question of substitution of activities; this is the extent to which there might be groups of activities within which one recreation might be regarded as an acceptable substitute for any other. In recreation planning where perhaps there are shortages of either space or other resources, knowledge about acceptable substitute activities would be particularly useful.

We have referred almost entirely in this chapter to recreation as an outdoor activity away from the home, and especially as a sport or pastime requiring the planned provision of facilities. As we have seen, there has been a concentration of research on the present and future use of facilities. There has been very little extension of this research interest into the Arts, a most neglected aspect of recreation. A local authority Development Plan is the basis for making provision for theatres, cinemas, libraries, museums and a host of public buildings, just as much as playing fields, swimming baths and golf courses, and there is the same importance of public investment in certain facilities. The use of these cultural buildings has been quite inadequately studied and the provision of new facilities is often made on very hazy assumptions. Work by Lee[17, 18] has shown the type of research possibilities with regard to social clubs and adult education.

Dramatic events often serve to highlight the need for research. For example, in central area redevelopment it is quite usual to find that major facilities such as cinemas or theatres are affected, demanding closure and perhaps re-siting. Decision to rebuild might depend on knowledge of existing and likely future use. Sometimes the onus falls on local authorities which become heavily involved, especially when a prestige building or reputation is affected. Catchment area studies can give essential data. Such a project has been carried out in respect of theatres for the London Borough of Havering; and in Newcastle, the Planning Department itself has undertaken a comprehensive study. This latter survey was carried out during 1967–8 to examine audience characteristics at three theatres in the City and to examine theatre-going in the context of general evening leisure habits. The findings have not yet been reported, but should make a significant contribution to a stock of knowledge where information is scanty.

To Oscar Wilde is attributed the remark that 'nothing succeeds like excess'. No one would claim that there has been an excess of recreation studies in local authorities. But a good deal of success has attended a large number of their projects. Local authority research workers can indeed be complimented on the contributions they have made in the last five years. To lay emphasis on what has not been done would seem ungenerous, and to say that the value of some repetitive studies is doubtful seems churlish; it is preferable to give due recognition to a series of important investigations undertaken by hard-worked officers in a local planning system already under manpower strain from other directions.

References

1. Joan Greaves, 'Trend Report: National Parks and Access to the Countryside including Coastal Areas', in *Planning Research*, The Town Planning Institute, 1968.

2. D. D. Molyneux, 'Working for Recreation', *Journal of the Town Planning Institute*, Vol. 54, No. 4, April 1968.

3. *Planning for Sport, Report of a Working Party on Scales of Provision*, The Sports Council, Central Council of Physical Recreation, 1968.

4. Gordon E. Cherry, 'Research in the Northern Region', in *Changing the North*, The Town Planning Institute Conference Handbook, May 1968.

5. *Surveys of the Use of Open Spaces*, Research Paper No. 2, Planning Department, Greater London Council, 1968.

6. *Surveys into Leisure Activities*, Report of City Planning Officer to the Town Planning Committee, September 26, 1966, City and County of Newcastle upon Tyne (mimeo).

7. D. M. Winterbottom, 'How Much Open Space Do We Need?', *Journal of the Town Planning Institute*, Vol. 53, No. 4, April 1967.

8. F. T. Burnett, 'Open Space in New Towns', *Journal of the Town Planning Institute*, Vol. 55, No. 6, June 1969.

9. *The Playground Study*, Council for Children's Welfare, 1967.

10. D. C. Nicholls and A. Young, *Recreation and Tourism in the Loch Lomond Area*, Department of Social and Economic Research, University of Glasgow, 1968.

11. *Public Swimming Baths in the North East*, Technical Sub Committee of Planning Officers, Northern Advisory Council for Sport and Recreation and North Regional Planning Committee, 1966.

12. *Survey of Golf Facilities*, North Regional Planning Committee, Northern Advisory Council for Sport and Recreation, 1967.

13. J. E. Palmer, 'Recreational Planning—a Bibliographical Review', *Planning Outlook*, New Series, Vol. 2, 1967.

14. For example, see Thomas L. Burton and P. A. Noad, *Recreation Research Methods: A Review of Recent Studies*, Occasional Paper No. 3, Centre for Urban and Regional Studies, University of Birmingham, 1968.

15. John Furmidge, 'Planning For Recreation in the Countryside', *Journal of the Town Planning Institute*, Vol. 55, No. 2, February 1969.

16. Thomas L. Burton, 'A Day in the Country', *Chartered Surveyor*, 98, 7, 1966.
17. Terence Lee, 'The Optimum Provision and Siting of Social Clubs', *Durham Research Review*, No. 14, September 1963.
18. Terence Lee, 'A Null Relationship Between Ecology and Adult Education', *The British Journal of Educational Psychology*, Vol. XXXVI, February 1966.

Part Three

Planning for Recreation

Chapter 6

Planning for Countryside Recreation*

B. CRACKNELL

Within a few years virtually every family in Britain will have a car, and will be able to enjoy the new mobility it brings. As a result recreational habits are changing and recreational pressures are becoming more widespread. Accessibility to the countryside round towns and cities is already an important aspect of planning for leisure, and this paper considers its implications for urban form and the distribution of population.

The monumental report of the United States Outdoor Recreation Resources Review Commission showed that car-driving for pleasure has become the foremost recreation activity in that country.[1] There has been no survey on such a nationwide scale or at such depth in Britain, but recent surveys by the British Travel Association (now the British Tourist Authority) suggest that in this country also car-driving for pleasure is a leading recreational activity. Their Whitsun 1963 survey showed that over half the population of Britain engaged in some pleasure travel during the three day period, and of these 60 per cent travelled by car.[2]

What do we know about this activity? Much of it, no doubt, is associated with holiday periods and holiday areas. These have their own problems, but in this chapter the emphasis is on the short-distance day or afternoon trip into the countryside.

Several surveys have been carried out recently which enable a tentative attempt to be made to analyse the nature of this activity. These include the survey of Box Hill, Surrey, by Burton, the survey of Berkhamsted Common by Wager, and the report to the 'Countryside in 1970' Conference on *Outdoor Recreation —Active and Passive*.[3] These, and other studies, examined

* First published as 'Accessibility to the Countryside as a Factor in Planning for Leisure', *Regional Studies*, 1, 2 (1967), pp. 147-61.

five key characteristics of day and afternoon travellers: traffic flow, length of stay at destination, distance travelled, place of origin and object of the journey.

Burton did his survey on Sunday, August 30, 1964 (the weather was excellent) and he made a count every hour of the cars in the car park at the foot of Box Hill. His results are shown in Table 6.1. To test whether Burton's experience could be

Table 6.1 *Vehicles in the Box Hill car park*

Time		No. of cars
a.m.	11	13
	12	39
p.m.	1	46
	2	87
	3	119
	4	178
	5	180
	6	117

Source: T. L. Burton, 'A Day in the Country',
Chartered Surveyor, 98, 7, 1966.

regarded as typical a count was made, from the results of the 1961 London Traffic Survey, of vehicles passing points on five A Class roads roughly 20 miles from London. Vehicles passing in both directions were counted. The results are shown in Figure 6.1. They suggest that Burton's figures are more or less typical, except that there is a minor drop in the traffic flow over the lunch period. Possibly this is not reflected in Burton's results because Box Hill is a popular spot for picnic lunches. The similarity of the slopes of the various graphs is remarkable. The opportunity was also taken to plot the average weekday flows at these points, and here again the various graphs are very similar in shape, although of course the pattern of traffic flow is completely different from that for the Sunday. The twin peaks, around 9 a.m. and 6 p.m., stand out very clearly.

An important feature of Figure 6.1 is the build-up of recreation traffic on a Sunday to a peak late in the afternoon and early evening, with homeward-bound traffic causing heavy flows late into the evening. It is also noteworthy that the Sunday volume of traffic is higher, on all the roads shown, than the weekday traffic.

Burton interviewed the occupants of ninety-seven cars between

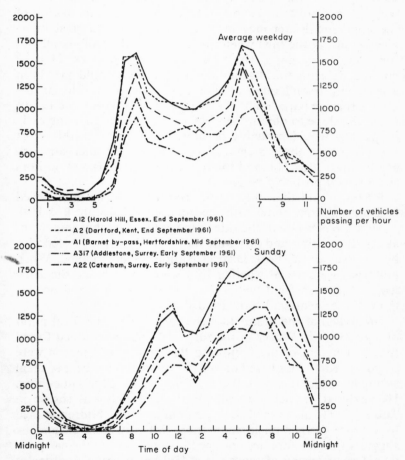

Figure 6.1.   Profiles of traffic flows during the day at points 15–20 miles from London (September 1961)

10.30 a.m. and 2.30 p.m. and he found that about two-thirds of them were staying part of the day at least at Box Hill, and the remainder only for a short time. It is interesting to compare this

I   129 with the results of a similar survey at Formby Park near Liverpool where it was found that 54 per cent of visitors spent less than 1 hour and 80 per cent of visitors less than 3 hours, with the result that there was considerable crowding near the car park and solitude a short distance away. An explanation of the apparent discrepancy may be that Burton stopped interviewing just at the time when the largest numbers of people out for a short afternoon trip were arriving at the park. Had he continued during the afternoon no doubt there would have been a marked preponderance of short-stay visitors. Another factor is that the car park lies at the foot of Box Hill and one has to climb the slope to obtain the view. Many of those arriving early in the day would probably be more likely to make this short excursion than those arriving later. There is another car park at the top of Box Hill and the proportion of short-stay visitors there would probably be greater.

Burton found that only 40 per cent of those he interviewed had set out from home with the intention of visiting Box Hill. Clearly the pleasure of the ride in the car is at least as important as the destination and probably more so. This is suggested also by a survey in the Peak District National Park in 1963. When motorists were asked whether they were going home the same way, 38 per cent said 'yes', 37 per cent said 'no', and no less than 25 per cent said 'not decided'.[4]

On arrival at the destination the car remains the focal point of activity. J. F. Wager in the survey already mentioned found that 78 per cent of the visitors to Berkhamsted Common were engaged in activities based on the motor-car, 55 per cent of them sitting in or picnicking by the car. Burton found the same thing. He analysed the activities of the people roughly as shown in Table 6.2. He also noted that the families with children tended to venture further afield than those without children and he suggests that for families cramped in small homes the car gives an extra dimension of space—Box Hill has become a garden at the end of a 30-minute car journey. He also noted the virtual absence of young teenagers in the 14–18 age group. There were a good number of older teenagers and young adults, most of whom stayed only a short time and then continued on their way to the coast.

The 'Countryside in 1970' Report, mentioned above, states that in a survey of visitors to thirty commons situated in all parts of England the average distance travelled by Sunday motorists was 12 miles. Burton found that the distance travelled at Box Hill varied from 10 to 30 miles, but this is consistent because the average inhabitant of London motoring out for a short trip in the country has to travel further than the average inhabitant of a smaller city. The survey carried out by the British Travel Association in 1963 showed that 45 per cent of all travellers over the weekend (i.e. including those on long-distance trips)

Table 6.2   *Leisure activities at Box Hill*

	All groups (per cent)	Groups with children (per cent)	Groups without children (per cent)
Sitting in car	15	6	20
Picnicking by car	46	50	44
Picnicking away from car	5	3	7
Playing, walking or sitting by car	5	—	8
Playing, walking or sitting away from car	29	41	21
	100	100	100

Source: T. L. Burton, op. cit.

remained within 25 miles of their homes while a further 25 per cent had reached a point 26–50 miles from home. It seems likely that the motor–car has not increased very much the average distance travelled for a recreational trip. Thus a survey of the recreational habits of some 4,000 people in four towns in the Rotterdam area in 1956 showed that people travelled in the morning by car, bus, and train to places 15–20 miles out from the city and returned in the evening. A second survey, in 1964, showed that although many more people travelled by car they still went to the same places, but now they generally left after lunch.[5] This suggests that the car is used more for flexibility in timing and route than to extend the distance travelled: it

131

enables the recreational belt to be more intensively used but has not noticeably extended its radius.

Burton found that about 75 per cent of the people interviewed had travelled down from Greater London, and most of them had come from the segment of London either side of the London–Worthing road. Less than 10 per cent of those he interviewed had come from places south of Box Hill. This suggests that recreational traffic from London has a pronounced linear shape; that is, people go out in the direction which gets them into the countryside quickest. The smaller the city the less likely it is that this will pertain until, with a small town, the likelihood is that the place of residence in the town will have virtually no influence on the direction in which people go for short car trips.

Implications of Pleasure Driving

Crowded though the roads already are in Britain, this country is only at the threshold of a tremendous increase in the number of cars. There were about 9 million cars in 1966, but by AD 2010 there are expected to be 25·9 million by which time the number of cars will be nearly 0·40 per head. The USA already has this proportion and it is expected to rise slowly to the 'saturation' point of 0·50 per head.[6] Ten years ago only 2 per cent of families in Britain had two cars, today it is 12½ per cent.[7] In Sweden 1·8 million families have a second home and the number is rising by 5 per cent per annum, whilst Denmark is planning for 1·3 million families to have a second home.[8] The second home, of course, adds greatly to the volume and dispersion of recreational traffic, as anyone can testify who has joined the queues of cars travelling northwards from Detroit towards the lakes and woodlands of the Michigan Peninsula on a Friday evening. Add to these factors the expected 20 million increase in population by AD 2000, the fall in the working week and the rise in real incomes, and one begins to have some idea of the extent to which car driving for pleasure is likely to grow. The impact on the countryside in a crowded island like Great Britain is certain to be drastic. In the 1930s for example there were 80,000 people visiting the Norfolk Broads annually; today there are 300,000;[9] what will the total be ten years hence? In 1963, the Peak District

National Park had 4 million visitors and there were 1·3 million cars. By the 1970s it is expected that there will be 8 million visitors and 3 million cars. These are typical figures for any attractive piece of countryside in Britain and, if the countryside itself is not to lose its character, the whole problem needs to be carefully thought out and planned for. The implications for urban planning will now be considered.

Access to the Countryside and Urban Form

If people want to drive out of cities as one of their principal forms of recreation and because it satisfies a deep urge to get into the countryside, it is important to consider what kind of urban form will achieve the objective of maximising this 'exitability'. When a city gets to the size of London millions of its inhabitants live so far from the countryside that they do not often bother to make the tiresome journey out. This is something which it should be an important objective of planning to avoid. This is no academic matter since new cities are already being planned to accommodate some of the expected increase of 20 million people and some of the existing cities will have to be greatly expanded to accommodate the bulk of the remainder. These new developments should be designed in such a way that people can get out of them quickly as well as into them. Figure 6.2 shows some of the possible ways of expanding a city of 1 million people to 1½ million with this problem in mind. These diagrams have been drawn on squared paper and are approximately to scale. Method 1 is the traditional 'onion' method—that is, layers of development accreting round an original core. This is how a city would normally expand in the absence of irregular physical features. It results in an increase in the average journey distance to the perimeter of 1¾ miles, and all the inhabitants of the city before its expansion will have their accessibility to the countryside reduced accordingly. With Methods 2 and 3 the expansion is concentrated in particular sectors to give a star-shape. Thus people who live in those parts of the city where expansion is to take place are worse off than by Method 1 in the direct line but better off diagonally. In a straight line they have to travel 3 miles further than with Method

1 to reach the countryside, but at the extreme diagonal they can reach the perimeter in 3 miles compared with 4 miles—although of course their choice of direction is limited. Those who live between expanding sectors are better off than they would be under Method 1 since their accessibility remains unchanged. Method 3 reduces the base line of each expanding sector thus improving accessibility a little all round, and Method 4 takes

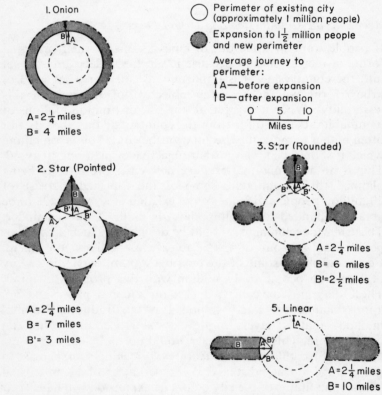

1. Onion

A = $2\frac{1}{4}$ miles
B = 4 miles

Perimeter of existing city
(approximately 1 million people)

Expansion to $1\frac{1}{2}$ million people
and new perimeter

Average journey to
perimeter:
A—before expansion
B—after expansion

0   5   10
Miles

2. Star (Pointed)

A = $2\frac{1}{4}$ miles
B = 7 miles
B' = 3 miles

3. Star (Rounded)

A = $2\frac{1}{4}$ miles
B = 6 miles
B' = $2\frac{1}{2}$ miles

5. Linear

A = $2\frac{1}{4}$ miles
B = 10 miles

this process to the ultimate by detaching the expansion altogether from the parent city. With Method 4 accessibility to the countryside remains unchanged but, of course, the total radius of 'urbanisation' has been pushed much further out than with Method 1, and if cities are already close together, as in South Lancashire and the West Riding, this sort of solution may not

134

be appropriate. Moreover, the temptation would be to use the green wedges for new motorways but this would defeat their purpose. Where existing towns and cities are close together one is driven back to Method 1, as this is the most compact form of urban development, but it could be modified with fast motorway exits as in Method 6. Of course, this also has its problems since the motorways channel recreation traffic in particular directions

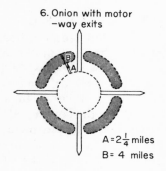

6. Onion with motor
   —way exits

A = 2¼ miles
B = 4 miles

Figure 6.2. The expanding city: accessibility to the countryside as a factor influencing the shape of a city

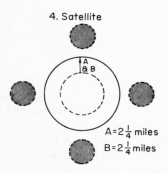

4. Satellite

A = 2¼ miles
B = 2¼ miles

and congestion is funnelled into corridors of countryside; but at least these are deep, even if they are narrow, since once on a motorway it is tempting to stay on it for a fair distance. The impact of the M6 on the Lake District, for example, is already a cause of concern. Method 5 represents a special case. It is the kind of solution Paris has adopted and seems particularly suitable where the physical features of the site (e.g. a river or range of hills) give a marked linearity.

135

This kind of approach cannot give definitive answers, but it focuses attention on an aspect of urban planning which has not received a great deal of study hitherto.

We turn now to consider the implications of motorised accessibility to the countryside so far as regional and national planning are concerned.

The Concept of Living Space

The surveys discussed earlier suggest that a relationship between a city and its neighbouring countryside is being established which is far more positive than is implied in the concept of the Green Belt. The surrounding countryside is now being used as an extension of life in the city—it is the garden for children to play in—a vista people can enjoy from their mobile room, their car. It is for some people a temporary return to the countryside they left not so long ago in the search for better employment, educational, or entertainment opportunities. For every city-dweller it has become, through the motor-car, an integral part of his environment; it is part of the subconscious contract he makes with city living; namely that whenever he wants to, he can get out and enjoy the country. In a very real sense the belt of countryside around a city has become its 'living space'.

Recreation Pressure on Living Space

It has become a matter of some urgency to find means of measuring both the pressures on the countryside round towns and cities and its capacity to absorb them. In essence, the pressures are mainly from people coming out by car for short trips, and the capacity to absorb is primarily a function of the density of the rural road network around the city. Of course the provision of car parks and access points is important, but it has been suggested earlier that it is often the actual driving along rural lanes that is the objective of the outing as much as any particular destination. If this is so it is important to consider the rural road network and its capacity to absorb this kind of traffic.

As a typical example of a large free-standing city, Leicester was chosen by the Ministry of Land and Natural Resources for a study of this kind. The first step was to plot the rural road network within 20 miles of the city and then to measure the length of classified roads in each 2-mile ring from the centre. The results are given in Table 6.3. The rather surprising fact

Table 6.3   *Road network within 20 miles of Leicester*

Miles from Leicester	Length of roads in each ring (miles)	Area of ring (square miles)	Length of road per square mile in each ring (miles)
miles from centre			
2–4	74·4	37·7	1·97
4–6	120·5	62·8	1·92
6–8	161·1	88·0	1·83
8–10	192·6	113·1	1·70
10–12	205·1	138·3	1·81
12–14	314·9	163·4	1·93
14–16	310·4	188·6	1·65
16–18	344·2	213·7	1·61
18–20	380·0	238·8	1·59

emerged that the density of the road network is remarkably even over the whole area and does not decline steadily with distance from the city centre. There is a small decline up to a radius of 10 miles, but then comes an increase which reflects the ring of smaller satellite towns round Leicester between 10 and 14 miles radius, and this is followed by a decline in the 15–20 mile belt. All this is a reminder of the excellent network of rural roads which Britain possesses, the outlines of which date from mediaeval times when the location of settlements was dictated by the pace of horse and oxen transport. Such an intricate network of secondary roads has a high capacity to absorb recreational traffic and is an asset which more recently developed areas often do not possess.

The next step was to look at the traffic pressures on this network. Unfortunately, traffic counts are related only to traffic on A roads and no traffic count data were available for the smaller roads. If further progress is to be made in measuring these recreational pressures it will be essential to carry out traffic surveys on B roads round towns and cities. However, the traffic data for the three trunk roads passing through Leicester are of interest. The data for the various counts along the three roads have been averaged in Table 6.4 to highlight the importance of the Sunday traffic (in summer) compared with the weekday. The flow of passenger cars is about 75 per cent greater, although the decline in the number of commercial vehicles at

Table 6.4 *Comparison between weekday and Sunday traffic flows*

Trunk road	Average weekday		Sunday	
	Passenger cars	Goods vehicles	Passenger cars	Goods vehicles
	(Average flow at various traffic count points— No. of vehicles per day)			
Rugby–Newark	5,840	2,080	8,630	860
Nuneaton–Uppingham	2,530	1,490	4,030	420
Kettering–Derby	4,010	2,660	7,220	590

Source: Traffic Census, Leicester, August 1961.

weekends goes some way to offset this. The recreational pressure on Sunday is probably concentrated on the east side of Leicester, where the countryside is prettiest, although of course one cannot be certain of this in the absence of data from origin-and-destination surveys. The fact that the Sunday flow of passenger cars on the Leicester–Nuneaton road was only a little higher than average weekday flow, whilst on the Leicester–Uppingham road it was almost two and a half times as heavy, certainly suggests, however, that most of the increase is recreational traffic originating in Leicester. But there are so many variables in the situation that one cannot interpret data of this kind with any confidence; what is needed is more traffic data related specifically to recreation traffic.

Living Space Zones

If one knew the length of rural roads round a city, and their

138

width, it would be possible to estimate the number of cars the road network could carry per square mile. If this were related to the number of cars the city is expected to generate it would be possible to estimate the total area required; that is, the radius of the living space area needed round the city to absorb its recreational traffic.

The formula is worked out as follows:*

Suppose that the population of a town is N, that a fraction p of the population make trips of duration t hours during some specified period and that the average occupancy of each car is n. Then the number of car trips is Np/n and the total of vehicle hours spent by vehicles on the roads in the neighbourhood of the town is Npt/n. It follows that if the average speed is v m.p.h., then the total distance travelled is $Npvt/n$ miles.

It is now necessary to consider what area of road is required to accommodate this traffic. Suppose that the capacity of a road of width W is C, then C vehicles can pass a given point on the road in unit time, and CT vehicles can pass in time T. It follows that CT vehicles require a width of road W in order to pass a point in time T. On this basis we may say that each vehicle requires a width of road W/CT. It is pointed out above that the total distance travelled during the period being considered is $Npvt/n$ and since each vehicle requires a width W/CT it follows that the area of road to accommodate the traffic is $NpvtW/nCT$.

Suppose now that all this travelling takes place within a circle of radius R around the town centre, and suppose that the fraction of this area devoted to the kind of road on which leisure motoring takes place is f. Then the total area devoted to the kind of road under consideration is $f\pi R^2$ and, if this is exactly equal to the amount required to avoid congestion, then

$$f\pi R^2 = \left(\frac{Npvt}{n}\right)\left(\frac{W}{CT}\right)$$

and

$$R = \sqrt{\frac{NpvtW}{\pi fnCT}}$$

* I am grateful to Professor Reuben Smeed, University College, London, for his help in formulating this concept in mathematical terms.

139

Values of the Symbols Used in the Formula

In order to make the maximum use of this formula, it is necessary to substitute for the various symbols in it. Suitable values for them will therefore now be considered.

(i) *f: The fraction of ground area devoted to roads.* Some figures relevant to the obtaining of this quantity are given in Table 6.5. The average mileage of road per square mile is about the same in England as it is in Wales, but is much less in Scotland.

Table 6.5 *Mileage of rural roads per square mile*

	England	Wales	Scotland
Miles of classified rural road	52,721	8,646	15,643
Miles of unclassified rural road	41,662	6,660	7,532
Total area (square miles)	50,056	7,967	29,795
Mileage of classified road per square mile	1·04	1·09	0·53
Mileage of unclassified road per square mile	0·82	0·84	0·25

Table 6.3 showed that the mileage of classified road per square mile in the neighbourhood of Leicester was about 1·75 (1·08 km./km.²). It seems reasonable to take this figure for the neighbourhood of towns and cities.

According to the *Road Research Laboratory Technical Paper No. 72*, the average road widths in rural areas are 23 feet (7·0 m.) for trunk roads, 21 feet (6·4 m.) for Class 1 roads, 18 feet (5·5 m.) for Class 2 roads and 14 feet (4·2 m.) for other rural roads. Weighting these figures by the length of the corresponding class of road in rural areas, it is found that the average width of classified (i.e. trunk and Classes 1 and 2) rural road is 20 feet (6·1 m.). Assuming that the mileage of road per square mile is 1·75, it follows that the fraction of ground devoted to classified road is about 0·007.

(ii) *p: The proportion of population making short car trips.* According to the BTA Survey referred to earlier, over half the population of Britain engaged in some form of travel during the three-day period of Whitsun 1963. Assuming there were equal numbers on each of the three days, the proportion taking a trip on any one day would be one-sixth, but some people make more than one trip and it seems more reasonable to adopt a value of one-quarter. Although all of these people do not travel by car at present, it will be assumed, for the restricted purposes of this paper, that they will travel by car at some time in the future.

(iii) *C, T and v: Time spent per journey.* An average journey time (*t*) of 2 hours at an average speed of 30 m.p.h. (50 km./hr.) (*v*) will be assumed. It will be assumed that all the travellers under consideration make their journeys during a period of 4 hours (*T*).

(iv) *n: Car occupancy.* According to *Economic Trends*, 116, June 1963, in a discussion on motor-car ownership and use, average car occupancy on a summer Sunday afternoon and early evening is 3·0.

(v) *C/W. Capacity of roads.* The capacity to be assumed for a road is to some extent arbitrary as drivers would find conditions unpleasant if roads were crowded to their ultimate capacity. The official capacity of a 24-foot (7·3 m.) road is 6,000 cars per day, corresponding to about 600 cars per hour. The capacity of roads of other widths would be expected to be approximately proportional to their width unless the road is so narrow that vehicles have difficulty in passing. *C/W* will therefore be taken to have a value of 25.

Substituting Values in the Formula

Substituting values in the formula, and measuring *R* in miles, it is found that:

$$R \text{ (miles)} = \frac{\sqrt{N}}{50} \text{ approximately}$$

Thus, neglecting the area on which buildings are situated in comparison with the rural area—a reasonable assumption in comparison with some of the others being made—it follows that

141

an urban population of 10,000 could have its recreation travel requirements accommodated in a rural area contained in a radius of not less than 2 miles (3·2 km.), a population of 100,000 requires a radius of 6 miles (9·6 km.) and a population of 1 million a radius of 20 miles (33·2 km.).

Significance for Land Use Planning in Great Britain as a Whole

The above mathematical formulation of the concept of living space is admittedly only a crude first attempt. In time it can be improved and more reliable data may become available as a basis for substituting values in the formula. However, there can be no questioning the basic idea that a town or city needs an area of countryside around it if its citizens are to enjoy a full and satisfying life. What the ideal radius of this living space zone should be will depend upon many variables; the attractiveness of the countryside, proximity of coast or mountains, the recreational habits of the people, the provision of 'country parks', and so on.

Assuming for the moment that the values substituted in the formula are nationally applicable, and applying the above formula to every town or city in Great Britain with 30,000 inhabitants or more, one obtains the picture in Figure 6.3. This diagram shows how the circles overlap in an intricate fashion in the six main conurbations (Southampton-Portsmouth being included on the strength of the proposed expansion scheme). Together, the living space zones of the five conurbations in England cover 11,910 square miles (30,846 km.²) out of a total of 50,056 square miles (129,645 km.²) and the South Wales zone covers 610 square miles (1,579 km.²) out of a total of 7,967 square miles (20,634 km.²). If the other congestion zones outside the main conurbations are added the English total becomes 16,180 square miles (41,906 km.²), that is, about a third of the total area. At a rough estimate, some 37 million people live in the six conurbation areas and the 12,520 square miles (32,426 km.²) represents about $\frac{1}{3}$ square mile (0·85 km.²) per 1,000 population. This is less than the 1·26 square miles (3·26 km.²) which the formula gives, because of the overlapping of the circles—the difference being some measure of the shortage of

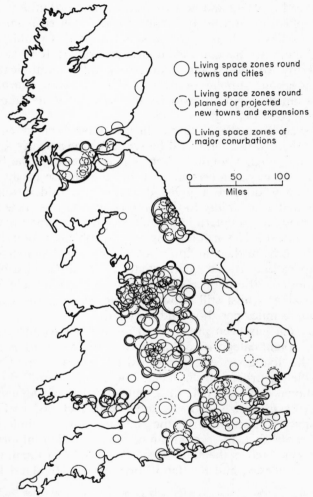

Figure 6.3. Living space zones round towns and cities in Britain

living space in South Lancashire, the West Riding, Birmingham and the other conurbations.*

One of the main problems which faces this country in the years ahead is where and how to accommodate 20 million extra people, plus say another 10 million to be rehoused from over-crowded cities. In looking for a solution to this problem the main factors to be considered are economic; for example, accessibility to ports and markets, good communications, adequate labour, supplies of raw materials and so on. Considerations of amenity and accessibility to the countryside take very much a second place at this stage.

However, once the economic factors have been taken into account there will usually still be scope for the amenity factors to be considered. Economic factors may determine the broad location of a city in a certain area, but the precise urban form selected may depend a great deal upon considerations of amenity and accessibility to the countryside. At this stage these factors may have a determining influence on the urban pattern. In this context it is worth looking at the problem of population distribution from the standpoint of 'living space' as defined in this paper; that is, to what extent it would be possible to accommodate 30 million people in Britain outside the existing built-up areas whilst still allowing living space at the scale of 1·25 square miles per thousand population.

Figure 6.4 has been prepared in an attempt to answer this question. Eight categories of land have been identified as either within the 'living space' zones of existing towns and cities, or unsuitable for urban development. These were identified in the order shown in Figure 6·4: thus, not all Areas of Outstanding Natural Beauty are shown, as some were included earlier in living space zones; similarly, the National Parks include some land over 800 feet. In recognition of the overriding importance of economic factors the counties of Cornwall, Cardigan, Caernarvon, Anglesey, and Scotland north of the Highland Line†

---

* London is a special case. The formula gives a radius of 60 miles (96·5 km.) but clearly only a small proportion of those living in the inner suburbs attempt to motor out at weekends, and an arbitrary radius of 35 miles (56·3 km.) has been assumed.

† Including Argyll, Banff, Caithness, Inverness, Moray, Nairn, Orkney, Ross and Cromarty, Sutherland, Zetland, and half of Perth.

have been regarded as so peripheral that no large-scale urban development is likely to take place there. Geographical

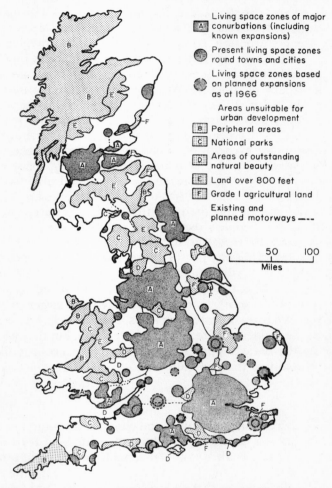

Figure 6.4. Factors affecting population distribution in Britain

remoteness was the only criterion for the selection of these areas. Other areas have been regarded as unsuitable for urban development because they are National Parks, Areas of Outstanding

Natural Beauty, over 800 feet (244 m.), or Grade 1 agricultural land (Sir Dudley Stamp's classification).

It is now possible to assess the capacity of the white areas of Figure 6.4 to absorb the expected 30 million people (or 28 million if one excludes the capacity of new towns and agreed expansions within the conurbation zones) and the results are given in Table 6.7. This shows that there is not enough space in England to accommodate 23·7 million extra people without transgressing the living space of other towns and cities or moving into the areas eliminated in Table 6.6. To some extent the latter would not matter (Grade 1 farm land might well constitute part of the living space of a nearby city, as it will do at Peterborough for instance), but even so the situation is extremely tight. And it must be remembered that if the available living space were utilised in this way it would mean the widespread urbanisation of rural areas on a scale that has not yet been contemplated.

It is necessary to add the rider that all this is based on the assumption that people's recreational habits in the future will remain unchanged. However, it may be that more people will be spending weekends away in the future, and country parks may be established that will channel the pressures into certain areas. It may even be that the motor-car will be superseded by some other form of transport, just as the car itself has largely ousted the bicycle as a form of recreation transport. Such changes might well alter the incidence of recreational pressures, but they do not invalidate the basic assumption that these pressures are likely to grow rapidly in the years ahead.

Conclusions

Deciding where to site new towns and cities for 30 million people is not primarily a question of finding adequate land for bricks and mortar. There is plenty of land capable of being built upon —that is not the problem. The problem is to choose a pattern of population distribution that will be basically economic and at the same time will satisfy as many as possible of the social aspirations of the people, that is, as to where and how they would like to live. Some new cities must go to particular locations for economic reasons—for example, accessibility to

Table 6.6 *Living space available for urban development*

	England	Wales (square miles)	Scotland
Total Area	50,056	7,967	29,795
LESS:			
Peripheral areas (B)	1,360	1,540	16,760
National Parks (C)	3,590	1,070	—
AONBs (D)	1,190	—	—
Land over 800 feet (E)	930	1,700	2,620
Grade 1 farm land (F)	1,380	—	340
Balance	8,450	4,310	19,720
	41,606	3,657	10,075
LESS existing 'living space' zones:			
Living space zones (A)	11,910	610	1,880
Other living space zones shown in Figure 6.4	4,270		330
Balance	16,180	610	2,210
	25,426	3,047	7,865

Table 6.7   *Comparison between available living space and population to be housed*

	England	Wales	Scotland
Rough estimate of population to be housed (million)	23·7	1·4	2·9
Living space available (thousand square miles)	25·4	3·0	7·9
Living space required (thousand square miles)	29·8	1·8	3·7
Deficiency (−) or surplus (+) (thousand square miles)	− 4·4	+1·2	+4·2

deep water or raw materials—but others can be sited, within reason, according to choice. But how do we choose? Do we put a high value on comparative economies of public services, in which case we might enlarge the existing towns and cities; or do we put a high value on accessibility to the countryside, in which case we might choose to locate new cities in areas not at present heavily urbanised? We might of course do both, but the important thing is that accessibility to the countryside is given its due weight in whatever decision is eventually arrived at. This paper has tried to show that living space ought not to be ignored as a factor influencing the planning of Britain's new towns and cities.*

* Acknowledgements—This paper expresses the personal views of the author and does not necessarily reflect the views of either the Ministry of Land and Natural Resources, when it existed, or the Ministry of Housing and Local Government. However, the author would like both to acknowledge the stimulus he has derived from discussions with official colleagues, and to express his thanks for being permitted to use material collected whilst he was in the Ministry of Land and Natural Resources.

References

1. ORRRC, *Outdoor Recreation for America*, US Government Printing Office, 1962.
2. British Travel Association, *Survey of Whitsun Holiday Travel*, 1963.
3. (i) T. L. Burton, 'A Day in the Country', *Chartered Surveyor*, 98, 7, 1966.
   (ii) J. F. Wager, 'How Common is the Land?', *New Society*, July 30, 1964.
   (iii) 'Countryside in 1970' Second Conference, *Outdoor Recreation —Active and Passive*, 1965.
4. British Travel Association, *Survey of the Peak District National Park*, 1963.
5. D. H. Stewart, quoted in a Lecture to the Institute of Advanced Architectural Studies, York, Conference on Recreation and Leisure, 1965.
6. Road Research Laboratory, *Road Traffic Research*, HMSO, 1962.
7. Automobile Association, *The Motorist Today*, 1966.
8. Report in *New Society*, November 18, 1965.
9. P. Hall, *New Society*, June 2, 1966.

Chapter 7

Planning for Outdoor Recreation in Urban Areas

D. M. WINTERBOTTOM

Many people argue that urban open space is not susceptible to standards. Requirements vary too much from place to place, and furthermore, recreation habits not only change as people become richer, but also with time and fashion. Nevertheless, the planner is required to make both gross overall long-term estimates (when planning a new town, for instance) and short-term allocations which will be built into the urban structure now under construction and which will be difficult to change in the future.

Changing patterns are making it at the same time easier and more difficult to estimate open space needs. It is easier, because man is so adaptable that the provision for open space must fall to a very low level before it inhibits his using it. Easier, too, because, except in the largest cities, if there is too little space he can either get into his car and go somewhere else where there is a surplus or else he can spend money and create hard surfaces or sports halls, which can be used very intensively, where previously there was only grass or mud. The estimates are more difficult in that the planner is called upon to make a judgment about how society will balance the expenditure of scarce resources of land and money to provide open space. Most criticisms by users of recreation facilities stem not so much from the absence of space as from its poor quality.

Apart from the recreational uses of open space, the aesthetics and visual qualities are, also, becoming an increasingly important element of the open space provision in towns. Wide reserves along main roads are one sign of this tendency, but the reservation of the Nene Valley in the Northampton Plan,[1] the village in the countryside parks in the Peterborough Plan[2] and the linear park and preserved woods in the Milton Keynes

Plan[3] are probably more significant. Whilst estimates have to be made of the local open space required, any underestimate can usually be provided for quite easily in a nearby major park.

One of the first attempts to revise open space standards on empirical rather than subjective lines was published in the April 1967 issue of the *Journal of the Town Planning Institute*[4] and much of what follows here is a revision of that article.

The Colchester Survey

In order to examine the validity of the then universally used, if not accepted, open space standard of 7 acres per thousand population, a survey was undertaken on the use of several specific open spaces in Colchester during July and August 1965. The survey was carried out on two weekends and two weekdays during the summer, when it was hoped that there would be maximum use of all of the open space facilities. The purpose of the study was to try to determine a standard for the provision of public open space by means of observed levels of usage rather than from the subjective methods employed by the National Playing Fields Association in its original standard first laid down in 1925.

A preliminary appraisal of the open spaces in Colchester revealed that Castle Park, the town park, was very well used, and that there were four major recreation grounds which were fairly well used, but that the remainder of the open spaces were used primarily as incidental areas and playgrounds for nearby housing developments, rather than as specific attractions in their own right. On this basis, it was decided to observe Castle Park and the two more important recreation grounds continuously during the survey period. To this end, counts at approximately hourly intervals were made of every person in each of the open spaces from 10 a.m. to 8 p.m. throughout the two weekends and from 12 noon to 2 p.m. and 4 p.m. to 8 p.m. on the two weekdays. These latter were an early closing day and a Friday.

The method employed was for each surveyor to use a separate record sheet for each open space (or section thereof, when the whole space could not be viewed at one time) on each day, and to record on it at each inspection the number of men and women, and children under school-leaving age, who were participating in various activities. This included

    (i) children's playgrounds with apparatus, hard areas, sand pits, and so on;

   (ii) informal activities such as games, walking and sitting;

 (iii) organised games such as cricket, football, tennis, and so on.

An attempt was also made to judge and record separately those people who were walking through the park. The time and weather conditions at each inspection were also noted.

The numbers of people using each open space on the various days were then compared. It proved nearly impossible to get any significant comparison at the most detailed level. If one tried to compare, for instance, the number of children using sand pits in sunny weather at about 3 p.m., there were so few occasions when this combination of circumstances occurred that the results obtained were just not reliable. In the first analysis, therefore, the results were compared on the basis of the total numbers of people participating in, first, organised games and, second, all other activities. For these an estimate of the 'significant' level of usage of each activity was made. This usually coincided with about the second highest number of people observed at any one time, but varied slightly, depending on the variation in the peaks from day to day.

The results were also inspected to see if at any stage any facility was used to capacity. This would be indicated by the early build-up of people and then little change in the number of people using the open space until late in the day. Although the present provision of open space in the Borough is only just about 2·5 acres per thousand population, there did not appear to be any instances where facilities were over-used. The Castle Park was overwhelmingly popular at all times and, as the other public open spaces in the town were laid out predominantly for organised games, though not necessarily used as such, calculations have been made on the basis of those taking part in such games.

The results were calculated by first dividing the town into five areas based on the five major open spaces and making allowances for such barriers to movement as were apparent. The population and open space provision for each of these areas was then estimated and significant levels of use for organised games were noted for the three areas where they were observed. Acres of open space per thousand population and significant users per thousand population were then computed for each area. Table 7.1 shows that the latter varied from 2·28 to 7·58 for the three areas for which data were obtained. The weighted mean of these figures is 5·27 and the difference between this and the recorded figure was used to compute the adjusted population estimate. This adjustment was made on the basis that a given population would tend to generate a given number of users. In other words, the preliminary breakdown of the town into five areas was revised so that the level of 'significant users per thousand population' was the same for each area.

As is shown in Table 7.2, this gives a remarkably similar provision of open space in acres per thousand population for each of the three areas tested—the East, South East and South West. However, although both the south-eastern and south-western areas are principally laid out for organised sport, the same cannot be said of the eastern area, where only about two-thirds are used in this way, so that the results are not quite as conclusive as they appear to be.

Whilst the differences between the 1921 and 1951 census demographic data would change the National Playing Fields Association's estimates from 200 to 166 persons participating in games per thousand population, this survey indicates that a maximum of only five to six persons will be playing at any one time. The involvement with public open space for playing fields seems to over-emphasise this side of the problem, but there is considerable use of what is basically a recreation ground for purposes other than organised sport. The difficulty with attempting to subdivide the sports grounds into their constituent parts and to calculate on the basis that, say, four persons per thousand population could play tennis at such and such a court, is that in calculating the area required for any particular facility, the overwhelming dominance of football and cricket pitches soon becomes apparent. Those areas used more intensively, such as bowling greens, take very little land per

153

Table 7.1

Area	Major open spaces (acres)	Population	Significant sports users	Major open spaces per thousand population	Significant sports users per thousand population	Adjusted population
North	18	3,200		5·6		
East	45	15,200	105	3·0	6·91	19,900
West	25	8,700		2·9		
South East	21	17,600	40	1·2	2·28	7,600
South West	39	11,900	90	3·3	7·58	17,100
	148	56,600		2·6	5·27	

Table 7.2

Area	Major open space (acres)	Adjusted population	Significant sports users	Major open space per thousand population	Significant sports users per thousand population
North	18	3,200		5·6	
East	45	19,800	105	2·3	5·3
West	25	8,700		2·9	
South East	21	7,500	40	2·8	5·3
South West	39	17,200	90	2·3	5·2

155

participant. The survey took place out of the football season as it was not anticipated that the main land-consuming use for out-of-doors open space facilities might be in the winter. In the event, the total number of people participating in organised games was grossed up and related to the total area of any given park, regardless of the fact that part of some areas was set aside as football pitches and was not being used as such.

The calculations seem to indicate that there is some relationship between the size of the open space and the population it serves, provided that it is reasonably accessible to the residential areas surrounding it. In the northern and western areas this is not the case since they are only on the edge of the areas they serve. From Table 7.2 it can be deduced that a provision of open space, to be laid out primarily for playing fields of the order of 2·5 acres per thousand population, is sufficient for Colchester at the present time. Obviously a radical change in its demographic structure or leisure habits would considerably alter this situation.

Winter Games Survey

The open space survey carried out during the summer in Colchester produced the tentative conclusion that 2·5 acres of public playing fields per thousand population was an adequate provision. It seemed possible, however, that there might be more players using more land in winter than in summer. In order to establish this, a postal survey was carried out during November 1965 in the Mid-Essex area.

The questionnaire shown on page 157 was sent to all association football, rugby football and hockey clubs in the County Districts of Chelmsford Borough and Rural, Burnham, Maldon Borough and Rural, Brentwood and Billericay without Basildon.

In all, eighty-one clubs were approached and details of nine who did not reply were estimated, using the reports of matches given in the local papers. Clubs were asked to distinguish between public and private playing fields, to state their total of playing members and, for each Saturday in November, the number of teams playing and the number of players available (Figure 7.1). Some indication of the past and future levels of

Essex County Council
Open Space Survey

Winter field games (Rugby Football, Association Football, Hockey)

Name of Club: ....

Please could you tell us:

1. Location of home ground: ....

2. Is this a private, public, or school/college playing field?........

3. Total playing membership? ....

	November 1965				
	6th	13th	20th	27th	
4. How many teams did you field on?					
How many members were available on?					
5. How many teams were playing at the same time at home?					
away?					

6. How many more teams could you field if more pitches were available?......................

7. How many teams did you field 5 years ago? ....
   10 years ago? ....

8. Please make any other comments which you feel might give a better overall picture of organised games in your area and help in assessing the future provision and distribution of the facilities in the County.

Figure 7.1 Open space survey questionnaire.

activity was also required. An analysis of the results is set out in Table 7.3.

There were sixty-five clubs playing association football on Saturdays (Sunday and midweek games were excluded). The maximum number of teams playing at any one time was 122: this is almost certainly an exaggeration of peak demand, since some games were played on Saturday morning and the peak days for each of the clubs over a period of four weeks will not necessarily have coincided. The figures have been worked out to show the difference between town and village clubs, by areas and by type of playing field. It will be seen that, on the whole, village clubs had fewer members, and ran fewer teams, but had a larger percentage of their members playing than town clubs. However, the percentage of available players not playing did not appear to depend on the type of club. About half the clubs played on public and half on private fields. Clubs using the latter appear to be marginally bigger than those using the former. As between sports it will be seen that nearly three-quarters of all winter sportsmen played soccer, but that, on the whole, the rugby and hockey clubs were bigger and offered a much better chance of a game.

All three games have been analysed, in Table 7.4, in terms of the population of county districts or groups of county districts. This is not altogether a just comparison as can be seen from the low number of players in Brentwood and Billericay. It can be assumed, however, that the excellent facilities offered by Basildon New Town have attracted people away from this area. Each club was asked to state how many *extra* teams it would be able to field if more ground were available. Of the extra thirty-one pitches suggested as being necessary only twelve appeared justified in terms of the clubs' membership and normal number of players available. Adding these additional needs to the number of teams playing and dividing by two gives a maximum number of pitches required. This divided by the catchment population yields the number of pitches needed per thousand population.

In order to arrive at an acreage, the minimum size of field for each game has been established and 50 per cent added to allow for odd-shaped grounds and other similar factors. This is shown

	Players	Maximum available	Played	Teams	Clubs	A	B	C	D	E
ASSOCIATION FOOTBALL										
Village, Public fields	490	440	330	30	17	25	67	29	26	1·8
Village, Private fields	328	305	209	19	12	31	64	27	25	1·6
Town	812	663	484	44	21	27	60	39	32	2·1
Closed clubs	540	463	319	29	15	31	59	36	31	1·9
TOTAL	2,170	1,871	1,342	122	65	28	62	33	29	1·9
Chelmsford Borough	619	504	352	32	17	30	57	36	30	1·9
Maldon and Burnham	468	422	286	26	15	32	61	31	28	1·7
Chelmsford Rural	538	474	341	31	18	28	63	30	26	1·7
Brentwood and Billericay	545	471	363	33	15	25	67	36	31	2·2
TOTAL	2,170	1,871	1,342	122	65	28	62	33	29	1·9
Public fields	1,093	927	660	60	35	29	60	31	27	1·7
Private fields	1,077	944	682	62	30	28	63	36	31	2·1
TOTAL	2,170	1,871	1,342	122	65	28	62	33	29	1·9
RUGBY FOOTBALL	360	316	255	17	6	19	71	60	53	2·8
HOCKEY	337	299	242	22	8	19	72	42	37	2·8

Key
A. Percentage of players available but not playing.
B. Percentage of members playing.
C. Members per club.
D. Members available per club.
E. Teams per club.

Table 7.4

	1965 population in thousands	Teams	Extra needs	Total pitches	Pitches per thousand population
SOCCER					
Chelmsford Borough	54·1	32	2	17	0·31
Maldon and Burnham	34·2	26	2	14	0·41
Chelmsford Rural	57·1	31	1	16	0·28
Brentwood and Billericay	98·9	33	2	17·5	0·18
TOTAL	244·3			64·5	0·27
RUGBY					
Chelmsford	111·2	7	0	3·5	0·03
Maldon	34·2	2	1	1·5	0·04
Brentwood	98·9	8	1	4·5	0·05
TOTAL	244·3			9·5	0·04
HOCKEY					
Chelmsford	111·2	16	3	9·5	0·08
Brentwood	98·9	6	0	3	0·03

in the first two columns of Table 7.5. Then the maximum number of pitches needed per thousand people (found in the last column of Table 7.4) is multiplied by the acreage figure to give the total land requirement for that sport per thousand people. The sum of these comes to slightly less than 2 acres per thousand population, which is below the Colchester summer requirement of 2·5 acres.

Table 7.5

Games	Minimum area (acres)	Adding 50%	Pitches per 1,000 pop.	Total land
Soccer	2·3	3·5	0·41	1·44
Rugby	2·8	4·2	0·05	0·21
Hockey	1·5	2·3	0·08	0·18
				1·83

A not dissimilar method to this was used recently, on a much wider scale, for establishing a revised standard for new towns.[5] The technique was to record the number of games played in eight new towns and two old towns during a season and to relate this to the number of playing fields available. The results were then scrutinised to see whether participation in games was related to the provision of facilities. It appeared that, for the small sample taken, once the provision of space exceeded about 1·25 acres per thousand people, the number of people playing games was related only in a random way to the volume of space available. However, below this level of provision, there appeared to be a decrease in the amount of sport played. It was suggested from this that an allocation of 1·5 acres per thousand people was adequate if pressures for further pitches were to be avoided. Also it was stressed that variations in quality of the pitches, ways in which the sports grounds were managed and the ownership of them played a large part in assessing the adequacy of the provision. This scale of provision may be slightly low, because new towns usually have fewer people in the 15–25 year age groups than most communities and it is from them that the heaviest demand for field sports comes. Also, preoccupation

L

RECREATION RESEARCH AND PLANNING

with a new home and new garden may erode, to some extent, both the desire and the need to play outdoor games, although so far there is no systematic evidence on this point.

The most elaborate attempt to compute open space, or rather outdoor sports space, was made recently, by the Sports Council.[6] Many of the calculations were based upon data derived from the same survey as was used to estimate the standards for new towns suggested above. Estimates were made of the numbers of participants in different games by age groups, so that towns with different demographic structures would have differing ratios of participants. It was then assumed that each player would play, *on average*, one game per week and that two games a week would be played on each pitch. From this, the number of pitches required for each sport could be calculated. The relationship between size of pitch and ancillary space was calculated from data provided by the National Playing Fields Association and assumed to be an additional 50 per cent over and above the size of the pitch itself (the same figure as was used in the winter games study above). An allowance was made for the dual use of some cricket and football pitches. It was then suggested that for soccer, rugby, cricket, lawn tennis, hockey, bowls and netball the total sports ground requirement would be about 2·4 acres per thousand people. By way of contrast, recreation centres and playing fields in the USA are estimated to be needed in groups of 10 to 30 acres at a rate of 1·25 acres per thousand population.[7]

The Sports Council's study also made an estimate of the land needs of that most land-consuming of all sports—golf. After examining the number of people who play golf, how often they play, and the capacity of golf courses they suggest that an eighteen-hole golf course is needed for every 20,000 to 30,000 people. This accounts for between 4 and 6 acres per thousand people. However, not all of these courses need necessarily be provided within the built-up urban area. Once again, the estimates represent the mean of a very wide range of provision in different places for different people at different times. For comparison, the United States study gives a figure of between 3 and 5 acres per thousand people for golf.[7]

If the limited studies on space allocation for field sports show wide variations and tolerances, those for parks are fewer and even less determinate. An unpublished study made in London indicated a need for local open space of 5 to 10 acres within a quarter of a mile of most homes to cater for the needs of old people and children. At suburban and new town densities, this implies a provision of between 1 and 2 acres per thousand population. A study of the actual levels of provision made in a number of new towns showed a range of from 0·2 to 3·1 acres per thousand persons.[8] Standards quoted by Chapin as current American practice, indicate local parks of at least 2 acres as a norm and the scale of provision as 1 acre per thousand persons.[7] However, they also recommend a major natural park of 100 acres for every 40,000 people (2·5 acres per thousand population.)

A further open space use for which a demand still exists in certain parts of the country is allotments. However, the current statutory figure of 4 acres per thousand people is being re-examined and as residential densities fall (those in county borough and large towns fell by nearly 20 per cent between 1950 and 1960), and judging by the present use made of allotments, the provision around existing settlements may well decline substantially and be negligible in new towns.

Playgrounds are also an important part of the open space provision in towns. A recent government publication indicated an allocation of about 0·5 acres per thousand people.[9] After a special survey, the Liverpool Interim Report suggested 0·7 acres, but as there is less garden space there, the need for play space may be greater than in less dense new development. Attention is increasingly being given to the older children too, although little quantifiable information seems to be available. Space is required for the provision of play parks, kickabout pitches and adventure playgrounds: perhaps 0·5 acres per thousand people would be adequate. The Americans suggest a figure for play-grounds of 5 to 10 acres each and a total provision of 1·25 acres per thousand population.[7]

These then, are some of the methods and some of the standards devised for the provision of urban open space. The most striking thing about them is the lack of consistency and the lack of correlation with any of the demographic or social indicators used to try to rationalise the differences. Whilst it has been shown, for instance, that, in general, people in social

163

classes I and II play more hockey than those in other social classes, the variation in the numbers of people doing so in different towns is usually much greater than the differences in the total percentages of people in these classes in the towns.[10] The dilemma is highlighted, perhaps, by the two suggestions— both published in 1968 and drawing on substantially the same survey data—that 1·5 and 2·5 acres per thousand population were reasonable levels of provision for sports grounds, even though both heavily qualified the estimates and stressed the limitations of the methods used to derive them.[5, 6]

What seems to be important, then, is that there is an adequate amount of land set aside for open space in the town and that decisions as to how it should be used and when those uses should be changed should be left to the local community to decide. It is a crucial part of such an approach that demands for change are recorded early and that measures are taken to ensure the proper management of the resources which are available. It also follows that one should be on the generous side when making allocations to allow for delays in achieving changes in recreation use. It further assumes that most towns have a 'reservoir' of open space, a river valley, park or maybe simply meadows on the fringe of the town, into which they can expand recreation activities should the occasion arise. Finally, if a quantitative standard must be given for new housing areas just being built, it is suggested that the local provision should be approximately 2·5 acres of playing fields per thousand population, 1·0 acres of children's play spaces and kickabout pitches and 1·0 acres for local parks, gardens, sitting out spaces or even allotments. One would hope, though, that the population for whom this local open space was being provided would be sufficiently vocal to register changing needs from time to time.

References

1. Wilson and Wormersley, *Northampton Draft Development Plan*, 1968.
2. Hancock and Hawkes, *Peterborough Draft Development Plan*, 1968.
3. Llewelyn-Davies, Weeks, Forestier-Walker and Bor, *Milton Keynes Interim Report*, 1969.
4. D. M. Winterbottom, 'How Much Urban Open Space do we Need?', *Journal of the Town Planning Institute*, April 1967.
5. Margaret Willis, 'Open Space in New Towns', *Town Planning Review*, July 1968.
6. Sports Council, *Planning for Sport*, October 1968.
7. F. Stuart Chapin, *Urban Land Use Planning*, University of Illinois Press, Urbana, USA, 1965.
8. F. T. Burnett, 'Open Space in New Towns', *Journal of the Town Planning Institute*, June 1969.
9. *Homes for Today and Tomorrow*, HMSO, 1961.
10. Ministry of Housing and Local Government, *Provision of Playing Pitches*, 1967 (restricted circulation).

Chapter 8

Planning for Tourism*

L. J. LICKORISH

Tourism is a part of recreation activity. It is a concept which is difficult to define precisely, but, broadly, it represents the movement of people, a market rather than an industry, and, in general, the incidence of a mobile population on any given reception area and its resident population. The external traffic to the area, which can be from within a country or from other countries, makes use of the services which are supplied, at least in part, for the residents. The tourist product is an activity at a destination with social participation—that is, an activity enjoyed with other people—although a small minority of tourists spend their holiday time on their own. Since it is a part of total recreation activity, the first approach to planning for tourism must take account of recreation as a whole. Leisure and the related activities of tourism, holidaymaking and recreation involve a total philosophy, raising questions of ethics; but they also represent a powerful economic force. Social attitudes, which set the conditions necessary to enable any community to exist and make progress, also have an important bearing on the matter.

The use of free time for recreation is as old as civilisation. The history of recreation is as long as that of trade. Greek theatres and Roman pageants, for example, provided a considerable volume of employment. Even in the Middle Ages, in the feudal or subsistence economy, there was a limited number of people who travelled, cultivated the arts or provided entertainment. In the nineteenth century, the first industrial revolution produced the railways and a substantial middle-class with time and money to spare for recreation. It was the demand generated by

* Based upon 'Planning for Recreation and Leisure', *Journal of the Town Planning Institute*, June 1965.

these two developments which brought into being the holiday industry as we now think of it. Even today the pattern of holidaymaking—the traditional week or fortnight by the sea— and the design of resorts—centred around the promenade, main street and railway station—reflect the habits and requirements of the nineteenth century.

Today we are in the middle of a much greater, technological revolution; and like the Industrial Revolution of the last century, it is based upon a transformation in systems of transport and communications. The aeroplane and the private car have made travel faster, easier and more generally available than ever before. In the nineteenth century, man harnessed the basic raw materials, coal, iron and steam; in the twentieth century, technology is leading to a more effective use of time. Time, in turn, controls production and the ability to create vast wealth. Transport affects our environment. This second revolution is taking us further from the age of scarcity into the age of abundance, making it certain that the demand for leisure-time activities will grow even more rapidly than in the past.

Holiday and recreation patterns have, until quite recently, been slow to evolve. There has been a firm tradition in the taking of holidays, based perhaps on a social conservatism, which has restricted demand from growing as fast as it might. The holiday trades are in a position to provide a much greater volume of services than is at present required. At the moment, nearly 50 per cent of the total capacity of all travel services is unused. The occupancy factor of aircraft and trains and the load factor of roads are low because of seasonal operation. The average annual sleeper occupancy rate of hotels in Britain was found, in 1968, to be only 53 per cent.[1]

The most important differences between present recreation trends and the recreation revolution of the nineteenth century stem from a massive growth in leisure time, in personal wealth and, above all, in personal mobility. It took nearly a century to extend the traditional one-day August Bank Holiday to two weeks. Now 50 per cent of the working population of Britain has three weeks annual holiday with pay and there is every likelihood of further rapid extension in holiday time. There has been a rapid expansion in the taking of second holidays, in

167

weekend and day trips away from home, and, for the wealthier members of the population, in the establishment of recreation homes, cottages, caravans, cruising boats and the like. It is in this area of multiple holidays that the biggest growth in the domestic movement in Britain is taking place. Mobility has resulted in the extensive practice of recreation and business activities formerly restricted to a limited area near the home being extended to a wider area. Physical mobility and improvement in communications generally has increased the desire for meetings of all kinds, and stimulated convention traffic, which is, in fact, a collection of a number of different forms of travel; business meetings, training meetings, seminars, educational meetings for pleasure, as well as for professional or profitable purposes. Sales incentive tours have grown rapidly. Mobility has created an evident increase in touring, both as a recreation in itself and as an additional activity, even for those who spend some time staying in one resort. Thus the hinterland of the resort has become as important to the resort itself as the reason for the visit, with accompanying expenditure being spread over a wide area.

Hobbies are becoming commercialised. In the past, sporting activities, such as camping, boating and riding, were available only to a relatively select few; sports and hobbies were regulated by organisations which were exclusive and non-commercial in character. Now many types of sporting club report an unprecedented increase in membership. The enthusiasm for active pursuits is being carried over into holidays. To give one example, it is estimated that in 1968 just about 6 million people took camping and caravanning holidays in Britain.[2] Demand for these holidays has long since outstripped the capacity of the old established voluntary organisations, so that provision of camping and caravanning facilities has become a substantial industry. The same is true of water sports. A recent survey of water sports discovered that sailing clubs have doubled their membership in the past twelve years; many also have waiting lists.[3] The volume of coastal sailing is said to have increased twenty times since 1945, and, according to the Royal Yachting Association, well over half a million people sailed in dinghies in coastal waters last year. Nevertheless, although the changes in tourist and holiday movement have become clear, they are at the beginning and not the end of their cycle of development. To a very large extent the holidaymaker and the tourist has not adjusted his own thinking to the new possibilities opened up to him by technological changes, by increasing leisure time and by wealth. There are many travellers by car who behave as though they were still subject to the limitations of travel by train with passive confinement at the destination.

There is still a strong tradition that certain forms of recreation which have an educational and social value should be provided free by government, as part of its social obligations, by charities or by institutions. Services that are provided free, however, are not always appreciated by a relatively wealthy public, and being removed from the stimulus of economic forces do not readily adapt themselves to change. Yet educational activities are greatly sought after and can be profitable. People are willing to pay for educational activity linked to recreation which they choose themselves, such as study tours, cultural courses, museum visits and the like. Such services linked to tourism are expanding and, as with the commercial development of hobbies, this growth is likely to accelerate in the future.

Tourism, holidaymaking and recreation are a function of wealth. Growing prosperity will inevitably bring a growth in demand for every kind of recreation facility. Already international tourism is the biggest single item in international trade. It is Britain's fourth largest export and one of the country's biggest dollar earners. In 1960 British residents paid £550 million on their holidays, of which £400 million was spent in Britain; by 1968 total holiday expenditure had risen to £890 million and expenditure in Britain to £570 million.[4] Overseas visitor expenditure inside Britain was £282 million in 1968. This makes a total expenditure of some £860 million on holidays in Britain. In England and Wales according to the 1961 Census about 4 million people—some 18 per cent of the employed population—were employed in travel and the trades providing travellers services.[*]

This provision of leisure services is already big business.

* Makers of food, drinks and tobacco; transport and communications; personal service.

Technological progress is bringing higher pay and shorter hours of work. Since the beginning of this century the working week has been reduced from 60 hours to 40, and from 6 days to $5\frac{1}{2}$ or less. It has been estimated that in the USA the standard working week will be reduced by 1976 to 36 hours and by the year 2000 to 32 hours. A comparable trend is expected in this country. In addition to this increase in leisure time and income, the population of Great Britain may well by the year 2010 have reached 67 million—an increase of almost 25 per cent.*

As we approach an economy of abundance and move further away from the economics of scarcity, many of the old economic virtues and vices are reversed. 'Waste and want not' is true of certain activities today. Recreation, which is the newest growth industry and perhaps the fastest growing of them all, has some important economic advantages. Yet it must be recognised that the ability to spend more time and money on recreation represents a potential and not an accomplished fact. Recreation services are a form of consumer product, and as such they have to be sold. Publicity and information services are not merely useful to the potential tripper, holidaymaker or hobby enthusiast; their use can in fact determine in advance the type of activity or destination he selects.

Changes in Recreation Behaviour

Tourism, holidaymaking and recreation are not industries. They are activities. In economic terms they provide a demand or market for a number of separate industries or trades. In certain areas they represent the major part of the demand, in others a complementary and often very profitable demand for catering, transport and entertainment and other services designed for a residential or industrial community.

The development of modern production techniques presupposes a knowledge of the present, and probable future, nature of the market. Behaviour patterns in modern society are becoming less individual and more of a mass movement. At the same time, the recreation product is becoming increasingly

* Based on the annual estimates prepared by the Government Actuary in consultation with the Registrar-General.

170

complex. In other words, more and diverse types of holiday are becoming popular: for example, the holiday camp, the coach tour, painting, riding, yachting and archaeological holidays. This growth in size of the travel demand and increasing range of variety of activity is leading to intense specialisation. Yet demand for each of these types is great enough to create a mass market. Successful development of this market depends essentially on improvements in publicity, in informing, educating and guiding people towards certain activities and organising or managing their leisure time.

The increasing range of tourist and holiday opportunities presents a problem for the potential traveller, just as a very elaborate and extensive menu may present a problem to all except the gourmet in enjoying the pleasure of good food. It is partly for this reason that the increasing tendency to organise and package both tours and entire holiday activities on a commercial basis is proving so popular. There is an added advantage in this mass production of services; the producers of the basic components of the tourist product—accommodation, transport and specialist activity—have been able to reduce prices to a remarkable extent. In 1949, a tourist wishing to visit Rome from London would have paid £53 for the air fare alone. Today he can enjoy at certain times of the year a whole week's holiday in Majorca for £25 inclusive of air travel.

We know in broad outline the kinds of holiday which are popular, and the types of activity—sport, motoring, the arts, listening to pop music and sitting in coffee bars—whose popularity is increasing. In order to plan effectively for the future much more detailed knowledge is essential, not only of the types of activity which are popular but of people's reasons for choosing them; whether, for example, people watch sport or drive in weekend convoys through the countryside because they really enjoy it, or simply because it is one degree less boring than staying at home. It will be necessary to predict the emergence of new activities, even to invent them. Demand for recreation is partly home-based and partly mobile, covering activities away from home in recreation as opposed to residential areas. The two markets are partly complementary and partly competitive. Both are affected by fashion, which in this field can prove more

171

upsetting than the traditional trade cycle for raw materials and capital goods.

It is possible, through research, to chart the tides of recreation behaviour, to isolate the separate types of activity, to predict their rates of growth, and to indicate their influence upon the environment and the economy. When this is done, it is possible to choose and promote the type of activity for which an area is suited.

Research in Recreation and Tourism

The purpose of research, as suggested in the Introduction to this book, is to provide a basis of knowledge for planners. An example is the survey of recreation activity carried out in the USA in 1960.[5] The most interesting of its findings was that which showed that the most popular activities are the simple ones— driving for pleasure, walking, swimming and picnicking—and that water is a focal point of much outdoor recreation. This survey recognised that the many recreation activities and facilities demanded by the public are often incompatible, and that different types of people, or the same people at different times, seek different types of recreation. In order to provide every kind of outdoor recreation in an environment in which it can best be enjoyed, a system of classification and zoning was proposed. There would be six classes of area. *Class 1* would consist of high-density recreation areas. These would be areas intensively developed for mass use, incorporating facilities such as bathing beaches, marinas, artificial lakes and playing fields, with a road network, parking areas and restaurants. They would be situated either near large cities or conurbations, or within national parks and forests. In the latter case they could do much to prevent overcrowding of the surrounding areas. *Classes 2, 3 and 4* would be countryside areas in progressively more natural condition with progressively fewer amenities, thereby attracting, it was hoped, proportionately fewer visitors. The other two types of area were sites of cultural and historic interest, and areas of outstanding natural beauty. The latter were to be preserved as far as possible in their natural condition, with food and lodging, roads and parking to be kept outside the area.

172

This system of zoning leads us to consider another problem which is becoming yearly more acute and which is immeasurably more serious in Britain than in the USA. Demand for recreation is growing; space for recreation is shrinking. National Parks and similar areas are becoming yearly more crowded. If the number of people visiting them continues to increase at its present rate, their beauty will be destroyed. Possible solutions include extension of the holiday season, extension of touring and holiday itineraries, invention of new pastimes, better organisation of existing services, and the creation of new recreation areas, including national water parks for boating, fishing and other water sports, all of which would help to alleviate the problems of peak-time overcrowding.

The zoning of facilities will come close to matching the segmentation in the movement of people. Already research in Britain shows broadly similar results to that in America. There is a similar recreation scale extending from the Blackpool man (noisy, cheerful, gregarious), to the Frinton man (quiet and semi-solitary), to the wilderness man who expects a mountain to himself free of charge. Wider areas can be zoned to accommodate angling, nature observation, speed boating and water skiing within the same area but not at the same spot. The conflict of interest can be resolved by directing and positively encouraging traffic separated into its constituent parts and grouped by compatible types of activity. An approach to this otherwise difficult problem then becomes simple. Rather than merely denying the majority of traffic to a particular area in order to cater for the minority user, each separated type of traffic is positively encouraged to go to the right destination. The public respond well to this treatment since they are naturally self-selecting according to their own likes or hopes.

The high-density recreation area is an important solution to the problem of overcrowding. A detailed scheme for just such an area has been drawn up by the Civic Trust in the Lea Valley. Such a scheme would provide a much needed outdoor recreation centre within easy reach of London, attracting large numbers of people who would otherwise have travelled much further, and probably enjoyed themselves considerably less, in the Home Counties.

173

One other feature of the Lea Valley project is worth stressing. The area to be converted into a park is at present derelict and unsightly. There is a great deal of such land in Britain—according to the Civic Trust, 150,000 acres of derelict land in England and Wales alone—while further industrial dereliction is forecast at the rate of 3,500 acres per year. Twenty years ago the cost of reconditioning and landscaping areas left derelict by mining, quarrying and tipping was prohibitive, and in many cases technically impossible, but today this is no longer the case. A special study undertaken by the Civic Trust has established that a comprehensive twenty year programme to renew all land left derelict by past industrial activities and to remedy the effect of current mineral workings would demand an outlay of only about £1 million per year—5d (c. 2p) per head of the population.

The Process of Tourist Development

The provision of recreation services can bring prosperity to an area, and benefit industries which could not grow so fast without the added component of leisure demand. Tourism is a new economic resource which often flourishes best in the areas that are poorest in industrial resources. Tourist expenditure can be an important source of revenue to an area for several reasons. When on holiday people tend to spend as if their income were two or three times greater than it is. Tourist expenditure is new money brought into an area from outside. Detailed studies of the circulation of the tourist pound have shown that each pound spent by visitors in an area results in between two and three pounds of local income. The US Department of Commerce reported in 1950: 'If a community can attract a couple of dozen tourists a day throughout the year, it would be economically comparable to acquiring a new manufacturing industry with an annual payroll of $100,000.' Even in times of depression holiday areas can be more prosperous than industrial areas. The wealthier the society the greater the proportion of total money and time devoted to service industries as opposed to physical commodities. Recreation creates a service industry concerned essentially with people. As automation proceeds, labour must move from manufacturing to service trades. Recreation has an almost insatiable demand for personal service. Modern techniques in production of services have a long way to go, but as these techniques develop and the price of services falls, the demand for labour increases.

Holiday development also affects the image of an area, with the result that new residents and other industries may be attracted to it. Holiday spending improves communications and utilities which can become the base for other trades. Moreover, the demand for travel and recreation is not easily satisfied; the appetite once whetted, the traveller will always travel without becoming bored by a surfeit of the product.

The recreation and tourist trade can be a profitable one. It is not a luxury trade. As a source of wealth it can prove a better investment in terms of land and natural resources than many manufacturing industries. Preservation and development of natural resources for pleasure have not been considered profitable until very recently. These have been traditionally fit subjects for charity. Yet, from the tourist point of view they should be regarded as a long-term investment in trade likely to show increasing returns in the future. There are examples of this happening and of the longer term being much shorter than originally supposed. An enormous increase in recreation demand can be met with a relatively limited increase in physical plant. Substantial investment is needed in publicity and information services and organisation to use existing resources. It is no use directing these efforts towards selling the old, traditional type of holiday. Of course, the summer holiday by the sea cannot be sold in the middle of December, but there is an increasing desire for new recreation pastimes. The growth of winter sports demonstrates the frustration and boredom of an increasingly wealthy population in northern winters. In the winter of 1968–9 there was an increase of no less than 24 per cent in overseas visitor traffic to London, due to the popularity of winter holidays of a different kind.

In creating and popularising new activities, the important fashion-forming or path-finding element does not necessarily come from the top level in society, as it did in the past. Improved communication makes it possible for fashions to start from any group. As increasingly each group in society has the economic

175

means to enforce its wishes, the trends can start from a number of social centres. Generally speaking, although by no means always, the active and participating leisure time activities are related to the younger element in society and the passive to the older. Because of their increasing wealth it is the younger element which is best able to turn its wishes into rapid reality. This explains the present growth in participation in active pursuits.

Increasing mobility extends the area within which leisure activities can be practised and is tending to produce the recreation region as a necessary complement, rather than the recreation centre, like the traditional holiday resort. The recreation region can be created either for the benefit of the resident population, principally at weekends, or for visitors. The Peak District National Park, for example, caters chiefly for the nearby resident population, but supplements its economy by accommodating visitor traffic staying for several nights in the slacker periods.

To supplement the income of an area which serves principally as a recreation area for residents by the introduction of the tourist and holiday trade can bring great economic benefits. Once the investment in plant and the outlay of resources is made to cover the fixed and operating costs, and unless the load factor or occupancy approaches 100 per cent, there is the increasing possibility of highly profitable business in selling the service which is manufactured and wasted. This is characteristic of a service industry. You cannot store unused accommodation. Although this complementary nature of tourism can result in a most profitable form of tourist and holiday traffic, the problem comes when, having reached a near 100 per cent capacity, there is pressure for new investment, not only in hotels and holiday towns but also perhaps in the public utilities serving the area. One therefore starts the cycle, entering the least profitable segment of tourist investment. It is at this point that government funds to assist investment have been injected in many countries. Recent legislation in Britain has provided for this kind of help for new hotel building.

The industries which together service the tourist and enable a region to provide a tourist product have certain difficulties akin to those in agriculture and the capital goods industries. Transport and its equipment, including airports, sea ports, roads and car parks, and hotels and accommodation centres, require very heavy fixed capital investment, where the return must be sought over a long period. The resulting equipment may not be capable of adaptation to alternative use. Yet the basic product does not lie in the provision of an aeroplane seat, a road or a hotel bed, but in the attractions of the countryside, in the delights of a hot, sunny beach, in the pleasures of visiting ancient buildings, monuments and museums particularly if they are situated, as they are in Britain, in delightful countryside. Some part of this total product may have no intrinsic value. A visitor who wants a mountain to himself expects to have it free although he may spend substantial sums of money on getting to it, and in the accommodation centre which may be some distance away. There is the further difficulty that tourism and holidaymaking, and indeed recreation as a whole, is a volatile activity, subject to fashion, a highly competitive business, with rapid rises and falls in traffic. Ten years ago it would have seemed most unlikely that Britain could have reached a position where its foreign traffic increased while that of France declined. But, in 1968, overseas visitors spent more in visiting Britain than British people spent in visiting other countries, whereas in France, a traditional tourist mecca, the French recently spent more travelling abroad than foreign visitors spent in enjoying the attractions of France.[6]

Planning for Tourism

If it is decided to develop an area for tourism, it is necessary to decide what kind of facilities are to be offered. Before making such a choice, there must be research in the area to establish two things: first, its existing facilities, and second, its natural resources which could be developed on a long-term basis. The survey carried out by the British Travel Association in the Peak District National Park has shown that, because of its relatively low hotel occupancy it would be possible to increase—perhaps two- or three-fold—tourist revenue in the area, simply by making fuller use of existing equipment. This fuller use could be achieved by increasing visitor traffic to the area through improved information services and better marketing.

Having carried out research into these two fields, the planning authorities will be in a position to decide which type of tourist development is to be their aim. There are two alternatives. They can either assume that the bulk of the area's income will be derived from some other industry, and cater for the local market by creating either a recreation centre within an urban area or a country recreation area adjoining an industrial area; or they can go in for tourism and holidaymaking, recognising that the holiday trade is fundamentally incompatible with a number of other industries. Under this second alternative they can seek external and foreign business to complement an existing local business, and develop the area primarily for tourism, with resorts becoming the centres from which a number of chosen recreation activities are practised. The resort can also play an important part as a local recreation area. It seems likely that Blackpool, for example, is now receiving a substantial part of its total business in the form of day visitors from the surrounding urban populations.

In selecting the type of recreation activity to be developed, it must be recognised that there is a high degree of competition, not least between different areas and different countries. There is a relatively secure form of recreation activity in which an area can invest, where it can be fairly sure of its market for a few years, and there is a very insecure form where changes in fashion can alter the economic outlook. Holidays on the Mediterranean coast, for example, are highly susceptible to variations in demand and price, because the attraction of such a holiday is not the unique and natural characteristics of a specific area or country, but simply hot sun and sea. In other forms of travel it is the area itself which creates the attraction. Britain has become known as the land of gardens, tradition, pageantry, sports and the arts, so that its image gives it a certain monopoly value. Another advantage we possess is that our climate is suitable for active pursuits, whereas the hot Mediterranean climate is not.

The result is that many of Britain's resorts and resort areas now enjoy a longer tourist season than some of the newer resorts in the warmer climates. Indeed, London may rightly claim to be an all-the-year-round centre. Its attractions are largely indoors. The Crown Jewels glitter as well in January as in July and can be more easily seen. Culture in an attractive setting can be a more powerful magnet than the sun. This could not be realised until there was an assessment of the unique factors in Britain's tourist and holiday attractions, as opposed to those abroad, and a recognition of those attractions, which if not unique, were at least competitive, which means as good as, if not better for the price than, the equivalent offered anywhere else. So far as Britain's resorts are concerned, they are competitive climatically with those in the long European coastline from Brittany to Scandinavia. Their equipment in many cases is better. They have shown a greater ability to hold on to their trade than many of the Northern European resorts, even though their business has changed not so much in the main attractions but in the activities of the people, the way they wish to be accommodated and the way they spend their money. It is a broad generalisation to say that people no longer swim in the sea. They do like walking by it, looking at it and practising sports on it. The rise in the standards of living has made heated swimming pools popular so that hotels built on the coast still invest in swimming pools in front of the sea. More important, it opens up great possibilities for the inland resorts to attract the kind of traffic for which their assets are eminently suitable.

In developing recreation facilities, planning is essential. But, once planning has been done, an organisation is needed to create and foster demand by providing information and guidance and by carrying out publicity. This is the highly specialised task of the tourist organisation, whether it be the local authority or a regional tourist board organised as a co-operative of interests. Although these organisations must guide and advise the service trades, as well as authorities and the public (the hosts) in their area, the task of actually providing the recreation facilities is best left, in a well-developed economy such as ours, to a competitive industry. It is a case of supreme delegation by the community to the commercial interest most likely to provide the kind of service for which the area has been agreed to be suitable.

Not all tourists in economic terms are equally good. Areas can go in for high-value, low-density traffic, and some should. It is not ministries of tourism and state tourist boards that can provide the tourist product. In developed countries 90 per cent of it is provided on a commercial basis, and it is on this basis that one must look for the massive expansion in facilities. The tourist organisation creates and thus controls the market, and must be in close touch with the providers of services who in turn are subject to the discipline of the market as their principal controlling force. It can and should devote resources to research to guide those in control of services, and particularly the planners, who are in control of the environment and can, with their connections with the government, create the conditions for expansion according to an agreed strategy of development for the area.

One of the tourist organisations' principal functions is that of co-ordinating activity, both in marketing and development of tourist services. The tourist product is a combination of a number of service components. These components are owned or controlled by a wide range of separate organisations such as state bodies, voluntary societies, commercial concerns. For each of them the tourist demand or tourist business is likely to represent a minority interest. These providers of basic components do not exist simply to cater for visitors. Thus, the co-ordinating task of the Tourist Authority becomes paramount. One failure in one component can stop tourist development or ruin the satisfaction of a holiday. Equally, one refusal by the Planning Authority to permit one of these components to develop can jeopardise the development of a flow of tourism to the area. Edinburgh City Council's reluctance to foster the development of substantial additional first-class hotel accommodation has, in the last ten years, undoubtedly cost that city, and Scotland as a whole, a great deal in tourist revenue. An overall strategy, based on research, implies, however, a choice as to the type of visitor which the area should receive and wishes to welcome and the type of activity which its assets will enable it to offer competitively. Above all, there is a requirement for a joint operation between tourist organisations and the planning authorities which must rest on one principle—that no area in this day and age of massive growth and change can tell the potential tourist what he should enjoy. There must be a realisation of the volatile and competitive nature of tourism and of the increasing offers from different tourist areas within a country or from foreign countries made yearly more accessible to the visitor. Thus the range of choice continually increases. The boundaries of the recreation area grow. Seasonal movement within a country from the hot, dusty cities to the cool mountains, from the industrial towns to the coast still exists, but this movement can cross several national frontiers and is increasingly less restricted by limitations of transport or available leisure time.

Tourist organisations and the planner have one common interest, that as recreation and holidaymaking become more international they alone can defend the interest of the area. The commercial enterprises can shift, albeit slowly, their investment to new countries, can concentrate on developing streams of traffic far away from the centre which provides the management, the know-how and the investment funds. Equally the tourist traffic itself can take off and move far away. Thus it is that a further common link binds the tourist organisation and the planners in defending their region in a competitive world. It is the planners' task to consider all possibilities of developing a region, which may or may not include tourist activity, but which cannot exclude, even if for the residents only, the need for recreation services. If the planners decide that tourism and holidaymaking is an economic activity suited to the resources of the region, then they must ally themselves with the tourist authority to seek from it the guidance as to the possible market, and to agree upon the selection of types of traffic to be attracted. They need for this purpose to create a strategy as a basis for a development plan embracing types of activity to be developed to cater for the kind of traffic to be encouraged. When the decision is made, a further period of close co-operation is required, whereby the tourist organisation, with its support from the tourist service trades, seeks to create the desired traffic and, in conjunction with the planners, seeks to encourage the expansion of the services and facilities which are needed. In certain cases state assistance in the early period of the cycle of

181

development will be required to stimulate the provision of long-term investment. The strategy will require continuous review. The time may come when the traffic to the area is considered to have reached saturation point so far as reception facilities are concerned. It is almost impossible in the tourist movement to hold traffic at a given level. There will always be tides of rising and falling demand affected by fashion so that the plan requires constant change. There is one consolation in that the provision of basic resources, accommodation and transport, can accommodate many forms of travel and, increasingly, tourist traffic can be attracted over a longer period, often enabling the area to increase its intake of people and to improve the profitability of its services.

Planners in democratic countries must take into consideration the wishes of the residents that they serve; but also, they must satisfy a national interest, which may at times conflict. Residents may resent the intrusion of the holiday traffic, often forgetting the resulting increase in wealth brought to the area and the provision of amenities and services which the area could not otherwise support. There are many cases of this problem in the resorts in Britain. While the group concept of tourism is generally unfavourable, it certainly is to the credit of Britain that the individual visitor, especially if he can make himself known by speaking the language, is received courteously and often with enthusiasm. The economic value of an external traffic is not readily understood. It is perhaps easier to compare adversely the relative affluence of the visitor, spending at two or three times his normal or 'residential' daily rate of expenditure while on his holiday, with the inevitably poorer resident. It may be forgotten that tourist and holiday wealth can preserve the countryside, maintain historic buildings, stimulate crafts, bring to life the tradition of the area which can so easily be lost in the growing conformity of modern industrialised society. All these things, generally speaking, residents approve, but they are rarely explained.

If leisure services are regarded as something 'consumed', then there is a need to consider who, in fact, is the producer. Hotels, restaurants and transport companies are all, in a sense, producers; but ultimately what is sold is something intangible—

the attractions of the destination. Of all the influences on the character of the destination, by far the greatest is wielded by the planners. Planners are dedicated to safeguarding amenity. Every tourist community must pay great attention to amenity. In tourist areas great economic activity is brought into being by an enormously increased demand for travel and leisure-time activities away from home. In these areas the local community and the planning experts are dedicated, not just to safeguarding amenity, but to producing great concentrations of it, where it has not only a social meaning but brings economic benefits.

The task of planning tourist development is a complex and professional job. It is no easier than undertaking development of any other massive industry. Yet the majority of existing resorts and resort areas do not approach the task professionally. They do not have a plan of development. Without this it is impossible for the tourist organisation and the planners to jointly encourage development of services, preservation of amenity, and specialisation in attractions, which together create tourist and holiday products and, in turn, provide the wealth of the region.

Planners must know about the demand for, and supply of, travel and recreational activities. For this reason they need contact with the travel industry; with the British Tourist Authority, the national tourist organisation, and with organisations such as the Scottish Tourist Board, the Northern Ireland Tourist Board, the Wales Tourist Board and regional tourist groups. These organisations are the focal points through which contact with the travel industry can be channelled. More research and joint action is needed in the following directions:

   (i) *National recreation studies* to indicate the types of activity for which facilities are required, and to forecast recreation trends, as, for example, the *Pilot National Recreation Survey* of 1965;[7]
   (ii) *Regional studies* to assess natural and economic resources and economic needs of specific recreation areas;
   (iii) *Development plans* to help each area to specialise according to its qualities;
   (iv) *Promotion plans* to mount joint operations by planners

and tourist organisations to develop existing holiday and recreation areas and to create new areas by stimulating demand for the chosen leisure product.

Tourist organisations and planners can together play a most valuable role in the important task of providing for the nation's recreation and for the profitable development of tourism.

References

1. British Travel Association, *Hotel Occupancy Survey*, 1968.
2. British Travel Association, *British National Travel Survey*, 1960 and 1968.
3. *Survey of Inland Waters and Recreation*, carried out on behalf of the Central Council of Physical Recreation.
4. British Travel Association, *British National Travel Survey*, op. cit.
5. Outdoor Recreation Resources Review Commission (USA), *Outdoor Recreation for America*, US Government Printing Office, 1962.
6. Organisation for Economic Co-operation and Development, *Tourism in OECD Member Countries*, 1969.
7. British Travel Association/University of Keele, *Pilot National Recreation Survey—Report No. 1*, 1967.

Chapter 9

The Organisation of Recreation Planning

THOMAS L. BURTON

The planning and provision of recreation facilities in Britain are the responsibility of a wide variety of agencies—central and local government, *ad hoc* public and semi-public authorities, private organisations and clubs, and commercial firms. In some cases, local government authorities and other public bodies may have a statutory duty to provide opportunities and facilities for recreation. In other cases, their provision is made entirely of their own accord and is, often, supplementary or subsidiary to their provision of some other service or good. Sometimes, public authorities are charged with a duty to provide recreation facilities, but are not given adequate powers with which to discharge this duty. Again, local and central government authorities will often choose not to provide recreation facilities directly, but will give financial support to clubs and organisations which are immediately concerned with the provision of facilities. These clubs and organisations range from small, local sports and social groups to the national sports federations, theatre companies and amenity societies. They are rarely governed by considerations of profitability, but usually by a need to balance income and expenditure. Commercial firms which provide recreation facilities, on the other hand, are, like all business undertakings, concerned with opportunities for profit. In short, then, the provision of recreation facilities comes from a wide range of agencies and organisations, with diverse motives and objectives.

These agencies can be grouped, however, into three broad categories: firstly, public and semi-public authorities, including Departments of the central government, local authorities and *ad hoc* organisations such as the Countryside Commission, the Forestry Commission, the Sports Council and its Regional

Sports Councils, the Nature Conservancy, and so on; secondly, (2) clubs and organisations, ranging from the many local youth clubs and community associations to the governing bodies of each major sport, and such organisations as the Central Council of Physical Recreation, the National Trust and the Royal Shakespeare Company; thirdly, commercial firms, ranging from (3) small independent operators of cinemas and dance clubs to the large multi-product firms such as Top Rank Limited and Mecca Limited. This chapter will consider the roles of each of these kinds of agencies in the planning and provision of recreation facilities at the present time, some of the problems with which they are faced, and the extent to which they work together and combine in providing for the leisure needs of the population.

The two main Departments of the central government responsible for recreation are the Ministry of Housing and Local Government (in Wales, the Welsh Office and, in Scotland, the Scottish Office) and the Department of Education and Science. The former is responsible for the activities of the Countryside Commission, while the latter has under its aegis the Sports Council and the Arts Council. In addition to these two Departments, the Ministry of Transport has an interest—particularly through its responsibilities for the British Waterways Board— while the Department of Employment and Productivity and Ministry of Agriculture are also involved with the problem. The Ministry of Housing and Local Government and the Department of Education and Science are also involved *indirectly*, by reason of their responsibilities *vis-à-vis* local planning authorities and local education authorities. Rather than try to assess the overall involvement and responsibilities of central government Departments directly, therefore, it is simplest to consider individually the main public bodies and organisations which carry responsibilities of various kinds for the planning and provision of recreation facilities, and to examine their particular relationships with Departments of the central government. The major bodies to be considered are the Countryside Commission, together with the various Park Planning Boards and Committees; the Arts Council; the Sports Council and its eleven Regional Sports Councils; the Forestry Commission; the Nature Conservancy; the British Waterways Board; and the British

187

Tourist Authority. In addition, consideration will be given to the roles that are played by local authorities, major voluntary organisations and commercial firms.

The Countryside Commission

The Countryside Commission was established under the Countryside Act, 1968. It took over the responsibilities of the National Parks Commission, established through the National Parks and Access to the Countryside Act of 1949, together with additional responsibilities which were laid upon it. It is simplest, therefore, to examine the Commission's powers in two sections: firstly, those that pertain to National Parks and derive from the Act of 1949; and secondly, those that pertain to the countryside generally and derive directly from the Act of 1968.

The National Parks Commission was created to play a predominantly advisory role in planning, the major planning duties within National Parks being retained by local planning authorities. The duties imposed upon the Commission were twofold:

(i) the preservation and enhancement of natural beauty in England and Wales, particularly in National Parks and designated Areas of Outstanding Natural Beauty;

(ii) the promotion of opportunities for public open air recreation within the National Parks.

From these duties spring a number of functions, of which the most important is to designate, after consultations with the local authorities concerned, areas in which National Parks and Areas of Outstanding Natural Beauty should be established, and to submit to the Minister of Housing and Local Government proposals for the creation of Long Distance Footpaths. The Commission's other functions are to provide information services relating to National Parks, Areas of Outstanding Natural Beauty and Long Distance Footpaths and to encourage, by suitable means of publicity, a proper standard of behaviour from people who visit these; to advise generally on matters relating to natural beauty anywhere in England and Wales; and to make recommendations to local planning authorities concerning the development of National Parks generally.

The National Parks are not vast areas of land given over primarily to recreation—as, for example, they are in America. They are simply designated areas in which ordinary rural life is carried on. They include within their boundaries farms, villages and even small towns. This multiple-use aspect of the Parks was emphasised on several occasions during the course of the debates in Parliament which preceded the passing of the 1949 Act: 'It is essential, and I think, very desirable too, that in our National Parks the ordinary rural life, such as farming, rural industry and afforestation, should continue to function. This is a small country, and we cannot afford, as can the United States, to set aside large areas solely for the purpose of public recreation, or of establishing a museum.' Furthermore, the designation of an area as a National Park confers no additional rights of access to that area upon the public, beyond those which it already possesses. The land is not nationalised, and designation effects no change in its ownership. Yet, despite this, the Commission was specifically charged under the Act with the task of promoting the provision of opportunities for open air recreation within the Parks. Obviously, if it was to carry out this task effectively, it would need some kind of legal powers in respect of public access to land which was to remain in private ownership.

Under Part V of the Act, therefore, local planning authorities are empowered to provide for public access to the countryside by means of *access agreements* and *access orders*. The Countryside Commission, through the planning authorities within each of the National Parks, can make agreements and orders providing for public access for open air recreation. But these powers are not restricted solely to National Parks. Any local planning authority in England and Wales may use them. The access agreement is made between the landowner and the planning authority and provides for access to the land which is the subject of the agreement. The access order also provides for public access, but is made unilaterally by the planning authority, subject to appeal by the landowner to the Minister of Housing and Local Government. Agreements and orders can be made in

189

respect of 'open country' only—defined in the 1949 Act as any area consisting 'wholly or predominantly of mountain, moor, heath, down, cliff or foreshore'. In so far as the land which is the subject of a proposed agreement or order is situated within the boundaries of a National Park, the Countryside Commission must be consulted; but the responsibility for making agreements and orders rests with the local planning authorities.

In fact, the Act of 1949 laid the major responsibility for planning in National Parks upon the shoulders of local planning authorities. The Countryside Commission fulfils a predominantly advisory role—towards both the Minister and the local planning authorities. The local planning authorities are responsible, however, for carrying out planning policies and, in those cases where a park falls within the areas of more than one local authority, this is done by means of a joint planning board or a joint advisory committee. It was intended that the normal form of administration would be by means of a joint planning board, but 'in fact, due to the strenuous opposition of local authorities, only two joint boards have been set up'.[1] The joint advisory committee has become the predominant form of administration for Parks which fall within the areas of two or more planning authorities.

The effect of access agreements and orders is to give a right of access to the land to the general public 'for purposes of open air recreation'. This right specifically excludes the playing of organised sports and games. The total area of land which is currently subject to access orders and agreements amounts to 66,839 acres—58,039 acres of which are within National Parks and Areas of Outstanding Natural Beauty. In addition, local authorities have acquired, by purchase or gift, over 6,500 acres of land for public access; about a third of this area is within National Parks and two-thirds within Areas of Outstanding Natural Beauty.

The total area of land within the National Parks which is the subject of access agreements and orders represents only a small fraction of the total area of the Parks—less than 2 per cent. But, it has been argued that this scale of provision is fairly adequate, because the public has *de facto* access to very large areas of the Parks already. Legal action to secure access is necessary, therefore, only in areas where this *de facto* access is restricted. Thus, in its evidence to the *Royal Commission on Common Land*, the Ministry of Housing and Local Government stated that there had been little need to use the powers available for making access agreements and orders in the National Parks, since the public is generally allowed to walk over the unfenced countryside without further action on the part of the local planning authorities.

The major weakness of the National Parks legislation was the creation of a Commission whose planning powers and financial resources are severely limited. The responsibilities for preserving and enhancing natural beauty in National Parks and Areas of Outstanding Natural Beauty and for promoting opportunities for open air recreation were laid upon the Commission; but the powers for achieving these objectives lie very largely with the local planning authorities. While, in practice, the Commission and local planning authorities have together fought strongly for the preservation and enhancement of natural beauty against heavy pressures for development, little attention has been given to the positive function of promoting opportunities for open air recreation. This is partly a result of financial difficulties. The various individual Park authorities rarely have the full-time qualified staff necessary to create and pursue positive policies for the provision of leisure facilities in the Parks; nor does the Commission. And neither the Park authorities nor the Commission will be able to obtain these qualified staff until they receive adequate financial resources. Exchequer grants are available to meet up to 75 per cent of the total expenditure on approved recreation projects in the Parks. But, until the planning authorities and the Commission obtain the staff needed to create projects, these Exchequer grants will be little used, and positive planning for recreation in the Parks will be minimal.

The establishment of National Parks as distinctive areas of the countryside in which opportunities for recreation are provided for the general public has, to some extent, been overtaken by events since it was proposed in 1949. The numbers of motor-cars in use in the community have trebled since that date. National income has more than doubled and non-working

191

Table 9.1 *Statutory access areas in the countryside, 1967*

National Parks and Areas of Outstanding Natural Beauty	Total acreage
Peak District NP	47,839
Lake District NP	105
Yorkshire Dales NP	2,349
Dartmoor NP	1,745
Exmoor NP	880
Northumberland NP	97
Snowdonia NP	1,186
Surrey Hills AONB	260
Cannock Chase AONB	2,096
East Hampshire AONB	317
Chichester Harbour AONB	265
Elsewhere (approx.)	8,800
TOTAL	66,839

Long Distance Footpaths	Date approved	Length (*miles*)
Pennine Way	1951	250
Pembrokeshire Coast Path	1953	167
Offa's Dyke	1955	168
South Downs Way	1963	80
South West Peninsula Coast Path:		
North Cornwall	1952	135
South Cornwall	1954	133
South Devon	1959	93
Somerset and North Devon	1961	82
Dorset	1963	72
Yorkshire and North York Moors	1965	93
TOTAL		1,273

Source: Seventeenth Report of the National Parks Commission, HMSO, 1967.

hours have increased substantially. The pressures upon the National Parks for recreation purposes have grown rapidly. Perhaps more important, these pressures have also been felt heavily in other areas of the countryside, outside the National Parks. This trend was recognised by the Government and led directly to the Countryside Act of 1968.* Under the provisions of this Act, the Countryside Commission was established, with a mandate to keep under review all matters relating to the provision, development and improvement of facilities for enjoyment of the countryside, the conservation and enhancement of its natural beauty and the need to secure public access to the countryside for the purposes of open air recreation. The most important section of the Act is that which provides for the creation of Country Parks in which facilities for open air recreation will be available to the general public.[2] The responsibility for the establishment of these parks lies with the local planning authorities, who will be advised and assisted by the Countryside Commission. In particular, it is intended that these parks should be established by joint arrangements between urban and rural planning authorities. Thus, urban authorities with large populations whose members visit the countryside, especially at weekends, are enabled to help finance country parks in adjacent (and distant) rural areas. The powers that the Commission and the local planning authorities have received represent an increased emphasis upon positive planning for recreation in the countryside, particularly for coping with the ever-increasing numbers of townsmen who visit the countryside for recreation.

The Arts Council

The support that is given by the Government to the Arts in Britain can be grouped into three broad categories—education, preservation and patronage. Educational support is the responsibility of the Department of Education and Science in England and Wales and the Scottish Education Department in Scotland. Most of this support is provided through the local education authorities and voluntary organisations and takes the form of financial support for the Arts in schools, colleges of further education, adult education courses and community centres. Preservation is primarily the responsibility of the Ministry of Public Building and Works, which cares directly for many historic buildings, ancient monuments and statues. In

* Similar legislation for Scotland—the Countryside (Scotland) Act—was enacted in 1967.

addition, the Ministry occasionally makes financial grants to the National Trust and its Scottish counterpart, the two main voluntary organisations concerned with the preservation of historic buildings and art collections. Patronage is channelled largely through the Arts Council. Some patronage is, however, made directly—to national institutions, such as the British Museum, which have their own boards of trustees and the management of whose affairs is in their own hands. The numbers of these institutions are, however, relatively few and, for the most part, financial support for the Arts is provided through the Arts Council.

The duties of the Arts Council, as set out in its charter in 1946, are to promote 'a greater knowledge, understanding and practice of the fine arts exclusively and, in particular, to increase the accessibility of the fine arts to the public . . . to improve the standard of execution of the fine arts and to advise and co-operate with . . . Government Departments, local authorities and other bodies on any matters concerned directly or indirectly with those objects'.[3] The Council is made up of sixteen members appointed by the Chancellor of the Exchequer after consultation with the Ministers responsible for Education in England, Wales and Scotland. These persons are chosen for their knowledge of and concern with one or more of the fine arts. The Council is responsible for the disposition of the grant-in-aid given to it through the Department of education and Science. This is now provided on a triennial basis, with an agreed annual increase of 10 per cent, in the second and third years. The Charter provided for the appointment of Committees of the Council, for Scotland and Wales, which are responsible for carrying out the Council's duties in these two countries.

The Council allocates funds to organise exhibitions and concerts, some of which tour the country. For the most part, however, it provides financial support, either in the form of grants or guarantees, to a wide range of national and regional organisations and events. Its role is, therefore, to act as a patron of the Arts, stimulating and encouraging interest by providing funds for diverse kinds of artistic groups, societies and individuals (Table 9.2).

It is in no way a governing body for the Arts, although its monetary resources obviously endow it with substantial authority. It is not concerned directly with standards or quality in the Arts; but, again, its ability to give and withhold financial support, especially in the form of guarantees, does allow it to make (indirect) judgments about standards, *if it wishes to do so.*

Table 9.2   *Major organisations supported by the Arts Council, 1965*

Opera and Ballet	Music
Covent Garden and Royal Ballet	Royal Festival Hall
Sadler's Wells	Scottish National Orchestra
Welsh National Opera Company	Halle Orchestra
Scottish Opera Society	Liverpool Philharmonic
London Opera Centre	Orchestra
Ballet Rambert	City of Birmingham Symphony
Western Theatre Ballet	Orchestra
	Western Orchestral Society
	Northern Sinfonia Orchestra
Theatre	*Art*
The National Theatre	Many local art exhibitions
Royal Shakespeare Company	
English Stage Society	
45 provincial repertory companies	
The Edinburgh Festival	
Various arts festivals	

Source: Compiled from White Paper, *A Policy for the Arts,* Cmnd. 2601, 1965.

The Sports Council

The Sports Council was established by the Minister with Responsibility for Sport in January 1965. Its terms of reference are 'to advise the Government on matters relating to the development of amateur sport and physical recreation services and to foster co-operation among the statutory authorities and voluntary organisations concerned'.[4] The Council is an advisory body with no executive powers. Its membership is variable but, at the time of writing, consisted of twenty-eight persons, including the Minister with Responsibility for Sport, who is the Chairman, and the Director and Deputy Director, the latter being a full-time salaried official. Until recently, it was *serviced* within the Department of Education and Science, but it now operates under the aegis of the Central Council of Physical Recreation, the major voluntary organisation concerned with amateur sport in this country and one which receives considerable government support.

In addition to its broad terms of reference, the Sports Council was given the responsibility of advising the Government on nine specific sports issues. These are:

   (i) Standards of provision of sports facilities for the community.

  (ii) Collation of information about the position of sport in other countries.

 (iii) Surveys of resources and regional planning.

 (iv) Co-ordination of the use of community resources.

  (v) Research.

 (vi) Development of training and coaching.

(vii) Likely capital expenditure.

(viii) Participation in sporting events overseas by British amateur teams.

 (ix) Priorities in sports development.

The Council has established four committees and allocated these responsibilities among them. The *International Committee* is responsible for advice concerning the development of amateur sport overseas and financial support for British teams going overseas. The *Research and Statistics Committee* is concerned to advise on matters of scientific research related to sport. The *Sports Development and Coaching Committee* is responsible for providing advice on the development of sport through national voluntary organisations, levels of capital expenditure and the development of training and coaching. Finally, the *Facilities Planning Committee* advises on matters relating to the provision and improvement of facilities for sport and physical recreation.

One of the most far-reaching proposals by the Sports Council has been the establishment of Regional Sports Councils throughout the country. It was the Council's opinion that the main responsibility for the development of sports and recreation

196

facilities, in both urban and rural areas, rested upon the local authorities—but organised into regional groups, and not specifically as individual authorities. Its proposals were accepted by the Minister, and eleven Regional Sports Councils established—one each in Scotland and Wales, and nine in England. As with the Sports Council itself, these Regional Councils are *serviced* by the Central Council of Physical Recreation, through its regional offices. Their members consist of persons appointed by local authorities, regional representatives of the Government Departments principally concerned with sport and physical recreation, and selected members of sports organisations in each region. Each Regional Council has a Technical Panel—made up of the planning officers from each local planning authority in the region and other people with interest and experience in sport and recreation—upon which it can call for expert advice.

The Sports Council itself is an advisory and consultative body, as are the eleven Regional Sports Councils. But the latter have direct representation from local authorities and can call upon the resources of these authorities to help with the administrative, research and planning tasks of the Councils. As a first priority, each Regional Sports Council was asked, by the national body, to make an initial appraisal of major needs and existing facilities within its region. This task was given to the Technical Panels and, hence, was carried out almost wholly by the local planning authorities. Ten of the Councils have now completed this task and have published their findings. Thus, although the Council and the Regional Councils are essentially advisory bodies, their close contact with local planning authorities has enabled them to take on a number of executive powers and to carry through specific executive tasks.

The Forestry Commission

It is essential to recognise that it is not a statutory duty of the Forestry Commission to provide facilities for recreation. The Commission's duties, outlined in the Forestry Act, 1945, are to increase the production of wood as a raw material for industry and, in so doing, to operate an efficient and economic forest industry. The Commission's primary objective, therefore, is to

197

build up a thriving forest industry by extending the woodland area in accordance with sound land use and efficient management. There are, however, two ways in which the Commission contributes to the development of recreation facilities. Firstly, it consults with the Countryside Commission and other interested bodies whenever any significant extension of the forest area is proposed in the National Parks and Areas of Outstanding Natural Beauty. This consultation has often led to the alteration of afforestation proposals, and in some cases to the complete withdrawal of proposals. J. B. Cullingworth cites a case, for example, in which a proposal by the Commission to afforest 1,200 acres in the Exmoor National Park was totally abandoned after objections by the Countryside Commission, the local planning authorities and local voluntary organisations.[5] It appears that, contrary to much public belief, the Commission is appreciative of the possible dangers to amenity caused by afforestation and works generally to limit these as much as possible.

The second way in which the Commission contributes to the provision of recreation facilities is a positive one, which, unfortunately, has tended to be overshadowed by public controversy over the effects upon amenity of its afforestation programme. The Commission has made provision for public access to all of its plantations, subject only to necessary restrictions arising from fire danger, sporting lettings and similar factors. It has, moreover, established seven National Forest Parks (Table 9.3) and several caravan and camping sites, nature trails and picnic areas within them. The provision of these facilities is not a statutory duty of the Commission, but one which it tries to combine with its legal obligations. The authority to provide such facilities is spelled out in detail in paragraph 17 of the Countryside Act, 1968: the Commission 'may on any land placed at their disposal . . . provide or arrange for, or assist in the provision of, tourist, recreational or sporting facilities'.[6] This is, perhaps, one of the few cases of a public authority receiving statutory permission to provide a service which it has, in fact, provided for many years. It is important to note, however, that the Act *permits* the Commission to provide these facilities; it does not *oblige* it to do so.

Table 9.3   *Forest Parks in Britain 1966*

Park	Area (acres)
Forest of Dean	34,000
Snowdonia	23,700
Border Forest	126,000
Glen Trool	130,127
Queen Elizabeth Forest	42,000
Argyll Forest	60,000
Glen More	9,200
TOTAL	425,027

Note: In addition to these, there is the New Forest which, although not a Forest Park, provides similar public access and leisure facilities. Its total area is 92,365 acres.

Source: J. B. Cullingworth, *Town and Country Planning in England and Wales*, Allen & Unwin, 2nd edition, 1967, p. 184.

The Nature Conservancy

The Nature Conservancy was established by Royal Charter in March, 1949, and was given additional powers under the National Parks and Access to the Countryside Act which came into force later in the same year. The Conservancy's main duties are to give scientific advice, to establish and manage nature reserves, and to organise and develop research into nature conservation. The Conservancy is, thus, conceived largely as a scientific body 'concerned particularly with research on problems underlying the management of natural sites and of vegetation and animal populations'.[7] This scientific emphasis in the Conservancy's work was reaffirmed when it was reconstituted as a part of the Natural Environment Research Council in 1965. The terms of reference of the latter are 'to encourage and support, by any means, research by any person or body in the earth sciences and ecology . . . and to carry out research . . . and to provide advice and disseminate knowledge in any field aforesaid'.[8] The Council is also required to 'appoint a committee, to be called the Nature Conservancy, for carrying out those activities of the Council that are concerned with the establishment of nature reserves, and with the provision of advice and the dissemination of knowledge concerning nature conserva-

199

tion, and for carrying out and supporting such research as the Conservancy considers appropriate having regard to those activities'.[9] Thus, the emphasis in the Conservancy's work remains on matters of scientific application and research.

Table 9.4   *National nature reserves in Britain, 1966*

	Number of reserves	Total area (acres)
England	52	36,892
Wales	24	11,280
Scotland	29	169,954
TOTAL	105	218,126

Source: The Nature Conservancy. Unpublished paper.

But, although it is scientifically oriented, the Nature Conservancy, like the Forestry Commission, has adopted a positive attitude towards the provision of recreation facilities. The primary objective in the setting-up of nature reserves is to protect certain plant and animal species. But the Conservancy has conducted a policy of allowing public access to these reserves, whenever this is compatible with proper scientific management. Access is of three kinds: firstly, there are some reserves to which the public has access at all times along footpaths and rights-of-way; secondly, there are reserves to which access can be obtained only by permits, which must be obtained in advance from regional and national offices of the Conservancy; finally, there are those to which access is possible only for scientific research. About half of the total area of nature reserves in Britain at the present time—more than 218,000 acres —is open to the general public at virtually all times (Table 9.4). The Nature Conservancy is, therefore, similar to the Forestry Commission in its position regarding the provision of recreation facilities; it is not a statutory duty of either body to provide these, but each does so whenever this is compatible with its primary statutory obligations.

The Water Resources and British Waterways Boards

The Water Resources Board was established through the Water

200

Resources Act, 1963. This Act brought into being a new water conservation system in England and Wales, in which the executive duties are the responsibility of twenty-nine river authorities. The duties of the Water Resources Board *vis-à-vis* these river authorities are mainly advisory and consultative in character. The Board is required to advise the river authorities about the performance of the new water resources functions that were given to them. It is also required 'to consider in what way action needs to be taken for the purposes of conserving, redistributing or otherwise augmenting water resources, or of securing the proper use of water resources', and, in connection with these matters, to carry out research and investigations.[10] The Board is, thus, an advisory and planning body, while the river authorities are executive bodies responsible for the management of water resources.

The 1963 Act permits the river authorities to allow the use of rivers and reservoirs by the public for any forms of recreation which the authorities consider appropriate, 'if it appears to them reasonable to do so'.[11] Thus, the river authorities have permissive powers to provide facilities for recreation, but no statutory obligation to do so. The Board has, however, taken the view that the provision of facilities for recreation is an important function of the river authorities and it has pressed this view firmly upon them. It has maintained that development planning should be both comprehensive and multi-purpose. Planning must take account of all water users, 'whether by abstraction for the public water supply, industry and agriculture, or by enjoyment of rivers and lakes for fishing and other forms of recreation and amenity'.[12] It is recognised that these different interests may often be in conflict, but this is seen not as an argument for ignoring certain users but, on the contrary, as an important reason for considering them in detail. This attitude on the part of the Board and the river authorities has begun to have visible results, such as the facilities for sailing, fishing and bird-watching provided on the recently completed Grafham Reservoir, in Huntingdonshire.

The British Waterways Board is an entirely separate body from the Water Resources Board. It was established under the Transport Act, 1962 and is responsible directly to the Minister of

Transport. Under Section 10 of the Act, the Board was required to review the manner in which the inland waterways owned and managed by it could be put to the best possible use. In doing so, it was instructed to carry on its business in such a way that it would obtain a revenue that would be 'not less than sufficient for making provision for the meeting of charges properly chargeable to revenue, taking one year with another'.[13] In other words, the Board was instructed to assess the future of its waterways with a strict eye to their economic potential. An interim report was published in December 1963, outlining the Board's initial reactions to this instruction.[14]

A considerable section of the Board's interim report was devoted to a consideration of pleasure craft, cruising, angling and other similar uses of the waterways. The view was taken that all of these activities had significant growth potential and, hence, could provide useful sources of revenue in the future. But, for the present, none of them appeared to contribute significantly to revenue. The Board felt, however, that certain broad decisions should be taken as soon as possible about the future provision of recreation facilities on the waterways. The nature of these decisions was outlined further in the White Paper *British Waterways: Recreation and Amenity* in 1967.[15] The latter proposed that legislation should make provision for two distinct groups of waterways. The first would be those which make up the commercial network; the second those which make up a network of *cruiseways*—waterways maintained primarily for powered pleasure craft. The commercial network, although maintained primarily for commercial transport, would still be accessible to pleasure craft. The effect of the proposals would be to ensure that more than 1,400 miles of waterways would remain open for pleasure cruising. These would consist largely of canals and would be additional to any rivers made available for pleasure use by the river authorities. These proposals were embodied in the Transport Act, 1968.

The British Tourist Authority

The British Tourist Authority was established under The Development of Tourism Act, 1969, which came into force on

August 25, 1969. It is, therefore, too recent for any assessment to be made of its progress. The Act established three regional Tourist Boards (one each for England, Scotland and Wales), in addition to the Authority. The full powers and duties of these four bodies *vis-à-vis* each other and the tourist industry generally were not clearly defined by the Act, so that there remains some scope for pragmatic development. It is clear, however, that the Authority will have at least three main tasks. First, it will be the co-ordinating body for the three regional Boards. Second, it will have the power and resources to make discriminatory grants and loans for hotel development and the right to institute a nation-wide system of hotel classification. Finally, it will take over the responsibilities of the semi-private British Travel Association (which it will absorb) in respect of the promotion of the tourist and holiday industry, particularly overseas. The latter was established by Royal Charter in 1947. Its terms of reference allowed it to collect information from official and other sources, with which to further its promotional objectives. In particular it was permitted 'to conduct surveys, inquiries, keep records and publish reports related to any aspect of the tourist and holiday industry'.[16] Its main functions, therefore, were research and promotion. It was not an executive body with powers over the various groups and institutions that make up the tourist industry.

The Association's major research activity during its twenty-two years of life centred upon national patterns of holiday-making and studies of the holiday industry within individual resorts. From 1960, it carried out a national sample survey of holiday patterns each year: prior to that date, surveys had been carried out in 1951 and 1955. These surveys provided (and still provide) the only means by which it was possible to trace changes in patterns of holidaymaking in this country from the end of the Second World War. In addition to these surveys, the Association carried out a number of studies of the tourist and holiday industries of individual resorts, such as Brighton, Plymouth, Bournemouth, Stratford-upon-Avon and the Isle of Man.

The second main feature of the Association's work was its promotional activity, both within Britain and abroad. The introduction of the £50 travel limit as part of the government's economic restrictions in 1966 led to an intensive advertising campaign by the Association in 1967 and 1968, which had as its main theme the virtues and pleasures that could be obtained from holidays taken at resorts within Britain instead of going abroad. In other countries, the Association consistently promoted the image of Britain as a tourist attraction steeped in tradition and history, but with modern accommodation and facilities. It is largely through the efforts of the Association during the past decade that the tourist industry is now such an important economic asset to the country. And, indeed, it was perhaps the work of the Association which most clearly demonstrated the need for an organisation with wider and more comprehensive powers and greater direct government support. Thus, in a sense, the British Tourist Authority was born from the labours of the British Travel Association. Whether it will justify its creation remains to be seen.

Local Authorities

A range of different local authorities is concerned, in one way and another, with the provision of recreation facilities for the general public. It includes urban and municipal authorities (in Scotland, Burgh Councils) county councils and local education authorities. In some areas, facilities may be provided jointly by, say, an urban district council and the local (county) education authority. In other areas, there may be no joint provision at all but, rather, a clear distinction between the responsibilities and functions of each. Again, in some areas, the local authorities may provide a very wide range of facilities; while, in others, provision may be restricted to a few *traditional* kinds of facilities. There do not appear to be any generally accepted standards relating to the kinds of facilities that the local authorities will provide; although certain kinds of facilities, such as urban parks and open spaces, have become accepted, by tradition, as the responsibility of the local authorities. But, whatever may be the variations between different authorities in the *range* of facilities which they provide, it is possible to distinguish three main *ways* in which they provide them.

Firstly, of course, local authorities engage in the direct

provision of a range of facilities, to which the public has free access; that is, individuals are not required to pay directly for the use of these facilities (although they frequently pay for them indirectly, through the rates). In addition, local authorities will often provide a number of different kinds of facilities for which users are required to pay a direct charge—although the level of this charge often bears no true relationship to the economic cost of providing the facilities. Examples of *free* recreation facilities are urban parks, public libraries, lay-bys and picnic areas, and, sometimes, allotments. The kinds of facilities for which *uneconomic* prices are usually charged include museums, art galleries, swimming baths and allotments. The main burden of providing these facilities falls upon urban district, municipal borough and county borough councils, although some facilities may be provided by education authorities and, occasionally, by rural district and county authorities.

The second way in which local authorities are involved in the provision of recreation facilities is through the support which they give to voluntary organisations. This support takes two basic forms: firstly, they can make facilities and equipment available for the use of voluntary organisations; secondly, they can make financial grants to these groups and organisations. The local education authorities are particularly active in providing both kinds of support. Many schools are available for the use of youth clubs and adult education classes, although there is still considerable reluctance on the part of many authorities to permit the use of school facilities by other kinds of voluntary groups. A number of education authorities also make capital and annual grants to community associations and similar kinds of social groups. These grants range in size from a few pounds to the total annual salaries of wardens and assistant wardens for purpose-built community centres.

The third and, perhaps, the most important way in which local authorities are involved in the provision of recreation facilities is by virtue of their planning powers. Even if they are not concerned, in large measure, with the direct provision of facilities, local planning authorities will be faced with development proposals and required to make development orders and give planning consents for recreation facilities provided by other bodies. Moreover, planning authorities cannot afford to consider planning proposals in isolation, since, once it has been developed for, say, industrial use, an area may never be capable of future conversion to recreation uses—or, at least, not for many years and then probably only at great cost. Thus, planning authorities really need to consider proposals for recreation facilities in the context of a broad overall policy for recreation. Moreover, it is rapidly becoming clear that the determination of an overall policy for recreation can no longer be conceived solely in local terms. There is a growing awareness that local authority boundaries often have little relevance to the patterns of participation in recreation pursuits. The growth of greater personal and family mobility which has accompanied the rapid increase in levels of car ownership during the past decade or so has enabled people to move more freely across local authority boundaries for their recreation. There are some kinds of facilities, such as parks and sports pitches, which can still be considered as satisfying mainly local needs and which, therefore, can be planned on a local basis. But many other facilities, such as swimming pools and sports centres, largely satisfy regional and sub-regional needs and should, therefore, be planned on regional and sub-regional bases.

The role played by local authorities in the provision of recreation facilities is likely to assume greater importance in future years. The growing pressures upon land from a variety of sources—industrial, residential, communications and educational—the high capital investment costs of such facilities as sports centres, swimming pools, theatres and concert halls, and the expectation of further increases in levels of participation in recreation pursuits, all point towards an increased involvement of the local authorities. Many facilities will be beyond the financial resources of voluntary organisations, while remaining unattractive to commercial organisations because of their probable low economic returns. If, therefore, they are to be provided at all, they are likely to become the responsibility of the local authorities and, sometimes, the central government. It seems probable, then, that the scale of the local authorities' threefold involvement in the provision of facilities will increase substantially. Certainly, their direct provision and involvement

206

in planning proposals are likely to grow. Perhaps, however, their support for voluntary organisations may not do so—at any rate, on the same scale.

Voluntary Organisations

Voluntary organisations which provide recreation facilities range from local youth clubs, community associations and sports clubs to the governing bodies of sport and such national organisations as the Central Council of Physical Recreation and the National Trust. In addition, there are many organisations which, although they do not directly provide recreation facilities, act as supporters of those organisations which do so, or as *guardians* of existing *de facto* facilities against encroachment for development purposes, or as pressure groups, continually exhorting local authorities and the central government to increase the amount and scope of the facilities which they desire. Such organisations include the National Playing Fields Association, the Council for the Preservation of Rural England (and its counterparts in Wales and Scotland), the Ramblers' Association and the Civic Trust.

Local voluntary groups are of two main kinds: community associations, tenants' estate clubs and youth clubs, which are usually supported financially by local authorities; and other groups, mainly sports and social groups, which are largely self-supporting. The latter may base their membership upon a local catchment area, or they may be restricted to some particular category of people; for example, sports clubs attached to factories and firms are restricted in their membership to the employees of these organisations. Community associations draw their membership from fairly well-defined geographical areas within cities and towns, as do tenants' associations and youth clubs. Almost without exception these organisations are given financial support, either directly, or indirectly, from local authorities. Thus, there were, in 1965, thirty-one community associations in the City of Birmingham, all of which received support, in some way or other, from the local education authority. Youth clubs are, of course, part of the Youth Service, which is fundamentally a partnership between three main groups:

207

the central government, by way of the Department of Education and Science; the local education authorities; and the numerous voluntary youth organisations themselves. It is, however, the local education authorities who are primarily responsible for making the partnership work. It is they who must interpret national policies in terms of local needs; set up the machinery through which they and the voluntary groups can work together satisfactorily; service local youth clubs and groups; and, in certain circumstances, provide buildings and centres for the use of clubs.

One of the most important national organisations which provides facilities for public recreation is the National Trust. It was founded in 1895 by a group of *practicable idealists* whose intention was to set up a body of responsible private citizens who would act for the nation in the acquisition of land and houses considered worthy of permanent preservation. It was intended that these individuals would act as trustees, holding areas of land, houses and property for the public, and protecting them from destruction or undesirable development. The Trust is controlled by a Council, part of which is appointed by various public bodies and societies and part of which is elected by the members of the Trust. It has, from time to time, received financial support and specific grants from the Government, and many of its properties are supported (and some managed) by local authorities. Its main source of revenue is, however, its members and the general public—by way of subscriptions, endowments, legacies and donations. There is a separate and identical National Trust for Scotland with a similar constitution and objective. The two organisations now own large areas of commons, moors, downland, hills, cliffs and woods, as well as houses, gardens, historic sites and collections of paintings, tapestries, furniture, books and china. Members of the public have free access to the Trusts' open spaces, subject to the requirements of forestry, farming and nature conservation. Entry to houses and gardens is generally available at relatively modest prices.

The Central Council of Physical Recreation is the major voluntary organisation concerned with the provision of facilities for amateur sport and physical recreation in Britain. It was established in 1935 (as the Central Council of Recreative Physical Training) by a group of teachers and local government officers concerned with physical education. Its emphasis, in its earliest years, was upon the value of sport and physical recreation as an instrument of training, discipline and character-building. From about 1944 onwards, however, when its name was changed to that which it has now, its attitude changed to a more enlightened approach: it was 'a major break-away from the idea of doing good to people and a step towards giving to the people what they wanted in the way of sport and recreation'.[17] The Council has always had close links with central and local government, and was one of the first voluntary organisations to receive financial aid from the Government under the Physical Training and Recreation Act, 1937. It is still, today, the primary recipient of current grants from the Government; together with its Scottish counterpart (the Scottish Council of Physical Recreation), it received nearly £420,000 in current grants in 1965–6—out of a total of £565,000 given to all national voluntary sports organisations. The Council maintains four national recreation centres in England and Wales, at which it operates a series of residential summer courses covering thirty-five different recreation pursuits.

In addition to its provision of facilities for sport and physical recreation, the Council has recently taken over responsibility for providing technical, administrative and research services for the Sports Council; and, from their inception in 1965, the Regional Sports Councils were *serviced* by the regional offices of the Council. The new arrangements mean that the Sports Council, while remaining an advisory and consultative body appointed by a Minister of the Government, will operate under the aegis of a voluntary organisation. It is a unique arrangement in the administration of a government organisation, the progress of which will be watched carefully by other voluntary groups.

This brief résumé of voluntary organisations concerned in the provision and administration of recreation facilities in this country is, of course, far from complete. The numbers of organisations whose purpose and interests lie in the field of leisure run to thousands. It would be beyond the scope and resources of the present work to even attempt to list these

o

organisations. Unfortunately, they will have to retain their anonymity.

Commercial Recreation

An important part of the provision of recreation facilities in Britain is made by commercial organisations whose interests are dictated, in large measure, by considerations of profitability. These organisations range from small firms consisting of the operator and, perhaps, one or two employees, to the large, multi-product companies. The facilities which they provide range from camping sites to motels, from coffee bars to restaurants, and from discotheques to ballrooms. They include fun-fairs and sideshows, riding stables, ice rinks, cinemas and public houses. Commercial interests are particularly important in the provision of holiday accommodation in the coastal resorts and, indeed, in the provision of holiday facilities generally. Often, commercial firms that provide recreation facilities do so in conjunction with the provision of some other good or service. This is particularly true of the small firm—for example, the farmer who provides camping and caravan sites on his land, or holiday accommodation in his farmhouse, or who operates a riding school as a supplementary enterprise to his normal farming operations. In many cases, the profitability of these enterprises is very low. In contrast to these small operators, there are the large firms and groups of companies, such as Mecca Limited, which provide a wide range of recreation facilities— dance halls, ice rinks, ten-pin bowling establishments, restaurants and cinemas. In some cases, many of these facilities will be provided in one multi-purpose recreation complex; for example, Mecca's *New Bristol Centre*, which includes an ice rink, a cinema, a ballroom, a restaurant, a 'teenage heartbeat club' and a multi-storey car park; or, again, the Aviemore Ski Centre, which provides a whole range of indoor and outdoor leisure facilities, thereby seeking to attract summer visitors as well as winter ones, by having a range of bad weather facilities.

In addition to the commercial firms that provide recreation facilities directly, there are many firms whose products are intended primarily for recreation use, but in private homes, sportsgrounds or other places which are not provided by these

210

firms. Thus, there are the television, radio and record manufacturers; the large number of firms that produce sports
equipment; toy manufacturers; book and magazine publishers;
and so on. Again, there are the firms that sponsor various kinds
of recreation events—motor racing, water skiing and arts
festivals. Often, considerable sums of money are put to recreation uses in this way.

The *raison d'être* of commercial organisations in the recreation business is, of course, that they be profit-making. They
should produce an adequate or sufficient profit for their owners
and operators and, in appropriate cases, a satisfactory dividend
for shareholders. (This does not apply, of course, to firms
sponsoring recreation events.) This statement begs a number of
questions, concerning definitions of what constitutes an *adequate*
profit and a *satisfactory* dividend; but its fundamental basis—
that commercial organisations are governed by considerations
of profitability—is accurate. What is, perhaps, less immediately
obvious is the fact that public authorities and organisations that
provide facilities for recreation may also be commercial
organisations in this sense. In general, it seems to be an assumed
principle at the present time that public organisations and, in
particular, local authorities should confine their interests to the
provision of those facilities which are, at least in direct monetary
terms, unprofitable. Thus, the provision of facilities by local
authorities tends to be confined to parks and open spaces,
library services, museums and art galleries, lay-bys and car
parks, picnic areas and a range of amateur sports facilities.
There may be, of course, restraints of a financial or statutory
nature which prevent public authorities providing commercial
facilities of many kinds. But there does appear to be, at present,
an attitude among public authorities and the general public that
the provision of profit-making facilities and services is the
prerogative of commercial organisations, while local authorities
should concern themselves only with the provision of goods and
services which are, in direct terms, uneconomic. This is an issue
which is currently receiving considerable attention from commentators and academics, but not yet among local councillors
and officers. It is one which will be touched upon again in a
later chapter.

Notes and References

1. J. B. Cullingworth, *Town and County Planning in England and Wales* (2nd edition), Allen & Unwin, 1967, p. 171.
2. *Countryside Act, 1968*, HMSO, London, 1968.
3. *Charter* of the Arts Council, 1946.
4. Statement of the Minister with Responsibility for Sport, February 1965.
5. J. B. Cullingworth, op. cit., p. 186.
6. *Countryside Act, 1968*, op. cit.
7. J. B. Cullingworth, op. cit., p. 187.
8. Natural Environment Research Council, *Charter*, 1965.
9. Ibid.
10. *Water Resources Act, 1963*, HMSO, London, 1963.
11. Ibid.
12. *Third Annual Report of the Water Resources Board*, HMSO, London, 1966.
13. *Transport Act, 1962*, HMSO, London, 1962, Section 18.
14. British Waterways Board, *The Future of the Waterways*, HMSO, London, 1964.
15. White Paper, *British Waterways: Recreation and Amenity*, Cmnd. 3401, HMSO, London, 1967.
16. British Travel Association, *Charter*, 1947.
17. P. C. McIntosh, *Sport in Society*, Watts, London, 1963.

Part Four

Contemporary Issues in Planning for Recreation

Chapter 10
Quality in Recreation

G. BROOKE TAYLOR

In a good deal of writing and talking about leisure pursuits there are underlying assumptions that some are more rewarding than others. By definition, these are the assumptions of the professionally concerned or the opinion-forming elite. They may derive from tradition—for example a view of drama, sculpture and athletics inherited from a long history of classical education; or they may be a direct or indirect response to the present shape of our society. Whatever their source, these value judgments, and any other preconceptions underlying our view of recreation, call for rigorous examination, especially at a time when we are beginning to prepare plans for leisure facilities on a considerable scale. These plans may even be said to institutionalise leisure to a greater degree than in the past. To the extent that this is so, or becomes so, preconceptions about the proper nature of recreation are the more important and potentially the more dangerous.

The value judgments about recreation which are current in our society relate to certain perceived characteristics of leisure pursuits. But these characteristics are by no means clear-cut or simple concepts and it may be valuable to probe some of them further before discussing the value judgments themselves

Recreation, the use of our leisure time, can be seen in practice to cover a wide range of activities and non-activities; some recreations can be a state of mind—for instance the state of mind of a man sitting on a headland contemplating the sea breaking on the rocks. We often talk about active or passive recreation. Active recreation may be swimming or playing golf or acting or playing bingo; passive recreation may be listening to a concert or watching Manchester United or having a picnic tea beside a main road or looking at a television programme. But either form can merge imperceptibly into work and for some

215

people can be their work. There is a continuum from the game of rounders on the beach to full time professional sport. (Recurring controversies over amateur and professional status merely illustrate one artificial critical point on this continuum.) The boy who shows footballing ability at school and also is selected for representative games may have a professional career in sport ahead of him; recreation becomes job. Recently the winner of the men's singles title at Wimbledon said he was going off on 'holiday' and did not intend to touch a tennis racket for several weeks. A similar continuum between recreation and work sometimes occurs in passive leisure pursuits, too. The dedicated amateur of music or spectator of sports becomes the paid critic; for example, Neville Cardus. Thus we cannot distinguish between work and recreation in our society merely by classification of the pursuits themselves.

Most people may, nevertheless, think of recreation primarily as a relief from the strain or unpleasantness of work. If one is comparing the Sheffield steel worker's labour in the blast furnace with his Saturday afternoon pint while watching a league cricket match, the contrast in both effort and tension is unambiguous, the distinction between work and recreation clear. If, on the other hand, one imagines a self-employed businessman running 50 miles a week with gritted teeth in preparation for competing in a 5,000 metres race, the contrast appears to lie in the nature of the activity, and whether there is a contrast in either effort or tension is more arguable. For this man, the distinction between work and recreation would appear to be less clear.

A further common factor between work and recreation in our society is the sense of achievement which results from hard endeavour. A man or woman who succeeds in winning a coveted prize for a sport may experience a greater sense of achievement than he or she will ever gain from paid employment. If it were possible to arrange for those with uninteresting or uncreative jobs to get their sense of achievement from active recreation, a lot of people would no doubt be happier; but it seems likely that many of those who are 'active' in recreation are also the sort of people who achieve in other directions and vice-versa.

Thus the apparent characteristics of recreation can themselves be misleading. For instance, we claim to recognise a distinction between work and recreation as complementary facets of our lives. But even the sketchy analysis possible here has revealed this distinction as, at best, only a very shaky assumption; and it is on insecure foundations such as this and with no clear view of the role of recreation that our society has built a number of widely accepted value judgments about its quality.

The first value judgment is that activities involving positive effort are superior to the contemplative or passive ones. For instance, although attitudes are now changing, until recently employers placed a value on the 'character building' effects of team games and tended to prefer young people who had a good record in this field. Committees assessing the work done in youth clubs and community centres tended to base their judgments on the number of active pursuits undertaken. Some youth clubs even required their members to take part in an 'activity' before being allowed to use the coffee bar.

A second value judgment is the belief in the superiority of the intellectual and aesthetic pursuit, whether active or passive. From time to time, ministers make speeches, when opening concert halls or inaugurating cultural organisations, about our cultural heritage and 'high culture' as the essence of our civilisation. (Ministers usually talk of 'culture' implying the Arts—the term 'high culture' is used here to differentiate the Arts from the rest of our culture, which, of course, really includes bingo and 'snogging' in cars as well as composing quartets.)

A third judgment is the view that in recreation, as in life generally, the individual should always be aiming to improve his or her standard of performance. Thus a pursuit which allows measurement of improved performance gains in value.

These value judgments are certainly not held by everybody but they have been, and are, influential in the shaping of recreation policy. For some people they have even been elevated to the status of moral judgments. This attitude can frequently be discerned in those who condemn 'pop' music or bingo; too passive, not 'high culture', no self-improvement involved and, therefore, altogether morally undesirable.

217

That anyone should be importing morality into the quality of recreation may appear to be a contradiction in terms and suggests that the source of these value judgments should be probed more deeply. Why is proficiency in active competitive sport so admired? That people who achieve in work will admire achievement in another field which also requires endeavour, determination and toughness is understandable. It is also understandable that the man on the terraces of Manchester United's ground, seeing a young man from his own background doing well in the forward line and seeing 'his' team win, will identify with the player and the team and get his sense of success and achievement by proxy.

It is more difficult to understand the value society attaches to the intellectual and aesthetic. It seems likely that only about 2 per cent of our population is directly interested in high culture. (This seems to be the proportion of people who regularly visit theatres, concerts and art galleries.) Above a certain level, the Arts require a wide general culture and some effort for understanding and appreciation. They are part of a complex inter-linked pattern of responses to the world. It helps in understanding Beethoven to have a working knowledge of the period in which he lived, to appreciate that he is poised between the classical, rigid society of the eighteenth century and the industrial and social revolution which was to come. Most people who appreciate the Arts come from homes in which this pattern of thinking and feeling is normal. The pattern is alien to the backgrounds of most children entering our schools today and, although some of them learn to comprehend and enjoy the pattern, it is simply a fact that a large part of our population is not interested in the Arts. Leaving aside the controversy over the effect of inheritance and environment in shaping intelligence, even if the education system and social environment were revolutionised in the next twenty years, for at least fifty years a majority of the population would remain unresponsive to certain kinds of music and books, to drama, ballet, painting and sculpture.

The value placed on self-improvement may perhaps help to explain the value given to a largely inaccessible high culture. But the value placed on measurable self-improvement itself needs to be explored. In sport it becomes a bias towards competition and seems to be a reflection in recreation of perhaps the dominant characteristic of the western, Anglo-Saxon way of life. From early childhood boys, in particular, tend to be thrust into competition. One can hear a mother say, 'Go on, you can run faster than he can', or (before the child), 'He's terribly strong, you know, you should have seen him holding down young Ted the other day.' And when he gets to school: 'How have you done with your sums today; did you come top again?' Of course, that mother is anxious because she knows that he enters a world which will judge him ruthlessly by comparison with others and that his earning capacity will depend upon his ability either at sums or English or on his force of personality or his skill at soccer or boxing as a profession. It is difficult to disentangle this general passion for competitiveness from the other human instinct to produce a craftsmanlike job. When one looks, in the Dordogne, at the elegance and certainty of the animal drawings done by our ancestors 20,000 years ago, one is aware that this is an ancient instinct. But only the few have the skill—the many can only applaud or imitate on an inferior plane of endeavour or opt out in frustration. There are, here, two different forms of competitiveness involved. There is, on the one hand, the struggle against the elements or the material or the man himself—his own internal critical voice. In this respect, the mountaineer tackling the almost impossible face and the artist fighting to separate from the obdurate stone the vision in his head have much in common. In interviews with great soccer players one has heard Bobby Charlton say: 'I just couldn't get it right—no; it wasn't good enough.' All are striving for an imagined perfection. On the other hand, there is the need for each individual human being to project himself forward in advance of his neighbour, perhaps in order to identify himself among the millions or to justify his existence. These rather different kinds of competitiveness, the craftsman instinct and the need to identify and project oneself or one's belongings, can be seen very clearly in the transformation of 'do-it-yourself' from a necessity of existence, a form of work, into a recreation.

Thus these judgments about quality in recreation, in so far as it has been possible to explain them, seem to relate to the

219

general structure of our society. They represent attitudes that one would expect to find emanating from a competitive society. In this context the adoption of similar attitudes to work and recreation is explicable; whether it is desirable is another question.

Before examining the effect of these attitudes on recreation policy it may be instructive to look at their operation in practice in a number of widely different leisure pursuits.

Soccer or rugby clubs may begin as a group of people in an area combining to play on a Saturday afternoon. They find a pitch and engage in some friendly matches. The more skilled players improve their standard of play and demand more skilled opposition. They attract other more skilled players or their younger players improve; they relegate the less skilled to a Second XI or XV and join a league (or in the case of rugby get accepted as opponents by more skilled opponents). This escalation of skill is the commonplace of team sports. But even in activities like mountaineering which began as one man against the natural rock there is now a recognised 'ladder' of difficulty and one is presumably classified as capable of tackling a 'difficult' climb or a 'very difficult' one, and so on.

Thus activities which begin as relaxations, with a man indulging in a light-hearted game in contrast to the strain of work, tend inexorably to become activities into which he has to inject effort and concentration and training if he is to retain his place. It could, of course, be argued that the individual not wishing to compete could continue to play his game at a lower level of skill and in the weakest team. It is to be doubted, however, that many sports clubs would encourage this sort of participant. The atmosphere tends to be one in which the casual is frowned upon: 'He doesn't take it seriously', is a revealing indictment.

A factor in the increasing complexity of sport is the tendency of organisers to elaborate rules and this may have something to do with the satisfaction some people gain from intellectualising sport. This is allied to the growth of professionalism. Some people begin as amateurs and end by gaining an income from teaching. The more complex the activity the more necessary is instruction; in this way there develops a built-in emphasis on complexity. The growth of competition ballroom dancing is an apt illustration of this syndrome.

Most people, however, do not play a game at all (except, perhaps, bingo and an occasional game of darts), but a considerable proportion watch one sport or other. In soccer or rugby crowds it is suggested that people achieve, as it were, by proxy. The fact that competitiveness enters strongly into watching sport can be demonstrated by the fact that the size of crowds drawn to games can be related fairly closely to success. The First Division soccer teams drawing the big crowds are the successful ones; and managers, notably, are paid by results. The success of the England team in the World Cup in 1966 led to a great revival of national interest in soccer. It could be said that one of the functions of sport is to compensate the non-achievers by allowing them to share directly in the achievements of others. That cricket no longer serves this function on any scale may be due to the fact that many people can no longer identify with an image which has undertones of class.

But if the operation of the competitive bias is fairly obvious in sport what about other recreations such as gambling, dancing, purely social activities like entertaining friends, and contemplative activities where other factors and attitudes can be expected?

One of the traditional bases for gambling in this country is horse racing, which began as an aristocratic activity related to the typically feudal pastime of hunting. Here the aristocrat raced his possessions—horses—against the property of other aristocrats and laid bets on the result. The aesthetic element which entered into the activity was the undoubted beauty of the animals; the skill emerged in breeding and then in training and riding. Superimposed on this original base is the national activity of betting, often by people who have never seen a racehorse in the flesh in their lives. While it is possible that those who bet on horse racing have some appreciation of the skill and quality of race-horses, it seems probable that the primary fever in gambling of any kind derives partly from the risk element inherent in it and partly from the fundamental fact that gambling is the great equaliser. Here the clever and the stupid, the beautiful and the ugly are equal in the arbitrariness of chance,

221

and here the humblest has the *possibility* of becoming rich and powerful.

Dancing is accepted as one of the basic forms of human expression and traditionally has a strong sexual connotation. Nowadays (ignoring it as a 'high art' form) it has a form closely related to the mating procedure between the sexes, and in this form it is probably the most popular adolescent activity. But it also has another form which has some of the characteristics of competitive sport, the modern ballroom and 'old tyme' dancing. The dance forms favoured by the young seem to maximise rhythm and sex attraction and minimise skill and a pattern which can be learned. These dance forms are particularly suitable for the younger adolescents and are particularly inappropriate for older people. It has, as a by-product, a marked division in social dancing between the generations. Whereas at one time a dance was an occasion at which the different generations could come together for a social purpose, dancing now tends to divide them.

Another equally basic and traditional form of recreation is the purely social occasion, though, of course, most forms of recreation have a lesser or greater social occasion content. With increasing affluence one of the growth sectors of this recreation is entertaining friends in one's own home and being entertained in turn. Here with growing interest in the preparation and presentation of food, in flower arrangement, in interior decoration, one can again see both the craftsmanship form of competition, that is, a competition with oneself or with materials, and the need of the individual to stand out from the crowd with a distinctive identity. No doubt on occasions the competition is of the direct form—'keeping up with the Joneses'.

The contemplative activities can be divided for our purposes into those connected with nature and those connected with art. In the first category can be placed driving a car into the country to look at scenery; sub-aquatics for the purpose of looking at the sea-bed and the marine life which inhabits it; walking; some types of sailing, in which the main pleasure comes from being on the water rather than from racing, and camping for the purpose of living in the open in attractive country. All these are activities which are growing in popularity, but apparently not solely because of the relief they offer from work or the urban environment—for even here there are those who convert the activity into a competition by claiming the achievement of a particularly long journey or a particularly arduous feat or who compete in terms of the complexity of expensive equipment which they acquire. The second type of contemplation (and perhaps this is the wrong word) has as its object works of art, the old Grand Tour in which people visited cities to admire painting, sculpture and architecture. This is still followed extensively, it seems, by Americans, Germans and Japanese, with guide books and cameras. As a recreation it is subject to both escalation and competition, as is obvious when listening to some people describing their holidays.

This review of a selection of leisure pursuits not only demonstrates the great range of opportunities open to people (as is often stressed by those who criticise lack of initiative), but it also emphasises the amount of competition that exists in recreation in our society as well as in work. It may be that this latter fact explains the large number of adults and young people who do not undertake any activity and yet complain of boredom. For, to the extent that recreation requires competitiveness and skill and application, qualities which are also required for success at work, it may be that a very large part of the population either has not got these qualities or feels that it has not got them, or alternatively, has tried to achieve them and failed and is not prepared to try again.

One is driven to the conclusion that the apparent shape of our society is given to it by the energetic strivers who sit (or stride about) on top of it; the writers, the businessmen, the professionals of all kinds who have pushed their way up the pyramid. Such people would no doubt argue that quality and refinement can only come from application, dedication and stress.

It is likely, however, that the successful in their various fields have a facility for whatever they do and that gifts of facility are not evenly distributed, either because of heredity or the disparate effects of environment. Thus there tends to be created a society in which a minority do and achieve, and a majority watch and advise, or become bored and apathetic. Most social agencies in the past have been convinced that the apathy could

223

be converted into energy if only enough money were spent on buildings and staff. In other words, they believed that people who took their recreation by sitting and chatting or playing bingo or drinking beer (with or without darts) or going to the dog track, could be induced to take up or take part in cultural activity or take an active part in a sport, if only these things could be made available in a sufficiently attractive form and convenient location. This discussion has tried to show that, where cultural activity is concerned, this is unlikely to happen for a long time and that, as far as sports are concerned, it is unlikely to happen while they retain such a strong competitive bias. It has also tried to ask whether it should ever be expected to happen. Surely thinking and planning for recreation should no longer be constrained by the puritan view that active competitive pursuits or cultural and aesthetic pursuits are necessarily morally superior.

It would be only too easy on these grounds to argue that it is sufficient to allow events to take their course without interference and people will somehow achieve the sort of recreation they want; but one is assailed by doubts. There is a good deal of evidence that a lot of people, particularly young people, are bored: newspapers tell this story as well as surveys in new areas where people claim that 'there is nothing to do'. While it seems quite wrong to bully or cajole someone into doing something he or she does not want to do on dubious grounds of a superior morality, it may be necessary to ensure that people have a knowledge of what is available so that they can make an informed choice. Whatever the schools try to do, many children from socially deprived areas take their life style from their parents and their peers. In so doing they arbitrarily cut down their choice of leisure pursuits. It may be that this negative attitude is strengthened by the very advocates of the activities which the children ignore. A young person from a deprived or limited background is likely to be among the non-achievers at school. If sport or entertainment is presented to him in terms of the same competitive struggle that has surrounded his other efforts at school and in life, then it may well be that he will turn away from these stress-inducing 'relaxations' in favour of the undemanding coffee bar or 'caff'. But the same considerations may well apply to a person from any background who has little or no facility for the activities on offer.

If we pursue this line of thought we come to the question 'to what extent is it necessary to perform sporting activities in a competitive manner?' Swimming is not necessarily connected with competition at all, and this is also true of sailing. These are activities pleasurable in themselves. A number of games can be played with enjoyment with a minimum of competition: golf and tennis in particular. Dancing, pleasurable in itself, has had competition artificially imported into it.

A related issue concerns not so much competition as skill. Competition discourages some people because they have little facility and play poorly; but they might still play if there was not so much insistence on quality and taking the game seriously. This is an aspect of recreation which needs a great deal of study. Is it possible to modify some games to make them interesting and enjoyable at low levels of skill? Can new activities be invented which demand low levels of skill and which do not lend themselves to escalation? Can we, through the administration of sports and arts centres, develop new attitudes to play and 'culture' by avoiding an insistence on excellence and high art forms?

We are, as a country, about to embark on a great programme of sports centre development to cater for the mass of the population. The programme will fail unless ordinary people with little or no sporting skill use these centres regularly. If they become, in effect, merely expensive clubs for the experts, then sooner or later they will be closed, for they will constitute an unjustifiable expenditure of public money.

This discussion has examined some influential preconceptions and value judgments about quality in recreation. It suggests that quality should not always be of prime importance; as a goal it may even mitigate against the overall aims of recreation policy, for what is or is not important in recreation depends on the viewpoint of the observer. If you are a person with a natural gift for tennis, a suitable temperament and physique, then for you this game may assume overwhelming importance in your life. You may come to feel that anyone not appreciating the game is moronic, uncivilised. If, on the other hand, you are a

P

person without facility for games, with a timid temperament and a limited intellect (and there are many such) then you may still have a desire to use your body in some activity, however clumsily. The important thing here is that the latter person should be given confidence, protected from sneers, coached to the limit of his or her ability. Recreation is for men; not men for recreation.

Chapter 11

Machinery for Local Government Recreation

D. D. MOLYNEUX

The recreation demands of an increasingly affluent and mobile
society are imposing pressures which challenge in radical and
far-reaching ways the existing machinery through which these
demands have been accommodated in the past. By far the
greatest part of leisure time is spent at home; but, outside of the
home, recreation demands require an increasing range of
sophisticated and specialist facilities, heavy in capital cost or
land requirement. Recent and current research has enabled
society to begin to understand more fully the pressures of both
urban and countryside recreation. Although much further work
needs to be done before demand can be more accurately
quantified, the outline of the total picture revealing the needs for
recreation centres in the urban context covering the Arts, sport
and physical recreation and many informal leisure pursuits,
together with a range of countryside requirements for both
active and passive recreation, is emerging quite clearly. Some
idea of this range has been indicated in previous chapters,
especially Chapters 2, 3 and 5.

Parallel to research designed to clarify and quantify recreation demand, there is a pressing need to examine critically the
machinery at local authority level through which recreation
opportunities for the community's existing and future population can be deployed more effectively and by which recreation
planning can be built into an authority's total physical, social
and economic plan. The need assumes greater urgency at this
particular period in the country's development when it is
remembered that both the size of local authorities and their
management structure have been under close scrutiny and are
the subject of continuing public debate.

Central and local government provision for recreation has

grown more by historical accident than by a clear understanding of modern requirements. But now the very pressure for space and for specialist facilities, if existing provision is to meet or approach current and future demand, requires that this haphazard approach must be discarded. Moreover, if society wishes to view seriously the future provision of recreation opportunities as a means of improving the quality of living whilst at the same time preserving and enhancing the physical environment, then it is of crucial importance to examine critically the present dispersed responsibilities for recreation management and administration. We must study ways and means by which recreation needs can be built into total local authority planning.

There are, broadly, three main providers of recreation facilities. First, there are private facilities owned and administered by private clubs and organisations; in this category one would include facilities owned by industrial or business concerns for the benefit of their employees. Second, there are commercial facilities, provided by individuals and organisations with the express purpose of making profit for a service rendered. They include small- and large-scale facilities, ranging from riding schools and boat yards to bowling alleys and skating rinks. Finally, there are public facilities, of which there are two main kinds: those provided by a public authority for general use; and those provided out of public funds for special purposes but for which certain restricted recreation use has been possible. Examples of the first category are urban parks, swimming pools, libraries, museums and, occasionally, facilities traditionally provided by the commercial sector. Examples of the second category include facilities in educational establishments, those administered by the Armed Services, forest areas, and certain types of water facilities, such as domestic supply reservoirs.

A closer look at the machinery through which local and regional public recreation provision is administered reveals marked differences between urban and rural authorities. These differences reflect, in large part, the powers which a local authority may invoke to increase recreation opportunities and the attitudes towards recreation prevalent at the time the relevant statutes were passed. In an urban authority, provision for sport and recreation emerges through three main departments—Baths, Parks, and Education (in which are included the Youth Service and Further Education). Occasionally, other committees, such as Entertainments or Estates, might be involved, but their provision is more marginal in relation to the other three—though they would assume greater importance in coastal towns or other resorts where tourism and the holiday trade form a major element in the community's commercial life.

The Baths and Washhouses Act of 1846, from which many of the present-day Baths Departments originate, was concerned primarily with personal cleansing; swimming pools were built alongside the washhouses, particularly in the last decades of the nineteenth century, and their instructional and recreation importance grew. Today, the recreation role is paramount in the baths service, and in many Baths Departments responsibilities embrace other physical recreation provision, such as sports halls and squash courts, as well as public entertainment facilities.

Many Parks Departments in the larger urban authorities also originated in the second half of the nineteenth century. Urban open spaces were, and in large parks still are, laid out with lawns, flower-beds, shrubberies, band-stands, greenhouses, ornamental gardens and water areas; 'green oases' and 'social lungs', Joseph Chamberlain called them in Birmingham in the 1870s, when many acquisitions were made and many bequests of land were received by that city (today, they still form the major part of its present system of parks). The same pattern was reflected in other towns and cities. Parks Departments went on to assimilate the organised team sports which grew up in the later part of the nineteenth century. Today, Parks Departments include in their provision not only facilities for team games, but provision for such activities as golf, tennis, athletics, boating and bowls, while the range of entertainments, shows and festivals which they stage continues to grow. Parks Departments now cater for active recreation and entertainment events to an increasing degree.

The third main department is, of course, the local education authority. Successive Education Acts armed the local authorities, first, with permissive powers (1918) to create facilities for social and physical training and then (1944), with specific responsibility to provide adequate facilities for 'social and recreative physical training' for primary, secondary and further education. These powers are interpreted through building regulations. The range of facilities frequently constructed in secondary schools today includes several facilities from among many types of sports grounds, swimming pools, gymnasia, sports halls or halls designed for dancing. The range of provision bears witness to the growth and importance of physical education, including sport, in the school curriculum between the two world wars and more particularly since 1945. This provision, particularly in respect of indoor facilities, is closely determined, however, by the cost limits of the building regulations themselves, which, particularly in the case of the medium- and smaller-sized secondary schools, mean that, unless monies are forthcoming from other public sources, the size of hall is unlikely to be able to accommodate the requirements of many indoor sports and activities. This point assumes greater importance when it is remembered that, at present, the provision in schools accounts for over 90 per cent of indoor recreation spaces (excluding swimming pools) developed by the public sector.

The effectiveness of school facilities for post-school recreation is largely dependent upon the interpretation by individual education authorities of their further education powers. In some cases there is support for an expanding programme covering a wide range of activities, including open or covert recognition of clubs and club activities on which so much community recreation depends. In others, the reverse applies and very limited schemes operate within the strict framework of further education classes offering little or no accommodation for post-school clubs or groups. Nevertheless, where local education authorities have developed a wide interpretation of further education through the schemes they operate, an astonishing interest in sport and other recreation activities has been revealed.[1]

Urban provision for recreation is spread among different departments of a single authority or, in the case of district councils, between different tiers of authorities. Liaison between departments making like provision, albeit for different sections of the same community, can and does prevent overlap and has led to much more effective provision. But, unless this liaison is present, the system allows and almost encourages within the same authority separate policies, separate budgets and, even, different attitudes and pricing policies towards recreationists, particularly clubs and societies.

There is a further feature which colours legislation affecting urban recreation and, to a lesser extent, the machinery through which recreation opportunities are created. Support for sport and physical recreation through the public sector has been forthcoming mainly on grounds of social and physical welfare, of 'character training', of the right use of leisure and of self-improvement. As one example, the Physical Training and Recreation Act of 1937, which at the present time is the main vehicle for direct central government assistance to the local voluntary organisations for sport and recreation, was based largely on a concern for the standard of physical fitness of the population at the period when the Act was passed. Those who, at the time, argued that the desire to play was a justification in itself were in a small minority.[2] But events since the Second World War, brought about by a rising standard of living and an increase in opportunities to participate in an ever-widening range of activities, have proved the minority right. Of course, there has been a gradual but marked change over the years and provision for recreation is now widely accepted as a desirable goal for any community. But, to give effect to this changed attitude, provision for urban recreation has to operate through a variety of departments with dispersed responsibilities and through statutes which, though utilised to best effect to meet modern requirements, are the product of an age which saw recreation activity in a different light and within much narrower confines than is general today.

Provision for countryside recreation differs from its urban counterpart in a number of ways. Effectively, powers for recreation provision in the countryside stem from the National Parks and Access to the Countryside Act of 1949. Though weighted on the side of conservation and preservation, the Act did make possible the creation of the National Parks. It also recognised an element of recreation enjoyment. It exhorted the (then new) local planning authorities to include recreation planning in their range of responsibilities, by such means as the development of Long-Distance Footpaths and the registration and mapping of local footpaths. This, however, was the limit of its concern with recreation. In defence of the framers of the Act, it must be admitted that very few people could have foreseen the growth of a general countryside recreation movement on the scale made possible by rapidly increasing car ownership. Nor could they have envisaged the explosive growth of active recreation, particularly in water-based sports. But the growth of actual numbers of recreationists, and the increasing conflicts among different kinds of recreationists and with other users of land and water, sharpened an awareness of a deteriorating situation.

The pressure for new countryside legislation gathered in the late fifties and early sixties and with it there came a healthier recognition of the needs of active recreationists in a balanced development with amenity and conservation. The Countryside Act of 1968, which resulted from this pressure, reinforces rather than replaces the Act of 1949.

The functions of the new Countryside Commission, itself an enlargement of the former National Parks Commission, are to conserve and enhance the natural beauty of the countryside and to encourage the provision and improvement of facilities for the enjoyment of open air recreation in the countryside. The new Act takes a more positive attitude towards recreation provision for a mobile population seeking enjoyment in the countryside. The Act gives local authorities the means to acquire, develop and manage land for certain forms of recreation, to relieve pressures on the remoter and more fragile parts of the country-side. The supply of grant aid, which may be up to 75 per cent of the cost of providing for country parks and picnic sites, is a stimulus to action on this front. Both local authorities and private agencies are eligible for this grant.[3] Within twelve months of the passing of the Act, some 13 country parks and 14 picnic sites had been recommended by the Countryside Commission for grant aid from the Ministry of Housing and Local Government.

The philosophy of the new Countryside Act is closely aligned to the recreation requirements of a modern society. Its powers, with associated financial provision, have established an initial framework from which to build further. Similarly, those parts of the new Transport Act affecting inland waterways are more in keeping with this forward policy for recreation provision. Henceforth, many hundreds of miles of waterways will be developed with recreational use as their main function and will operate as 'cruiseways'. Doubts concerning the future of the waterways have been resolved and their future as a recreation resource assured.[4]

In so far as any specific machinery has emerged in local government in very recent years to implement countryside amenity and recreation provision, including sport and physical recreation, two types stand out. The first is the establishment of new *ad hoc* authorities, such as the Lee Valley Regional Park Authority. This authority, established by Act of Parliament in 1966, has powers to raise revenues in order to develop a large multi-purpose regional park from what is, at present, an area of dereliction.[5] Currently, consideration is being given in several parts of the country to the establishment of similar regional park authorities. It may be that when the Countryside Act and the Planning Act of 1968 are both fully made use of, and with the restructuring of the local government which is discussed later in this chapter, the need for specific Acts to establish new authorities will be obviated. The important point to note is the recognition by individual authorities and groups of authorities of the need to create recreation parks, and of the potential which exists in certain areas for such development.

The second development, in county authorities, has been the creation of main or sub-committees of the county council with specific responsibilities for amenities and recreation provision in the countryside. By early 1968, twenty-three county authorities in England and Wales had established countryside committees or their equivalent. More specifically, some county councils have established specific departments to handle the management and administration of open space areas owned by the authority and developed for recreation, whilst being involved with other matters related to countryside recreation. Hampshire and Cheshire are among counties which have made moves in this direction. The Hampshire County Council established its Open

233

Spaces Committee in 1958, it being responsible at that time for the management of areas totalling 124 acres. By 1968, the Countryside Committee, as it had become, was responsible for twenty areas totalling 3,060 acres and had appointed an officer with special responsibilities to serve the widening objectives of the Committee. Their present objectives are:

(a) to provide and improve facilities for the enjoyment of the countryside.
(b) To alleviate recreational pressures on agricultural land, woods and peaceful villages . . . by establishing country parks capable of withstanding intensive use.
(c) To conserve and enhance the natural beauty and amenity of the countryside.
(d) To safeguard existing public rights of way and to improve, where desirable, public access to the countryside for the purposes of open air recreation.[6]

It would be wrong to assume that these developments in countryside recreation machinery have not been paralleled in the urban context. In recent years several county and non-county boroughs have made moves to bring together under one committee various recreation responsibilities which previously were dispersed among a number of departments. In other cases, liaison machinery has been established.

Many of these changes have stemmed directly from the thinking put forward in the Redcliffe–Maud report on the *Management of Local Government* published in 1967. The report made a number of recommendations which are pertinent to the present discussion. The Maud Committee was particularly concerned about the absence of unity in the work of many authorities. It recommended that the numbers of committees within authorities should be reduced and that similar or related services should be grouped and allocated to one committee. It recommended, too, that the management board be part of a new organisation and that the functions of the board should include the formulation of the principal objectives of the authority and the presentation of plans to reach these objectives.[7]

It is doubtful whether the Maud Committee had the case of recreation in mind when it was formulating its recommendations;

but the case for recreation as one example for rethinking and re-alignment in the light of modern requirements is very strong and has been acted upon in very recent years in the changes and restructuring undertaken by a number of urban authorities. Other than liaison committees bringing together separate departments with responsibilities for certain aspects of recreation development, several authorities, such as Liverpool and Sheffield, have gone further to establish new recreation departments, fusing under one committee what were formerly separate Baths and Parks departments.

Some authorities have gone still further by establishing Departments of Arts and Recreation. One example is the Department of Arts and Recreation in the new county borough of Teesside, where a chief officer heads a service which includes the Arts, entertainment, sports and physical recreation, museums and art galleries, libraries, baths, parks and catering. This department is now the third highest spending committee of the Teesside Council with net expenditure in excess of £1,400,000 in 1968–9, to be substantially increased in 1969–70.[8] A similar type of restructuring took place in the Basildon Urban District Council in 1968 and, in the same year, the non-county borough of Spenborough established a new appointment of Recreational and Cultural Organiser for the town.

The inclusion of departments for libraries, museums, art galleries and so on within a department of recreation may, at first sight, appear anomalous; yet, basically, other than their general educational function, facilities offered by these departments are essentially concerned with providing opportunities for the purposeful use of leisure. As one example, the traditional function of the library service is being drastically reappraised. Traditionally the library has had three functions: to act as a book depository or a museum of written culture; to provide entertainment of the kind that can be obtained from reading books; and to exert an educational influence upon adult society.

Wainwright is among several writers who have argued for a change in the emphasis given to these basic functions, so that the library service as a whole can follow the lead already given by more progressive libraries and begin to plan for an age of greater leisure with a service providing increased opportunities

235

to meet this challenge through fuller information, education and entertainment services. As such, libraries could become even more vital cells of community life.[9]

The case for the composite Recreation Department or Office can be argued on several grounds. First, it could achieve a much better use of existing resources and a more effective development, siting and administration of new facilities. Next it could work effectively with planning departments and planning committees in drawing up the social and physical requirements of a comprehensive plan for a community recreation provision. Thirdly, by bringing together into one major leisure service what were formally a series of 'Cinderella' departments, recreation provision could be more effectively promoted as a major factor in the financial structure of the authority. Finally, the Recreation Office can provide the focus for increasing leisure opportunities, interpreting closely the roles of departments which were created originally with other objectives, but where the recreation function has now assumed major importance, and monitoring changing interests to feed back into the total social and physical plan. In this light the Recreation Office could serve the community much more effectively. It could generate more positive policies to serve the varying recreation aspirations of the community, making known existing opportunities for leisure participation and creating new ones. It would work closely with, and utilise, voluntary organisations. In some sectors of recreation provision it could bring into fuller use private facilities, and blend commercial capital and management expertise into the authority's overall recreation plan. In short, it would be more closely aligned to and in tune with the leisure needs of a modern society.

The establishment of separate Recreation Departments, fusing former baths and parks committees, or, as in the case of Teesside and Basildon, covering a wider range of recreation responsibilities, encourages the belief that the Recreation Office can justify one distinct element in an authority's restructuring and streamlining of committees. The Maud report advocated a reduction to about six committees and within this number it might be necessary to accept the Recreation Department as one section of a larger department of, say, education or social welfare. However, there are signs from county boroughs who have taken steps during 1967–8 to reduce the number of committees that the optimum operational number will be between 10 and 15.[10] Within this number of committees it would seem that the case for the Recreation Department, particularly of the wide-ranging type developed at Teesside and Basildon, can be fully justified.

The development in urban authorities of close liaison between different departments with limited responsibilities for recreation, and in some cases, of comprehensive Recreation Offices themselves, and, as we have seen in some county authorities, the growth of countryside committees and even a type of Countryside Recreation Officer, leads naturally to discussion of the proposals put forward in the main report of the Royal Commission on Local Government. Implicit in both the main and dissenting reports is a recognition of the need to regard town and country as an entity.[11] Recreationists have long acknowledged this situation and have paid no regard to administrative boundaries when seeking their recreation in either town or countryside. All of the Commissioners, including the author of the dissenting report, accepted that the map of local government must be completely redrawn in such a way that town and country are fused. One of the Commission's major objectives was to identify a set of local government units which were large enough, without becoming unnecessarily remote, to handle all of the functions of local government. If, in the 1960s in separate urban and rural authorities, some signs of a comprehensive Recreation Service are emerging, will the seventies, bringing in clear possibilities of new and enlarged authorities covering present rural and urban authorities, see the development of a Recreation Service spanning town and countryside? The hypothesis is worth close examination; for the establishment of new administrative boundaries presents a unique opportunity to create within the new authorities the right structure and machinery by which the enlarged units of local government will be managed and administered.

Specific countryside and recreation areas, whether they be water sports centres, areas of outstanding natural beauty, nature trails, regional parks, country parks or picnic areas, have one

237

common factor with urban facilities such as swimming pools, theatres, urban parks or museums. They are established to provide, in various ways, for the enjoyment and satisfaction of individuals, groups and organisations in their leisure time. They each have particular problems of management and control and they frequently require a more sophisticated interpretative service to guide the participant or the visitor in his use of the facility. They differ from urban recreation facilities, which are essentially man-made, in that they are generally developed from a resource which has several other uses, often primary or well-established uses, besides recreation: these other uses may be, for example, agricultural, industrial, conservation, ecological, transport or water supply. As such, they present special problems over and above the usual run of man-made urban recreation facilities. Countryside recreation facilities are also established and managed by a variety of statutory organisations including local authorities, the Nature Conservancy, the Forestry Commission, and the British Waterways Board.

However, looking to a future of new and enlarged authorities covering town and countryside, one can envisage a role for the Recreation Office extending to cover aspects of countryside recreation. In some areas of provision there is a clear relationship between certain features of urban and countryside provision. As one example, country parks should be seen as an extension of the traditional urban park, situated in many cases within reasonable proximity to large centres of population. Their management in a new unitary authority could be undertaken by a 'parks wing' of a Recreation Office which is already well experienced in the management of a wide variety of forms of open space and estates. Where other facilities and amenities are managed by statutory bodies other than the local authority, or by private agencies, there could be an important interpretative role for the Recreation Office as a medium for information and education for the community it serves. In some cases, the statutory bodies might welcome a sharing of the management role. They would certainly welcome the opportunity which the new enlarged authorities offer of directing finance for the development of rural recreation facilities. Many rural authorities are at present both unwilling and unable to finance recreation amenities in the countryside for the benefit of visitors drawn predominantly from their richer urban counterparts.

The detailed role of the Recreation Department in countryside recreation is less clear than the urban function, where already there are several examples pointing the way ahead. Details will become clearer when firm decisions are made on the lines which the reshaping of local government boundaries will take.

Whatever the range of recreation responsibilities any new enlarged authority decides to bring together under a new Recreation Department, there will continue to be specialist roles for heads of sub-departments, such as baths, parks, museums, art galleries, libraries or countryside areas. The Recreation Department itself will be subject to the major objectives established in the authority's overall social, physical and economic planning policies.[12] The speed with which the department can put forward its own policies will be determined not only by available finance, but by the efficacy with which it can argue its case in the context of the leisure needs of a modern society. The important point, however, is that the Recreation Department can articulate these needs into the authority's physical, social and economic development plans.

Many other problems, it is acknowledged, are raised by this argument for a Recreation Department as a focal point within the management of local government affairs. They include implications for the machinery of central government itself and the disparate powers of grant-aid at present operating for different elements of recreation provision, urban and countryside, through government departments and agencies.[13] Officers of new and enlarged Departments of Recreation, with responsibilities for a wide range of sophisticated and specialist facilities catering for varying needs of individuals, groups, clubs and societies, will be seeking specialist management training over and above their initial professional education, if they are to succeed in running their departments or sections efficiently and effectively.

Additionally, there is the special case of education facilities and the further education service, and the relationship of these elements of education facilities which offer recreation opportunities to the community's total plan for recreation provision. The advances made in recent years, through joint planning schemes whereby other local authority monies are added to local education authority projects to develop a facility or group of facilities to serve both the school and the post-school community, represent major advances in thinking and attitudes. In the autumn of 1969 some twenty-six projects of this kind, ranging from swimming pools to indoor sports centres, had been built and over ninety other similar schemes were at various stages of construction or advanced planning. These later schemes included not only sports facilities but concert halls, theatres, craftrooms and workshops, with firm supporting social facilities. This welcome upsurge of interest in joint planning schemes emphasises that the fullest exploitation of all resources and the better planning and administration of new facilities demands that education facilities, where applicable, should be related to the community's total recreation planning.

Yet while conceding that there are many problems and difficulties, the ultimate goal of an improved social and physical environment with increased recreation opportunities adding to the general quality of living fully justify the changes which are argued. There is no doubt that there will be changes in the boundaries and the management of local government in the 1970s. The case for a new deal for recreation should be debated, outlined and implemented within the context of those changes.

References

1. D. D. Molyneux, 'Working for Recreation', *Journal of the Town Planning Institute*, Vol. 54, No. 4, April 1968, Tables 6 and 7, p. 153.

2. *Hansard Parliamentary Debates*, Official Report, Fifth Series, 1936–7, Vol. 322, columns 193–284, and Vol. 324, columns 2,172–3, 192.

3. See *Policy on Country Parks and Scenic Sites*, Countryside Commission, March 1969.

4. *British Waterways: Recreation and Amenity*, Cmnd. 3401, HMSO, September 1967, and *Leisure and the Waterways Board*, September 1967, published by the British Waterways Board.

5. Lee Valley Regional Park Act, 1966.

6. *Future Policy of The Countryside Committee*, Hampshire County Council, 1969.

7. Ministry of Housing and Local Government, *Management of Local Government*, Vol. 1, 1967, HMSO. See especially paras. 93–8, 162, 169 and 435.

8. J. W. Pinches, 'Recreation in Teesside', *Sport and Recreation*, Vol. 10, No. 1, January 1969, pp. 20–5.

9. Gordon Wainwright, 'Libraries—Tomorrow's Community Centres', *Municipal Review*, Vol. 40, No. 477, September 1969, pp. 434–5.

10. University of Birmingham, Institute of Local Government Studies, *Occasional Paper No. 1*, Series A, pp. 12–20.

11. *Royal Commission on Local Government in England 1966–1969*, Vol. I, Report, Cmnd. 4040, HMSO.
Royal Commission on Local Government in England 1966–1969, Vol. II, Memorandum of Dissent by Mr D. Senior, Cmnd. 4041, HMSO.

12. See also J. D. Stewart, 'The Case For Local Authority Policy Planning', *Proceedings of the Town and Country Planning Summer School*, Nottingham, 1969.

13. As for example the powers accorded to the Ministry of Housing and Local Government through the Countryside Act 1968 for grant-aiding country parks and picnic sites on the advice of the Countryside Commission. Conversely, since the passing of the Local Government Act, 1968, grant-aiding of specific urban facilities ceased when the new fiscal arrangements came into being.

Chapter 12

The Shape of Things to Come

THOMAS L. BURTON

When, in 1933, H. G. Wells wrote his now famous history of the future, *The Shape of Things to Come*,[1] the science of forecasting, as we now know it, did not exist. Man has, of course, been making forecasts of one kind and another for centuries. Knowledge of what is to happen in the future would be the key to power for anyone who had it. Hence, people in positions of power, and those who would hope to supplant them, have long wanted at least some indications of what was to happen in the future. But the extent to which they have been prepared to trust the forecasts of prophets and oracles and to act upon the basis of them has fluctuated widely from time to time and from place to place. At the present time, the demand for forecasts is high, particularly in the economic sector of society. This is due, in large measure, to the complexity of modern industry, which often requires the investment of very large amounts of money, with no very clear indication of the levels of likely returns to the investor. This applies not only to those investments which produce direct monetary returns, but also to those which produce only indirect benefits and which are undertaken as public or social services.

This increased demand for forecasts has not been without its hazards—or, indeed, its serious failures. It has become almost commonplace for public reaction to government forecasts about development costs of (in particular) aviation projects to be one of outright disbelief and, even, wry humour. The estimated development costs of the Anglo-French Concorde project for a supersonic airliner, for example, more than trebled between 1962 and 1966—from about £150 million to about £500 million.[2] Admittedly, these figures do not allow for inflationary effects during this period; but, even when allowance is made for

242

these, the discrepancy is one of a very high magnitude indeed. The Concorde example is only the most spectacular failure in recent years. There have been others of lesser, though still considerable, significance—notably in the forecasting of changes in the levels of population and motor-car ownership, and in the levels of demand from students for places in institutions of higher education, especially in the universities.

But, despite these failures—or, perhaps, because of them—the demand for forecasts continues to grow. Those people who are responsible for making decisions, whether in government, industry or commerce, will have to continue to plan and provide for the future. It is hardly possible to do this without making some attempt to forecast that future. What, perhaps, is likely to change is the attitude towards forecasts, the degree of sophistication in the methods employed for making them, and the amount of confidence that is placed upon them by decision-makers. Already, there is a strong tendency among planners and others to reject the single forecast as a basis of action, and to seek, instead, to have a range of different forecasts related to a range of different assumptions. The implication of this is, of course, that planning itself will become more flexible, both in attitude and in application.

It is pertinent at this point to distinguish between several different concepts of forecasting which are often loosely assumed to be identical—such terms as *estimate, extrapolation, projection, prediction* and *prospective*.

An *estimate* implies the use of judgment. It represents a subjective 'hunch' on the part of the person who makes it. Such an estimate may be based upon a great deal of detailed information and experience; or, alternatively, it could derive from one single but powerful experience on the part of the forecaster. Generally, estimates are more credible when made by persons with experience of the subject for which a forecast is required. In the case of future demands for recreation facilities, such persons might be officials of sports clubs, community organisations and social groups of one kind and another, managers of swimming pools and sports centres, librarians, curators of museums and art galleries, managers of commercial facilities, academics, and so on.

243

Extrapolation consists of the extension of past trends into the future. Its chief advantage is, of course, its simplicity of operation. Its major disadvantage is its assumption that past trends will continue into the future: that is, that causal factors will continue to operate in the future *in the same ways and to the same extent* that they have operated in the recent past. Its value is, therefore, greatest for short-term forecasting. The longer is the period for which forecasts are required, the greater is the possibility for error in those based upon extrapolation.

Projection and *prediction* are, essentially, two different terms used to describe the same process—the forecasting of trends based upon the extrapolation of more than one variable. The forecasting of population levels, for instance, can be carried out either by the simple extrapolation of past trends in population levels themselves or by the forecasting of past trends in the component determinants of population change—birth rates, mortality rates and migration. The forecasts of these component variables are then related to each other, in various ways, to provide forecasts of future population levels. The advantage of this approach is that it recognises that there is rarely one single and 'correct' interpretation of the cause of any event. A steady increase in total population over a period of, say, ten years could be the result of a high birth rate or, equally, of a high level of inward migration. An extrapolation of the one rather than the other would give quite a different figure for the level of the total population, say, ten years ahead.

What distinguishes this approach from the extrapolation of a major causal variable described in the previous section is, of course, its concern with more than one causal variable; and, hence, the need to utilise a technique or techniques whereby these variables can be related to each other. If follows from this that it is impossible to make predictions without a model of some kind which combines the causal variables in such a way that the population can be divided into meaningful groups. The purpose is to seek an understanding, in quantitative terms, of the interrelationships between two or more variables: in recreation, for example, to establish not only the extent to which such factors as population increase, rising incomes, increasing standards of education and longer periods of paid holiday each influence levels of participation in recreation pursuits, but also the extent to which they operate *through each other*. It constitutes an attempt to discover the relative significance of each of the causal factors in recreation.

A *prospective* is not really a forecasting technique at all, but, rather a planning tool. It is mentioned here, however, because there has sometimes been confusion as to its precise nature and its relationship to forecasts generally. Essentially, a prospective is deterministic. It embodies a definite—and often quite specific—purpose. Boudeville has described it particularly well: 'It aims at establishing an objective . . . and at determining the ways and means necessary to reach this objective. . . .'[3] Most recent economic forecasts, for example—such as *The National Plan* of 1965 —have really been prospectives. They have established desirable objectives and have then considered the instruments and policies that will be necessary to achieve them. Thus, although a prospective is concerned with the future and is, in a sense, a forecast, it is fundamentally different from the other three techniques of forecasting which have been described above.

Most recreation forecasting to date in this country has consisted of projections of recreation-related variables which have then been considered subjectively to produce *informed judgments* of future developments; and, although there have been a few experimental attempts to make predictions based upon analytical models, this is still by far the most usual method of forecasting. It is the method that will be used in this chapter. An analysis will be made of the major factors which seem to have been significant in shaping recreational patterns in the immediate past. These were identified in the Introduction as being of three main kinds: socio-economic factors; technological factors; and institutional factors. Each of these will be considered with particular emphasis upon the changes that they have undergone since 1945 and the possible implications of these for the future.

Socio-economic Forces

One of the key socio-economic forces influencing levels of demand for leisure is, of course, the size of the total population. This increased in England and Wales by about 2·5 million

(5·3 per cent) in the decade from 1951 to 1961. In the quinquennium 1961–6, it rose by a further 4 per cent.[4] The latest official projections suggest that, by 1981, the total will have risen to 52·4 million, an increase of about 17 per cent over the figure for 1961.[5] Projections beyond 1981 are less reliable, but the general expectation is that the total population will have risen to between 62 and 65 million by 2001, representing an overall increase of about 40 per cent over the total for 1961. The figures for Scotland also show a rise in total population during the past decade, but at a much slower rate. The total figure in 1966 was 5·2 million which will probably rise to a level of about 6 million by 1981. These forecasts should be treated with caution, however; they are based upon such factors as mortality, marriage and fertility rates, and levels of migration. Knowledge of the

Table 12.1   *Projected growth of the population of Britain, 1961–2001*

Year	Projected population (*thousands*)
1961	51,287*
1971	54,762
1981	58,306
1991	64,810†
2001	69,500†

* Actual figure for 1961.
† Official Projections for England and Wales; author's estimate for Scotland.

Sources:
1. *Registrar General's Quarterly Return for England and Wales*, December 31, 1967, HMSO, 1968.
2. *Quarterly Return of the Registrar General for Scotland*, December 31, 1967, HMSO, 1968.

social forces underlying changes in these factors is still inadequate and it is difficult to establish the precise effects of those forces which are suspected of being significant. Moreover, small changes in the rates of such factors as mortality and fertility can have significant effects on the absolute size of the projected population. An increase of 1 per cent in fertility rates, for example, could easily alter the projected total population twenty years ahead by a figure of several million. But, despite these difficulties, the official projections are valuable, especially when they are made for a period which is only, say, five or ten years ahead. Here, the knowledge of changes in contributory factors during the immediate past has more relevance. It takes time for major changes in fertility rates, for instance, to take effect. Thus, while not ignoring the weaknesses and difficulties associated with the above projections, they can be accepted as a general basis for planning—at least for the next decade or so.

While the size of the total population is obviously a fundamental determinant of the levels of demand for recreation the *distribution* of the population and its *age structure* are probably more immediately important. There are wide variations in the distribution of the total population among the different regions of the country at the present time; and, more important, there have been wide disparities in growth rates in recent years. About a fifth of the total population in 1961 was to be found within the Registrar-General's London and South East Region and about a tenth in the Midland Region. In contrast, the Southern Region held only one-twentieth of the population in an area of approximately the same size as the London and South East Region. Similar discrepancies arise from a consideration of the growth rates of the regions: the population of the Southern Region rose by nearly 16 per cent between 1951 and 1961; that of the Midland Region by about 8 per cent; and that of the London and South East Region by less than 2 per cent. These growth rates are, however, misleading, since the absolute size of the populations within each region vary tremendously. The total population of the London and South East Region in 1961 was nearly four times as great as that of the Southern Region. On a smaller areal basis, there was a fall of about 3 per cent in the proportion of the total population living within the six conurbations in England and Wales, although the total numbers remained more or less constant. The greatest change was in the proportion living within urban areas with populations of between 50,000 and 75,000 persons.

Also significant have been changes in the age-composition of the total population. The proportions of people in the youngest

247

Table 12.2　The population of Britain, 1951 and 1961, by regions

Region	1951 Numbers (thousands)	1951 Per cent	1961 Numbers (thousands)	1961 Per cent	Change 1951–61 Per cent
North	3,141	6·5	3,252	6·3	+3·5
East and West Ridings	4,097	8·4	4,172	8·1	+1·8
North West	6,447	13·2	6,567	12·8	+1·9
North Midland	3,378	6·9	3,634	7·1	+7·6
Midland	4,423	9·1	4,757	9·3	+7·6
East	3,098	6·3	3,736	7·3	+20·6
London and South East	10,906	22·3	11,104	21·6	+1·8
South	2,441	5·0	2,826	5·5	+15·8
South West	3,229	6·6	3,411	6·7	+5·6
England	41,159	84·3	43,461	84·7	+5·6
Wales	2,599	5·3	2,644	5·2	+1·7
England and Wales	43,758	89·6	46,105	89·9	+5·3
Scotland	5,096	10·4	5,178	10·1	+1·6
Great Britain	48,854	100·0	51,283	100·0	+5·0

Sources:
General Register Office, *Reports on the Censuses of 1951 and 1961*, HMSO.

(0–14 years) and the oldest (60 + years) age groups increased significantly between 1951 and 1961. The numbers in the age groups 20–24 years and 25–29 years declined not only as proportions of the total population, but also in absolute terms. Moreover, the official projections suggest that the rise in the proportions in the youngest and oldest age groups will continue during the next twenty years or so. It is likely that the *proportions* in the middle age groups will continue to fall, although the *absolute* numbers will probably rise again.

Table 12.3   *Age-structure of the population of Britain, 1951 and 1961: with projections to 1981*

Age-group	Population (thousands)		Projected population (thousands)	
	1951	*1961*	*1971*	*1981*
0–14	10,948	11,923	13,189	14,529
15–19	3,066	3,575	3,710	4,564
20–24	3,291	3,211	4,232	4,191
25–39	10,778	10,080	10,145	11,593
40–59	13,073	13,733	13,262	12,602
60 and over	7,701	8,765	10,224	10,827
TOTALS	48,857	51,287	54,762	58,306

Sources:
1. General Register Office, *Census 1951: England and Wales* and *Census 1961: England and Wales*, HMSO.
2. General Register Office, *Census 1951: Scotland* and *Census 1961: Scotland*, HMSO.
3. Registrar-General's *Quarterly Return for England and Wales*, December 31, 1967, HMSO.
4. *Quarterly Return of the Registrar General for Scotland*, December 31, 1967, HMSO.

A second important socio-economic characteristic affecting levels of demand for recreation is education. The *Pilot National Recreation Survey* noted that interest and participation in many recreation pursuits, particularly the Arts and cultural pursuits, is closely related to the amount of full-time education that people have received. The American studies by the Outdoor Recreation Resources Review Commission were even more

249

specific about this: 'education findings reflect, in part, age and income differences . . . [but] education itself does have a distinct bearing on interest in outdoor recreation even after the influence of these other factors is taken into account'.[6] In the light of the evidence from both of these studies, it seems worth while examining recent relevant trends in education in this country, and the prospects for the immediate future.

The numbers of children at school increased by about 600,000 between 1955 and 1965, but this rise reflected, in part, the increase in the numbers of the total population who were of school age during these years. What is, perhaps, more significant is the increase in the numbers of children staying at school beyond the age of 15 years, who represented 7·3 per cent of the age group 16–18 years in 1955, and 11·6 per cent in 1965.[7] This is particularly significant since several studies have recently shown that it is among this age group that recreation interests tend to be most diverse and strongest; and, by staying on at school, they receive greater exposure to, in particular, cultural and sporting activities.[8] Similarly, the numbers and the proportion of young people in full-time higher education (beyond the age of 18 years) increased during this decade. Moreover, all the indications are that these trends will continue in the immediate future. By 1985, the proportion of the age group 16–18 years still at school will probably have risen to about 24 per cent and, by 2000 to about 28 per cent. The numbers of students in full-time higher education will probably rise by about 240 per cent between 1965 and 1985; and, by 2000, they will be more than three times the figure for 1965.[9]

Income levels have also been shown to be among the most crucial factors affecting levels of participation in recreation pursuits. The *Pilot National Recreation Survey* showed that 'in almost every pursuit, participation increases with income'.[10] The increase in the incidence of participation occurs at different levels of income for different pursuits—it is at a much higher income for golf, for example, than for ten-pin bowling—but there are very few pursuits where participation does not increase with rising income. This again reflects the findings of the American studies of outdoor recreation, although there are differences between the relationships among different pursuits

Table 12.4 *Numbers of pupils in full-time education, Britain, 1955 and 1965; with projections to 2000*

	1955 (thousands)	1965 (thousands)	1985 (thousands)	2000 (thousands)
Pupils at school	8,064	8,659	12,700	14,750
Pupils in full-time higher education	128	290	697	1,012
TOTALS	8,192	8,949	13,397	15,762

Sources:
1. Department of Education and Science, *Statistics of Education*, HMSO, 1967.
2. *Report of the Committee on Higher Education* (The Robbins Report), Cmnd. 2154, HMSO, 1963.

and different levels of income for the two countries. In general, though, the relationship is clear and unmistakable; increasing income leads to increasing participation in recreation pursuits. In this context, it is useful to examine the present distribution of incomes in Britain, and the prospects for the growth of incomes in the immediate future.

Table 12.5 *Distribution of personal disposable incomes* in the United Kingdom, 1959 and 1966*

Income (£) (lower limit)	Number of incomes (thousands)		Number of incomes as percentage of total	
	1959	1966	1959	1966
50	6,200	2,480	23·4	9·0
250	7,440	6,598	28·1	23·8
500	6,630	5,581	25·0	20·2
750	3,880	4,810	14·6	17·3
1,000	2,052	7,411	7·7	26·8
2,000	287	762	1·1	2·7
5,000 and over	11	58	0·1	0·2
TOTALS	26,500	27,700	100·0	100·0

* Personal disposable incomes are incomes after tax.

Source:
Central Statistical Office, *National Income and Expenditure*, 1968, HMSO.

The distribution of incomes for the years 1959 and 1966 is shown in Table 12.5. This refers to personal disposable incomes; that is, net incomes after tax has been deducted. The major import of the Table is that, in 1966, a third of incomes were still below £500 per annum, and nearly three-quarters below £1,000 per annum. This compared with a half below £500 per annum and 90 per cent below £1,000 in 1959. Only about 3 per cent of incomes are currently over £2,000 per annum after tax.[11] (Perhaps, this reflects most clearly the progressive element in our tax structure rather than any general equality in earnings.)

Table 12.6   *Recreation expenditures in the United Kingdom 1956 and 1967*

Item	Expenditure (£ million)*	
	1956	*1967*
Books	48	61
Newspapers	145	131
Magazines	49	45
Miscellaneous recreational goods	278	429
Entertainment and recreational services	275	379
TOTALS	795	1,045

* At 1958 prices.

Source:
Central Statistical Office, *National Income and Expenditure*, 1968, HMSO.

It is much more difficult to ascertain how these incomes are spent, particularly in relation to recreation expenditures. Known recreational expenditures increased by about £250 million in real terms between 1956 and 1966; but, as a proportion of Gross Domestic Product, they remained more or less constant.[12] This expenditure is, however, only a crude measure of the demand for recreation. It consists of expenditure upon books, newspapers, magazines, 'recreational goods and equipment' and 'entertainment'. It does not include items of expenditure which might reasonably be classed as recreational; for example, motoring costs incurred in making day trips to the countryside at weekends. Furthermore, it cannot take account of increased

252

participation in recreation pursuits for which the individual incurs no direct costs; for example, the use of parks and open spaces in urban areas. It is, therefore, merely a broad indicator of trends in the demand for recreation and not a measure of them. With this general proviso, however, it seems that recreation expenditures have risen more or less proportionately to the growth of Gross Domestic Product.

Table 12.7 *Index of the projected growth of Gross Domestic Product of the United Kingdom, 1964–85, at high and low rates*

| Year | Gross Domestic Product at growth rates of | |
	(i) 2 per cent	*(ii) 3·75 per cent*
1964	100	100
1970	111	121
1975	122	145
1980	135	174
1985	149	210

The prospects for the growth of incomes during the next twenty years or so are not very clear. So much depends upon the financial and monetary policies of the Government of the day. The National Economic Development Council suggested, in 1962, that a reasonable long-term rate of growth which would be within the capacity of the economy was about 4 per cent per annum.[13] *The National Plan* took as a target for the period 1964–70 a figure of about 3·75 per cent per annum.[14] This latter figure was only slightly greater than the rate which was obtained during the period 1959–64. The country's recent economic difficulties have, however, severely prejudiced the chances of achieving rates of growth of this magnitude, at least during the next few years. For the immediate future, therefore, it is probably realistic to think in terms of rates of growth between about 2 per cent, representing a low figure, and 3·75 per cent, representing a high level (and the target figure in *The National Plan*). These rates suggest that Gross Domestic Product will rise by an amount between 50 per cent and 110 per cent in the period from 1964 to 1985.

Occupation is another socio-economic characteristic which appears to have considerable effects upon levels of participation in recreation pursuits, although the scale of influence is not clear. Occupations are reflected, in part, in income levels, and are likely to influence recreation patterns indirectly through the latter. But there are indications that occupation has an independent effect as well. The *Pilot National Recreation Survey* found that persons in higher occupational groups have a greater recreational experience than persons in lower groups. Nor were the differences in their experiences confined to those recreational pursuits which are relatively expensive and for which participation was found to be closely related to income levels: 'Families in the higher occupation (i.e. professional) groups often report a greater interest than manual workers in the inexpensive recreations, especially camping, youth-hostelling and the like.'[15] In general, it appears that participation rises as people move up the occupational scale, as distinct from the income scale.

It is, of course, difficult to relate this to the future demand for recreation by forecasting changes in the distribution of the population among different occupational groups. The latter depends so much upon the needs of each industry for professional, administrative, skilled and unskilled staff. What can be done, however, is an analysis of changes in this distribution in the recent past (Table 12.8). The five occupational groups shown correspond to those used by the Registrar-General for the Censuses of 1951 and 1961.[16] There were some small changes of definition between the two dates which removed some occupations from one category to another; but it is thought unlikely that these have had a significant effect on the figures. The Table shows, beyond doubt, that there has been a relative and absolute decline in the numbers of unskilled workers, and an increase in the numbers in the semi-skilled category. The professional group has risen rapidly. It is likely that the trend will continue, particularly with increasing automation in some sectors of industry; but there is no way of forecasting the extent of this change in the immediate future.

What, then, do all these recent and projected changes in socio-economic factors add up to? A population which is likely to

254

increase by about 17 per cent between 1961 and 1981, which is increasing at widely varying rates in different regions of the country, and which is made up of an increasing proportion of 'dependants' (young people under 15 years of age and old people over 60 years of age). The numbers of these dependants are likely to be increased further by the growth in the numbers of children staying on at school over the age of 15 years and the numbers of students in full-time higher education. Income levels, too, are expected to rise, although it is difficult to forecast exactly how the distribution of incomes will change. Finally, there is likely to be a continued redistribution of the working population among occupational groups—in particular, a

Table 12.8   *Social class in Britain 1951 and 1961*

Class	1951		1961	
	Numbers	*Per cent*	*Numbers*	*Per cent*
(i) Professional	983,895	3·0	1,167,480	3·1
(ii) Intermediate	5,120,475	15·6	5,947,190	15·9
(iii) Skilled	17,183,464	52·3	18,911,900	50·5
(iv) Part skilled	5,624,240	17·1	8,342,430	22·2
(v) Unskilled	3,958,225	12·0	3,106,280	8·3
TOTALS	32,870,299	100·0	37,475,280	100·0

Sources:
1. General Register Office, *Census 1951: England and Wales*, and *Census 1961: England and Wales*, HMSO.
2. General Register Office, *Census 1951: Scotland* and *Census 1961: Scotland*, HMSO.

reduction of the proportion of the total labour force in unskilled occupations. The known relationship between these factors and levels of participation in recreation pursuits suggest that the latter, too, will increase significantly in the immediate future.

Technological Factors

One of the most significant technological innovations which has influenced patterns of recreation activity during the past decade or so has been the growth of car ownership. In 1951, there were

255

about 2·4 million cars in use in Britain; by 1961, the figure had risen to about 6 million, and, by 1965, to nearly 9 million.[17] These figures represent a rise of about 270 per cent in the fifteen years (1951–65).

There is a wealth of evidence relating to the positive effects of increased car ownership upon patterns of recreation activity. A survey by the Automobile Association in 1965 showed that, apart from the journey to and from work, about three-fifths of all car-owners in Britain used their cars for non-business purposes only.[18] More than half of owners drove at least 5,000 miles a year on social, domestic and pleasure outings. The *Pilot National Recreation Survey* showed, in the same year, that public transport is little used for recreational purposes. Even in the cases of sports for which there are usually local facilities, about half of respondents travelled by car.[19] Perhaps more important, however, is the direct effect that car ownership appears to have upon the frequency of participation in recreation pursuits. All of the empirical evidence suggests that frequency of participation increases significantly with car ownership. This is particularly true regarding the use of the countryside for recreation, where the rapid growth in levels of car ownership has created an entirely new kind of recreation pursuit—the day or afternoon trip into the countryside from the cities and towns. In view of the strength of this relationship between car ownership and patterns of recreation it is imperative that consideration be given to potential developments in the immediate future.

Levels of car ownership are, of course, closely related to income levels, but there are strong indications that the former is not entirely dependent upon the latter. Moreover, the quite independent effects of car ownership upon *types* of recreation activity make it important that it should be discussed separately. J. C. Tanner has estimated that the 'saturation level' of ownership will be about 400 cars per thousand population, which he expects will be reached soon after the turn of the century.[20] The level of ownership at the present time is about 170 cars per thousand population; so it is likely that the level will more than double in the next forty years or so. Allowing for the expected increase in population during this period, this means that the

256

total number of cars in use will increase by more than three times. Moreover, the rate of increase in total numbers is likely to be at its highest in the immediate future—during the next fifteen years. The total will rise from about 9 million cars in 1965 to about 13 million in 1971 and 20 million in 1981.

The extent of the use of the car for recreation purposes in the future is much more difficult to predict than the mere growth of ownership. It depends upon a much wider range of factors, including traffic congestion, the extent to which recreation facilities that are provided in urban areas can act as alternatives to visits by car to the countryside and, not least, unknown

Table 12.9 *Number of Private Cars in Use in Britain, 1951–65: with Projection to 1981*

Year	Number of cars (millions)	Population (millions)	Numbers of cars per thousand population
1951	2·4	48·9	49
1955	3·5	49·6	71
1961	6·0	51·3	116
1965	8·9	53·1	168
1971	13·0	54·8	256
1981	20·0	58·3	345

Sources:
1. British Road Federation, *Basic Road Statistics, 1967.*
2. J. C. Tanner, 'Forecasts of Future Numbers of Vehicles in Great Britain, *Roads and Road Construction*, September 1962.

technological innovations in forms of mass transport. For the present, it is clear that the car is a significant element in shaping recreational patterns and is widely used by a majority of owners for recreational purposes.

The motor-car is not, however, the only technological factor which has significantly influenced patterns of recreational activity. Radio and television have also had a very clear impact. About 75 per cent of all respondents in the *Pilot National Recreation Survey* reported that they had listened to the radio or watched television during the weekend immediately preceding the survey; 10 per cent had listened to the radio while 65 per cent had watched television.[21] While it is impossible to predict how this type of activity will develop in the future, it is fairly simple to forecast trends in the availability of radio and television sets. There is, in effect, almost universal household ownership of television sets at the present time; and there is little doubt that what 'slack' there is will be taken up in a very short period (see Chapter 1, Table 1.1). The major change during the next decade is likely to be in the ownership of colour sets, which are presently owned by a small fraction of households (easily less than 1 per cent).

Of the other technological forces that may influence developments in the future, the most important is probably the increasing levels of automation in modern industry. The major effects of this trend will probably be seen in changes in weekly hours of work and in the length of the period of paid annual holiday for employees. These two factors have undergone considerable change in recent years, but it is probably fair to say that this has been the result of pressures from the trade unions and organised labour generally, rather than a consequence of increased automation. They will be considered, therefore, in the context of the institutional forces that have influenced patterns of recreation since about 1945.

Institutional Forces

Two broad groups of institutions have had a major influence upon patterns of recreation activity in the past century—the law and social organisations. The law has been particularly important in redistributing the balance of time between work and recreation: for example, by defining statutory hours of work in certain industries. This kind of influence will probably continue, but there are indications that legislation is gradually taking on a more positive attitude to recreation. The Countryside Act, 1968, and its predecessor the Countryside (Scotland) Act, 1967, are two examples of this positive approach.

Of the major social institutions, the trade unions have probably been the most instrumental in influencing recreational patterns. In particular, they have achieved notable success in reducing the length of the standard working week in many

258

industries and in extending the length of paid annual holidays for many employees. The length of time available for recreation is governed, in large measure, by hours of work. Some time is necessary for sleeping, eating, washing and similar activities and, indeed, these often take up a very large proportion of each day. But the time taken up by these activities is fairly stable and, even for the most somnolent of people, it is rarely more than about 10–12 hours. The remainder of each day is distributed between work and leisure. Generally speaking, if one declines the other will increase.

Table 12.10 *Weekly hours of work, United Kingdom 1951–65*

Year	'Standard' or 'normal' hours of work per week	Actual hours of work per week
1951	44·6	46·3
1955	44·6	47·0
1959	44·4	46·6
1961	42·8	45·7
1963	42·4	45·4
1965	41·4	45·3
1966	40·7	44·3
1967	40·5	44·3
1968	40·5	44·5

Source: Ministry of Labour, *Statistics on Incomes, Prices, Employment and Production*, June 1969, HMSO.

There are no detailed figures available of weekly working hours for the whole of the employed population. The length of the standard working week in 1951 was, on average, about 45 hours. (By standard working week is meant the length agreed between employers and unions for each category of work, or that which is defined by statutory instrument.) It remained at about this level until 1960, at which time a steady reduction began which is still continuing. By 1966, the length had fallen to about 41 hours.[22] But, although the length of the standard working week has fallen considerably, the number of hours actually worked each week has declined much less—from an average of about 46 hours in 1960 to about 45 hours in 1965. The increased free time made available to employees by the

R*   259 reduction of the length of the standard working week has been taken up largely in the form of increased overtime and, hence, increased incomes. We cannot predict the extent to which this trend will continue, but it is clear that the changes in the length of the standard working week during the past five or six years have had very little influence upon the length of time available for recreation.

Table 12.11   *Annual holidays with pay in Britain, 1963 and 1966*

Length of basic holiday	Percentage of firms*	
	1963	1966
1. MANUAL WORKERS		
Up to 2 weeks	85	44
More than 2 weeks but less than		
3 weeks	13	39
3 weeks and more	2	17
ALL	100	100
2. OFFICE WORKERS		
Up to 2 weeks	76	35
More than 2 weeks but less than		
3 weeks	15	27
3 weeks and more	9	38
ALL	100	100

* Figures refer to sample of member-firms of the Industrial Society.
Sources:
The Industrial Society, *Holidays: Current Practices and Trends 1963*, and *Holidays: Current Practices and Trends, 1966*, Reports Nos. 110 and 134.

Information about trends in the length of paid annual holidays is woefully inadequate. It has been estimated that, in 1950, about 80 per cent of all industrial workers received an annual holiday with pay of at least one week. By 1965, the figure was virtually 100 per cent. There is, however, no indication of the proportions of these employees that received one week, two weeks, three weeks, and more than three weeks. The only data available come from two studies made by *The*

Industrial Society in 1963 and 1966, and from the *Pilot National Recreation Survey*. The former studies showed that there has been a significant increase in the length of the paid annual holiday received by employees, particularly among office staff. In 1963 about 76 per cent of member-firms gave a basic paid holiday of two weeks to office staff; 15 per cent gave between two and three weeks; and 9 per cent gave three weeks or more. In 1966, the proportions were 35 per cent, 27 per cent and 38 per cent respectively. A similar, though less significant, trend had occurred in the length of paid annual holiday given to manual workers. There also appears to have been an increase in the practice of dividing the paid annual holiday into two separate parts, although there is not sufficient direct evidence about this. The increase in recent years in the numbers of people taking a second holiday away from home suggests, however, that the practice is growing. The *Pilot National Recreation Survey* showed that 44 per cent of respondents received up to two weeks annual holiday with pay; a further 19 per cent received between two and three weeks; and a further 8 per cent between three and four weeks.

Prospects for the Future Growth of Recreation

There seems little doubt that levels of participation in recreation pursuits generally will rise dramatically during the next twenty years. There are very few people who would not agree with this broad statement. But there is much greater scope for controversy whenever an attempt is made to encompass the scale of future growth and to predict, quantitatively, the levels of change. A warning was given at the beginning of this chapter of the difficulties and pitfalls of forecasting. These difficulties are still apparent. But, despite this, forecasts and predictions must be made. Government and industry will have to continue to plan and provide for the future; and, to do this, they must have forecasts of one kind or another. Those which have been made in this chapter, based partly upon extrapolation, partly upon an analysis of socio-economic characteristics and partly, perhaps, upon the informed hunches of people who have become expert in these particular fields of study, represent the best that are currently available. They make thoughtful reading.

By 1981, the total population of the country is likely to be about 17 per cent greater than the figure for 1961. Unless policy measures are taken to the contrary, the regional distribution of this increased population will continue to be unbalanced geographically—with the largest proportions concentrated in the South East, Southern and Midland regions. There will certainly be an increase in the proportion of dependants in the population, both those within the age group 0–14 years and those over 60 years of age. This latter trend will be further accentuated by an increase in the numbers of children staying on at school beyond the age of 15 years and in the numbers of students in higher education; the former is likely to rise by about 40 per cent and the latter by nearly 200 per cent. Real income per head, the most difficult of all factors to forecast, will probably rise by an amount somewhere between 50 and 100 per cent. There is likely to be a continuing reduction in the proportion of the working population employed in unskilled occupations and an increase in the proportion in professional careers. The numbers of private cars in use will show one of the largest proportionate increases—about 280 per cent. The length of the standard working week will probably continue to fall, although the extent to which this will be reflected in the number of hours actually worked each week is unclear. Finally, there seems little doubt that the average length of paid annual holiday will rise significantly—perhaps by as much as 100 per cent.[23] These trends are likely to continue, though probably at very different rates, into the more distant future to the turn of the century. The precise significance of these forecasts for future changes in the volume and patterns of recreation activity is difficult to judge, but a number of informed guesses by people who have become deeply involved in the study of recreation in our society suggest that, broadly, the total volume of activity will double between 1960 and 1985, and probably treble by the end of the century.

But forecasts of this kind, though valuable as indicators of the likely scale of change in the total volume of recreational activity, are of limited practicable value. In the final instance, government agencies, local authorities and commercial firms will wish to know what specific recreation facilities they will be

262

Table 12.12 *An Index of projected changes in recreation related factors at quinquennial intervals 1960–1985*

| Factor | Year | | | | | |
	1960	1965	1970	1975	1980	1985
1. Population	100	103	106	110	113	117
2. Home students in full-time higher education	100	165*	195	240	315	395
3. Real income per head	100	115*	130	155	180	200
4. Numbers of cars in use	100	165*	220	280	330	380
5. Length of standard working week	100	95	90	85	80	75
6. Average length of annual holiday with pay	100	110	125	150	180	200

* Actual figure for 1965.

Source: T. L. Burton, *Economic Aspects of Selected Outdoor Recreation Enterprises in Rural Britain,* unpublished Ph.D. thesis, University of London, 1967.

required to provide in the immediate future. They will be concerned to discover whether they should provide, say, more football pitches in a given area or more tennis courts; whether recreational spending will increase most rapidly for consumer durables, such as record players and television sets, or for entertainment services, such as 'live' concerts, plays and films; whether more free time will be spent in making visits to the countryside or whether the cities and towns will prove more attractive. At some point, therefore, the projected increase in the recreation-related factors outlined above will have to be translated into projections of demands for specific recreation facilities and groups of facilities.

There has been little detailed study of how this might be done, although attention is increasingly being given to this in Britain and, more especially, the United States of America. The range of methods is wide—from simple extrapolations of existing levels of participation in individual pursuits to sophisticated computer models employing multivariate analyses. Until much more work has been done on these, however, planners will have to rely on their own hunches and the informed guesses of people directly involved in the provision and management of facilities—officials of sports clubs, community organisations and social groups of one kind and another, managers of swimming pools and sports centres, librarians, curators of museums and art galleries, the managers of commercial firms, and so on. Such people can examine past trends in their own particular fields of interest and, perhaps, on the basis of experience, suggest broad changes that would appear likely for relatively short periods ahead (say, five years at a time). It is unlikely that any much better procedure than this will be available for several years ahead. In the long term, however, we need to pay less detailed attention to statistics of the relationship between participation in recreation pursuits and major socio-economic variables, and to concentrate more on the motivations and aspirations of people with different socio-economic characteristics—to try to understand the forces which impel them to use their free time in particular ways. For the present, however, we must rely on informed judgments. It is in this spirit that the following suggestions are made.

In all likelihood there will be a sustained growth in levels of participation in those recreation activities which stress individuality and personality, as distinct from those which emphasise teamwork and discipline. Naturally, the professional, whose work consists of sport or some other kind of (ordinarily) recreation pursuit, will devote much time to practice and discipline. But for the majority of amateurs, not dedicated to a particular activity but concerned only to increase the range of their recreation experiences, the key element is likely to be individuality. We may, therefore, expect to see increases in levels of participation in such activities as golf, sailing, water skiing, climbing and camping; also in many small-group sports, such as tennis, badminton, squash and volleyball. In social recreation, we are likely to see a continued rise in the popularity of parties, dining out, dancing and home entertaining. Places such as the pub and the club should continue to be particularly popular. They stress individuality, but within a gregarious setting. Most of us, it seems, like to act in a highly individual fashion, but to retain our sense of social identity and 'belonging' by doing so within a crowd! In this context, it would be precipitous to dismiss the recent rapid growth in the popularity of bingo as a whim of fashion. The bingo club gives a sense of social identity to women in the skilled and unskilled manual classes which is akin to that given to professional people by the tennis and rugby club and to manual male workers by the working man's club. The bingo club is much more than an assembly of gamblers!

In contrast to these increases in popularity, we can expect to see a fall in the relative, though not necessarily the absolute, popularity of organised team sports, such as football, cricket and rugby. Nor, in spite of the recent increases in the numbers of people watching professional football, do I expect these sports to maintain their popularity for spectators. Professional football has received a stimulus from the World Cup and European competitions and it is not unlikely that these individual competitions will continue to attract large crowds. But mass spectator sports in general are likely to continue to face dwindling crowds and falling revenues. The cinema and theatre, too, look like continuing to decline in popularity. The major companies have, however, recognised this and have taken steps to reduce their scale of operations to accommodate a smaller, but viable, market.

These brief thoughts, set out more specifically in Table 12.13,

Table 12.13 *Suggested changes in selected recreation activities, 1968–85*

A. *Activities which may be expected to increase in popularity*

Tennis	Fishing
Golf	Mountaineering, Climbing
Archery	Pot-holing
Winter sports	Horse riding
Flying, Gliding, Sky diving	Camping, Youth-Hostelling
Squash	Caravanning
Badminton	Picnicking
Fencing	Driving for pleasure
Ice and roller skating	Amateur dramatics
Judo, Karate	Parties, Dining out
Keep fit	Dancing
Water skiing	Bingo
Sailing, Boating	Hobbies, Do-it-yourself
Rowing, Canoeing	Home entertaining

B. *Activities which may be expected to decline, at least relatively, in popularity*

Soccer	Ten-pin bowling
Rugby	Boxing
Cricket	Wrestling
Hockey	Rambling
Netball	Cycling
Lacrosse	Visit to cinema
Athletics	Mass spectator sports

represent one person's perspective on recent changes in recreational patterns and in recreation-related factors. They are by way of being *guesstimates* and, as such, are open to dispute. But there is one trend which few will challenge. There seems little doubt that the volume of recreation activity will increase significantly in Britain during the next twenty years and that it will be expressed in a demand for a much wider and diverse range of recreation experiences for the whole population.

Notes and References

1. H. G. Wells, *The Shape of Things to Come*, Hutchinson, 1933.
2. M. Young (ed.), *Forecasting and the Social Sciences*, Heinemann, 1968.
3. J. R. Boudeville, *Problems of Regional Economic Planning*, Edinburgh University Press, 1966.
4. *Registrar-General's Quarterly Return for England and Wales*, December 31, 1967, HMSO, London, 1968.
5. Ibid.
6. Outdoor Recreation Resources Review Commission, *Outdoor Recreation for America*, US Government Printing Office, Washington, 1962.
7. Department of Education and Science, *Statistics of Education*, HMSO, London, 1967.
8. White Paper, *A Policy for the Arts*, Cmnd. 2601, HMSO, London, 1965.
9. *Report of the Committee on Higher Education* (The Robbins Report), Cmnd. 2154, HMSO, London, 1963.
10. British Travel Association/University of Keele, *Pilot National Recreation Survey–Report No. 1*, British Travel Association, London, 1967.
11. Central Statistical Office, *National Income and Expenditure 1968*, HMSO, London, 1969.
12. Ibid.
13. National Economic Development Council, *Conditions Favourable to Faster Growth*, HMSO, London, 1963.
14. Department of Economic Affairs, *The National Plan*, HMSO, London, 1965.
15. British Travel Association/University of Keele, op. cit.
16. General Register Office, *Census 1951: England and Wales* and *Census 1961: England and Wales*, HMSO, London.
17. British Road Federation, *Basic Road Statistics*, 1967.
18. Automobile Association, *The Motorist Today*, 1965.
19. British Travel Association/University of Keele, op. cit.
20. J. C. Tanner, 'Forecasts of Future Numbers of Vehicles in Great Britain', *Roads and Road Construction*, September 1962.
21. British Travel Association/University of Keele, op. cit.

22. Ministry of Labour, *Statistics on Incomes, Prices, Employment and Production*, HMSO, June 1969.

23. T. L. Burton, *Economic Aspects of Selected Outdoor Recreation Enterprises in Rural Britain*, unpublished Ph.D. thesis, University of London, 1967.

Index

Department of Employment and Productivity, 187
Dereliction, 174
Detroit, 132
Development of Tourism Act 1969, 202
Development Plans, 104, 121, 183
Devon, 72
Dower, M., 101
Dudley Stamp, 146
Duke of Edinburgh, 71
Dunbarton, 115
Durham, 110

East Sussex, 119
Economic Planning Regions, 65
Economic Trends, 141
Edinburgh, 180
Education, 19, 20, 29, 50–1, 249–50
Education Act, 1918, 229
Education Act 1944, 103, 230
Education Department, 56, 103, 229
Education Officer, 109
Emmett, I., 7, 65
Estimate, 243
Exmoor, 17
Exmoor National Park, 198
Extrapolation, 243, 244

Family Structure, 19
Feldstein, M., 99
Finance, 56
Football Association, The, 32, 34
Football League, The, 33
Forecasting, 23, 242–5
Forestry Act 1945, 197
Forestry Commission, 47, 58, 106, 186, 187, 197–9, 200, 238
Formby Park, 130
France, 177
French Culture, The, 28
Furmidge, J., 119, 120, 123
Future Recreation Prospects, 261–6

Gambling, 221
Garland-Compton Limited, 43
Golf Survey, 117
Government Social Survey, 63
Gloucestershire, 110, 118
Grafham Reservoir, 93, 201
Grand Tour, 223
Greater London, 111, 112, 113, 132
Greater London Council, 110, 118
Great Exhibition, The, 15
Great Ouse Valley, 115
Great Ouse Water Act 1961, 82, 98
Great Ouse Water Authority, 82
Greaves, J., 57, 63, 64, 123
Green Belt, 136
Gross Domestic Product, 252, 253

Hall, P., 149
Hampshire, 110, 233
Havering, 121
High Culture, 217
Highlands, 40
Hobbies, 168
Holiday and Tourist Industry, 38–40
Holiday Expenditure, 169
Holidaymaking and Tourism, 27
Housing, 9
Human Resources, 107
Humperdinck, Engelbert, 72

Ince-in-Makerfield, 66
Income, 19, 35
Income Distribution, 252–3
Income Elasticity of Demand, 95
Income Growth, 253
Income Levels, 29, 39, 250–1
Industrial Location, 9, 78
Industrial Revolution, The, 167
Industrial Society, The, 261
Inferior Goods, 95
Institution of Water Engineers, The, 83, 98
Institutional Forces, 14, 17–8, 258–61

271